QUALITY LEARNING FOR POSITIVE AGEING

Quality Learning for Positive Ageing explores the views of older adult learners to understand the factors that contribute to 'quality' in later-life learning and how these relate to wellbeing, positive ageing, and gaining protection against cognitive decline.

Through capturing and considering the viewpoints of learners, facilitators and learning organisations, the author outlines the specific characteristics of quality that they associate with informal learning and how it can be enhanced through the adoption of simple strategies. Key topics covered include the implications of an increasing ageing population and barriers to older people learning as well as the cognitive, mental wellbeing, health, and social benefits of learning in later life. Illustrated throughout with vignettes of real later-life learners, this thought-provoking text unpicks how learners can maximise the benefits of learning in later life for themselves, how tutors can create learning opportunities that embody the characteristics of quality for them, and how providers can offer an environment that simply allows quality learning to flourish.

This accessible and comprehensive text will be of great interest to researchers of gerontology and ageing, educational gerontology, adult education, and lifelong learning as well as those engaged in dementia research.

Dr Alan Potter is a former teacher, adviser and Director of Education. His passion for learning, and research into understanding quality learning in later life, has led to him become a Later Life Learning specialist at Long Life Learning Ltd. (www.longlifelearning.co.uk) based in the United Kingdom.

QUALITY LEARNING FOR POSITIVE AGEING

Voices of Older Learners

Alan Potter

Routledge
Taylor & Francis Group
LONDON AND NEW YORK

Cover Image: © Getty Images

First published 2024
by Routledge
4 Park Square, Milton Park, Abingdon, Oxon OX14 4RN

and by Routledge
605 Third Avenue, New York, NY 10158

Routledge is an imprint of the Taylor & Francis Group, an informa business

British Library Cataloguing-in-Publication Data
A catalogue record for this book is available from the British Library

ISBN: 978-1-032-21665-2 (hbk)
ISBN: 978-1-032-21664-5 (pbk)
ISBN: 978-1-003-26989-2 (ebk)

DOI: 10.4324/9781003269892

Typeset in Galliard
by codeMantra

Access the Support Material: www.routledge.com/9781032216645

My thanks go to my wife and family for their
support and encouragement
and my obeisance to later-life learners everywhere.

CONTENTS

FOREWORD

Life expectancy is increasing and so more and more people will be exposed to the challenges that ageing brings. Fortunately, there is growing evidence from research in fields such as health, psychology, and neuroscience, that has identified learning as contributing to the wellbeing of those in later life as well as offering protection from cognitive decline (Field, 2009; Frith, 2011). This book outlines such rewards but goes further by examining what kind of learning best enables those participating to gain the benefits from doing so.

Using an empirical inquiry the views of older adult learners with regard to the factors contributing to 'quality' in informal later-life learning are captured and explored. There has been little research focusing on the qualities of informal later-life learning that are valued by older learners but using a critical geragogical lens, the perceptions of later-life learners were privileged in this case. A three-phase sequential methodology involving an exploratory Feasibility Study, followed by the main study comprising a series of focus groups, a follow-up questionnaire and participant observations, explored older learners' experiences of perceived 'quality' learning environments in which access to wider benefits could, potentially, be maximised. In doing so, a 'Quality Cirque' theoretical model for quality informal later-life learning emerged, which summarises this research in one key diagram.

Overall, the study identified three key stakeholders in the provision of 'quality' informal later-life learning – the tutor or facilitator, the learning organisation, and the learners themselves. Twenty-eight specific characteristics of quality associated with these stakeholders were identified, clustered around four dimensions of learning. The consistency and strength of the participant responses highlighted how informal learning could, and should, be enhanced through the adoption of simple strategies to enable and enhance the quality of later-life learning. As a case study, it offers vicarious significance for other providers, suggests some key messages regarding later-life learning practices for policy makers and furthermore points to the need for future research that is focused on developing quality provision in informal later-life learning.

In this book, the voices of later-life learners themselves can be heard loud and clear and are brought together to discover what 'quality' in later-life learning means to them. In this way not only the participants, but all their fellow learners, can glean the benefits arising from it. Over recent years, raising the standards of teaching and learning in schools and universities has been a strong focus for many from parents and educationalists to government ministers and appointed inspectors. If the quality of learning is of such importance for some members of society, shouldn't it be important for all?

CONTENTS SUMMARY

1 Introduction

A personal perspective
The need for the study
The benefits of the findings
How the book may be approached and used
Who might find the book of interest

The introduction sets the scene outlining how much later life teaching and learning is simply ad hoc, is often by voluntary tutors and charities, and is seldom underpinned by guidance or direction. Consequently much time is, and many opportunities are, lost that could be used to make the lives of older people better. This book provides just such guidance from the mouths of learners themselves and enables learning for those in later life to be of the 'quality' they have come to expect and which they deserve.

2 Researching the Quality of Learning

Research design
A case study
Focus groups
Questionnaire and findings
Participant observation

This chapter outlines the way the research was undertaken to identify the outcomes of this study and was designed so as to maximise the opinions of those taking part in later-life learning. An anonymised learning organisation is used to provide a context for both the research and the findings. A Mixed-Method approach is explained to show how it underpinned both how the outcomes were captured and analysed and then identified through participant observations.

This section outlines the demographic changes occurring both globally and in the United Kingdom illustrating the increasing ageing of populations, the implications for the societies arising from it, and the involvement of older people in learning. The forms of learning being undertaken are explained together with both the motivations for, and the barriers against, participation. Finally the chapter contrasts geragogy, the teaching of those in later life, with pedagogy in schools and the vital role of continuing learning to enable older people to play a full part in the life of the country and their local communities. This chapter also stresses the need to capture the thoughts and feelings of those in later life if actions that involve them and their welfare are going to be both valuable to them and valued by them.

This section of the book outlines the research into the benefits of learning in later life and four areas in which they can be considered. The scientific language underpinning the findings is made accessible without losing the rigour. Examples are used to show how such benefits would translate to aiding everyday living. Finally, the role of the learning environment is critiqued to outline how and where we learn is as important to many older people as what we learn including interpersonal and intrapersonal factors.

This part of the book provides an understanding of what is meant by quality and how it can be defined in different ways and for different reasons. A person-centric definition is expressed, reflecting on the notion of 'qualia', which champions the opinions of individual learners. The context of learning is then dissected to discuss quality before, during and after the learning sessions. Finally, the role of evaluation is considered to understand the ways in which quality in learning can be both identified and assured for all participants, including the learners.

In this seminal chapter, the newly identified twenty-eight characteristics of quality later-life learning are set out including their association with each of the three 'stakeholders' involved (the learners, the tutors, and the providers). Each characteristic is explained in some detail and is accompanied by comments from learners to bring them to life. Finally a brief summary stresses both their importance and their uniqueness.

In this chapter the characteristics are grouped under the four 'dimensions' of later-life learning (again a unique finding) indicating how they readily associate themselves with the lives of all those taking part. Reflecting on research in each of the key areas, the role of novel initiatives such as 'social prescribing' is discussed. Finally, research findings on key features of the quality learning sessions, such as group size or time of day, are also revealed.

8 What Does Quality Later-Life Learning Look Like?

Context
Observations
Learner comments
Explaining missing characteristics

My observations as a participant in learning sessions are used to elaborate on, and exemplify, the 28 quality learning characteristics. Such observations are embellished and brought to life through the comments made by the learners taking part. Explanations are espoused for the times when quality later-life learning characteristics were not present or, by their very nature, were hard to determine.

9 Good News for Learners and for Providers

For learners
For tutors
For providers
For policy makers
For society

This research has revealed a lot of new information, which has implications for all those involved in the learning process. Learners can identify how to maximise the benefits from learning themselves, tutors can identify how to create learning opportunities that embody the characteristics of quality, and providers can understand how to provide an environment that allows quality learning to flourish. Finally, those making policy for later-life learners, whether locally or nationally, can take note of both the characteristics and methodology that predicates the voice of learners themselves if they are to promote 'quality' learning for the good of society.

10 Concluding Remarks

The Contribution of this research
The limitations of this research
The need for further research
Reflection

A relatively brief final chapter provides an opportunity to summarise the findings and restate their value while also reflecting on up-to-date research or commentary on later-life learning. A case for the need for further investigation is made by identifying areas in which that might take place, such as with men or learners from ethnic minority groups.

APPENDICES

FIGURES

TABLES

1

INTRODUCTION

My passion for learning, and later for research, emerged from my training as a teacher and subsequent experience of teaching in secondary schools over many years. As an advisory teacher, I taught both primary school pupils and a wide variety of adults too. Later, as Director of Education, I was responsible for adult education in a large London borough that incorporated both formal courses leading to qualifications and training and also informal learning characterised as being for enjoyment and betterment.

During such a career, I naturally began to identify teaching and learning that were very positive for the learners and that where little learning took place. Different classes often looked equally interesting and enjoyable but some were far more productive than others in achieving the learning expected to be gained at the outset. Over the years, I embraced some theoretical perspectives relating to 'pedagogy' such as the suggestion by Knowles (1970) that pedagogy involves a teacher who is fully accountable as to what should be learned and both how and when it should be learned too. Later on, this led to an understanding of 'andragogy', defined by Knowles (1984) as 'the art and science of helping adults learn' and became more aware of critical debates concerned with distinctions between pedagogy for young people and andragogy for adults (Knowles, 1984; Jarvis, 1985; Hanson, 1996).

However, although andragogy was useful in some respects in informing my approach to learners in later life, for example, taking into account the maturity of adults, their life experience, and their capacity for independence in learning, it remained limited in others. As has been argued by Jarvis (1985), Knowles' theory was constrained in the extent to which it could fully embrace the relationships between learners, viewing learners in isolation, while Hanson (1996)

DOI: 10.4324/9781003269892-1

questioned Knowles' theory for focusing on age and stage of development rather than questions of purpose or the role of the individual and society.

As an education adviser, I was also interested in the relationship between the teacher's approach to teaching and the positive effect it could have on the quality of the learning outcomes (Trigwell et al., 1997). In fact, one study in Australia by Trigwell and Prosser (1991) highlighted that learners' perceptions that they were simply experiencing 'good teaching' was a factor that precipitated approaches to learning that were related to high-quality learning outcomes (Prosser and Trigwell, 1999). In those studies, good teaching was defined as teaching that involves giving helpful feedback, making an effort to understand the difficulties students may be having, being good at explanations, making subjects interesting, motivating students, and showing an interest in what the students have to say (Ramsden, 1992).

Later on I began to consider if my experience and background could be used to improve the provision for later-life learners. In the UK, much time and effort has been put into devising ways in which the quality of teaching and learning in schools, colleges, and universities can be measured, compared, and improved. This is not the case in the world of adult learning in general and where the learning is informal in particular. It is equally important though as Schuller and Watson (2009), in their book Learning Through Life, point out: '... learning is intimately connected with the achievement of freedom of choice, control over individual and group destinies, health and well-being, cultural identity and demographic tolerance' (p. 1).

Looking at Learning

As an adviser or director, some of my experiences of the features of the learning environment that impact on the outcomes of learning were very positive; other experiences, however, raised questions in my mind that would help to motivate me to explore learning in later life more deeply. In one informal adult learning class, for example, I noted the following:

> *Six older adults sit in a windowless room. It is warm, too warm but the learning centre had had trouble with the boiler, which is 'playing up'. Four participants stare ahead where painting after painting is rapidly shown on the screen from a power point presentation as part of an art history session. The two other participants doze. The paintings flash by with comments on colour and appreciation. One learner asks; 'Who painted that one?' 'It's alright', says the tutor, 'you don't need to know that.' The learner is not so easily placated. 'Oh, it's just that as a printer, I'm sure I came across that one over many years. I really liked it, I found it hard to get the blue colour right, but I can't for the life of me remember its name'. 'What do you expect' says a fellow learner 'at your*

age'. There are chuckles of laughter in the class, including from the tutor, and the next painting is flashed up, then the next, then the next ....

It is questionable if the participants represented in this vignette remembered much from the session (especially those asleep) and the 'lesson' was one that is often referred to colloquially as 'edutainment' where the emphasis is particularly on enjoyment. Enjoyment can promote positive attitudes to learning (Wlodkowski, 2008) and enjoyment is also a necessary condition of 'flow' in learning – meaning very deep and absorbed learning (Csikszentmihályi, 1990). However, Csikszentmihályi also distinguishes 'enjoyment' from 'instant gratification', and argues that it is related to the experience of personal growth and striving towards challenges. It is possible, therefore, that learning sessions such as the one described, could be simply 'filling time' with limited regard to factors contributing to quality 'learning' experiences. In such scenarios, valuable learning opportunities, with potential wider benefits, were, in my view, being lost.

As a result, I decided to carry out research to identify just what is it that makes some teaching and learning in later life 'better' than others. This book arises from that research, which was an empirical investigation into older learners' views of 'quality' in informal later-life learning. My intention was to develop an understanding of the nature of the learning sessions that they perceived to be most effective in meeting their needs as learners. The research used a mixed-method approach, capturing perceptions through a Feasibility Study and focus group discussions and then triangulating these findings through a questionnaire supported by participant observations. My overarching aim was to gather and understand the views of a sample of later-life learners concerning the characteristics that they perceived as underpinning quality in their informal learning environments. An objective of this study was to then contextualise these perceptions within the wider field of research concerned with the teaching and learning of older adults in general and the evidence of the benefits of learning in later life in particular.

Some research into the influences on effective learning has identified teacher quality as the most important school-based factor in student achievement (McCaffrey et al., 2003). In the specific context of later-life learning, Duay and Bryan (2008) reported that the instructor played a vital role in positive learner experiences. Similarly, studies exploring the social, emotional, and cognitive benefits of participation in informal learning during community-based music classes for older people, also identified that facilitators played a key role in fostering effective outcomes for the participants (Creech and Hallam, 2015).

Much research into later-life learning has focused on levels of participation (McNair, 2012), the motivation of older adults to learn (Dench and Regan, 2000; Ahl, 2006) and the barriers to learning they experience (Darkenwald and Merriam, 1982). Some research has looked at associated aspects of later-life learning such as the gender of learners (Formosa, 2005) or the social class of those participating (Formosa, 2007). Other research has focused on the role of the teacher in facilitating effective learning for older people in specific subjects, music-making for example (Creech et al., 2014b), and what seniors, over 64 years old, want from learning experiences in general terms (Duay and Bryan, 2008). Some research on quality has been carried out in the field of 'formal' learning associated with adult education classes (Boshier, 2006) and into the factors aiding the participation of older adults in Higher Education (Findsen and McCullough, 2007; Phillipson et al., 2010). However, at the time of undertaking this study there was no research, to my knowledge, that had focused specifically on the older learners' perceptions of the characteristics of 'quality learning' across a range of informal later-life learning activities.

Origins of the Study

For the purposes of this case study, older people, as later-life learners, were classified as 'post-work' i.e. no longer employed in the workforce on a full-time basis or no longer having any major responsibilities for raising a family. All those participating in the study were aged 50 years or over as that was a criterion for enrolling on learning programmes at the charity, based in a large multicultural city in the UK, where the fieldwork took place. The charity provided opportunities for older people to engage in informal learning each day by offering a range of learning activities in a number of different centres. The rapid increase in the population of older people (Findsen and Formosa, 2011) and the associated increase in numbers participating in forms of learning (McNair, 2012), led to my interest in the nature of what was being provided for them.

Participants in this research included a wide range of people from those living independently to those in need of some physical, social, or emotional support but did not include those in receipt of full-time care. Although the latter were outside the scope of my research, it is acknowledged that informal learning in care settings has been found to have benefits both for the residents and for their family and friends as care givers. Withnall (2012) purports that the availability of appropriate opportunities to learn maximises each resident's independence and wellbeing.

A Question of Research

It has been argued that there is a growing need for more informal learning in society, for it to be accessible and for it to take place over longer periods of time (Schuller and Watson, 2009). Such accessible and sustained informal learning for older people could benefit from being informed by recent and relevant research into later-life learners' perceptions and experiences of their learning (Maginess, 2017). Informal learning opportunities could be structured with the needs of the older learner at their centre, thus facilitating older people in continuing to learn into later life and to enable them to be truly 'empowered' to take, or maintain, control of their own lives and so retain true independence for longer (Findsen and Formosa, 2011). My research sought to capture, and to privilege, the voice of those in later life, which is too often not sought and consequently not understood. My overarching research question, which emerged from the initial Feasibility Study, was simply:

What Are Older Learners' Perceptions of Quality, in Informal Later-Life Learning?

In answering this question it was important to find out just what the learners' perceptions were of the environmental factors that underpin quality learning experiences and then find out if the informal learning that they experienced actually reflected the principles of quality as defined by the participants themselves. This was done in three specific stages:

First of all, a review of the literature concerned with the context of later-life learning both in the UK and further afield was undertaken. In doing so, the qualities of the informal learning environments they were involved with that help to sustain wellbeing and active ageing were investigated. Secondly I explored the beliefs and experiences of quality learning amongst older people in informal learning contexts so the voices of older learners could be captured directly.

Finally, time was taken to observe how the characteristics of quality learning, as identified by the informal later-life learners, were articulated in practice. To pursue this I participated as a learner in some informal learning sessions and, at other times, was present as a non-participant. In observing a wide range of learning activities, it proved possible to interact closely with the learners to create an atmosphere of trust and openness enabling me to gather a significant amount of evidence about quality learning in practice.

Book Organisation

In Chapter 1, the Introduction, the background to this study has been set out and the rationale for the focus on both later-life learning in general and informal learning in particular. I have also given some indication of who may find this book both interesting and useful.

In Chapter 2, I present my research questions, which emerged from an initial Feasibility Study and underpinned the subsequent main study. In addition, how the study was designed to enable the final research question to be answered has been set out. In providing a rationale for both the methodology adopted and the methods used, I describe them in some detail including how they changed as the research proceeded.

In Chapter 3, the context in which learning takes place in later life, including the rapid growth in numbers of older people, is presented. I go on to outline the cognitive, physical, and emotional changes that might be experienced in older age, exploring how learning might offer older people some relevant support and benefits. Finally, there remains a focus on the theoretical frameworks, including critical geragogy, which underpin this research.

In Chapter 4, I outline and discuss the literature associated with research into the benefits of later-life learning from the cognitive, health, social, and psychological standpoints, focusing on the characteristics of later-life learning environments that have been shown to contribute to fostering these wider benefits.

In Chapter 5, the notion of quality is examined; how it can be defined in a variety of ways and why 'quality learning' really matters. I also discuss the ways in which 'quality' can relate to characteristics and standards set internally and externally and lead to a variety of approaches to evaluation.

In Chapter 6, the research findings are presented revealing the characteristics of later-life learning. In doing so, I prioritise the authentic voices of the later-life learners themselves through their comments, opinions, and expressions.

In Chapter 7, the quality characteristics of later-life learning are interpreted within four dimensions, which also add depth to their relative importance. Understanding the context that the research took place gives a good understanding of the parameters surrounding quality learning in later life.

In Chapter 8, there is a focus on what quality learning in later-life looks like using examples of practice that resonated with my understanding of the later-life learners' perceptions, as well as examples that were surprising or unexpected.

In Chapter 9, I reflect on the implications of the findings from my research, interpreting these findings within a critical geragogy framework and contextualising the research within the landscape of literature concerned with the wider benefits of later-life learning.

In Chapter 10, the ideas presented throughout the book are drawn together and, while understanding the limitations to any one study, set out some recommendations for possible new practices as such findings have something to say to individual learners, to both local and national providers of learning and also to policy makers and leaders the world over.

Who Might This Book Be For?

Maginess (2017) propounds that accessible and sustained informal learning for older people could benefit from being informed by recent and relevant research into the application of their learning to, and the articulation of their learning by, later-life learners. This book, based on such research and concerned with the 'quality' of informal learning, seeks to contribute by identifying and revealing the perspectives of older people actively engaged in learning.

Such characteristics, I attest, would help an individual to reap the benefits from learning. This publication is based on just one study and represents just one context for informal later-life learning in the UK. In doing so, it does not claim to be representative of the population of older people or, indeed, the population of later-life learners, as a whole.

However, it does offer the potential to gain an in-depth account of the perceptions of older learners who were active participants in informal learning and whose voices can resonate across the whole later-life learning sector. In this way, the research findings described in the following chapters have implications for a range of people involved with informal later-life learning from policy makers and providers, at both local and national levels, to practitioners and to learners themselves.

For policy makers, the outcomes could help to guide social policy so that the agreed benefits of learning in later-life become a significant part of more older people's lives. For providers the responses of the later-life learners can be used to inform and improve the learning 'environment' in which learning can take place and suggest ways in which the needs of those learning can be best met to maximise the benefits from learning in later life.

For practitioners, those given the privilege of teaching older learners, from qualified facilitators to peer tutors, it is possible that the characteristics of quality provide a 'checklist' which can be used as a reflective tool to ensure the perceptions of learners on what they value, and especially the needs of individual learners, are taken into account both in planning and in delivery.

For learners, in general, the outcomes can be considered a set of guidelines on the learning provision learners, like them, say are valuable and likely to benefit them in later life. Therefore they have a set of expectations they can share with their providers including facilitators and organisations. Identifying and promoting an understanding of how learning could be supported by practices considered to be 'quality' in the minds of older adults themselves, could be a way of encouraging those in later-life learning to remain, those in learning in isolation to partake in social learning and those not partaking in learning at all to do so.

The research set out in this book, also contributes to the identification of how the teaching and learning environment for those in later-life could be enhanced so that they can gain the benefits from such learning; it has done so by engaging and privileging the voices of the later-life learners themselves.

Mahatma Gandhi said, 'Live as if you were to die tomorrow, learn as if you were to live forever.'

In this simple way the value of learning, and its place within a well-rounded life, is valuably espoused. This applies to learning in later life in general and, I believe, to informal later-life learning in particular. If that learning was of the 'quality' identified here by later-life learners themselves, how much better would that learning be and, arguably, how much better that life.

2

RESEARCHING THE QUALITY OF LEARNING

Introduction

This chapter outlines the approach to my research and provides both an explanation and a justification for the methodology employed. It presents the rationale for the practical steps, or methods, taken and includes the reasons for changes as the research progressed. This chapter also outlines the selection of samples, the forms of data collection, and my analytical framework.

I began the process of formulating a research design by carrying out a Feasibility Study (see Phase 1 later in this chapter), which focused on what older learners valued in informal learning. From that fieldwork emerged my specific questions, which were:

What are older learners' perceptions of quality, in informal later-life learning?

a What are the learners' perceptions of the environmental factors that underpin quality learning experiences?
b How does informal learning reflect the principles of quality as defined by the participants themselves?

and my approach to the main study, which included focus groups, a questionnaire, and observations.

Research Design

Developing a research strategy involves devising a clear path taking the researcher from the initial research question to valuable answers (Blakie, 2007). Educational research has been considered to be twin-focused – a systematic

DOI: 10.4324/9781003269892-2

inquiry that is both (1) a distinctive way of thinking about educational phenomena, that is, an attitude; and (2) a distinctive way of investigating those phenomena, that is, an action or activity (Robson, 2011). Brown and Dowling (1998) dubbed this approach 'a mode of interrogation for education', which involves making a connection between the empirical field and the theoretical field. To do so involves choosing the most appropriate approaches and reflecting on the lessons from previous research and associated literature. The research question is at the heart of the enquiry and influences the choice of research methods. Responses to my research questions were obtained using a mixture of methods involving both qualitative (explored through discussion and observation) and quantitative (measured by a questionnaire) approaches.

My study can be described as a mixed-method sequential study where first one method is employed and the findings from this method serve as an input to the next method. The specific ordering of these components gives rise to the type of study. In my research, the study involved three phases where the qualitative components, the Feasibility Study and the focus groups, were followed by a larger quantitative component, the Quality Learning Questionnaire (survey). This is known as a 'sequential exploratory design' (Hesse-Biber, 2010), rather than a 'sequential explanatory design' where the quantitative data are collected first and, in doing so, it gives priority to the qualitative aspects of the research project (Creswell, 2003).

A Mixed-Method Approach

The research study adopted a mixed-method approach, which began with a Feasibility Study, which focused on what older learners valued in informal learning. From that fieldwork emerged my specific question identified previously. This determined my approach to the main study, which included focus groups, a questionnaire, and observations (Figure 2.1).

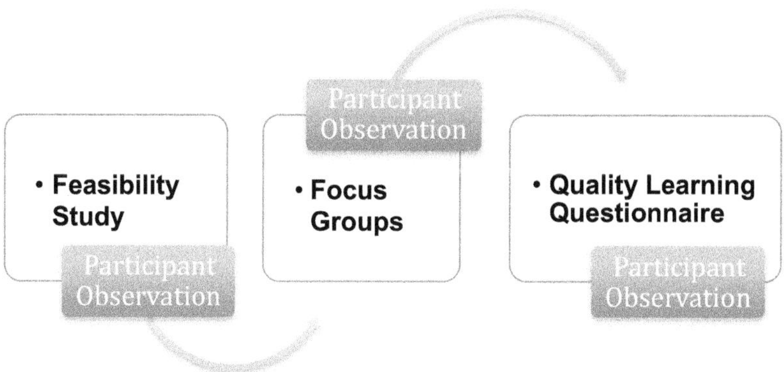

FIGURE 2.1 The mixed-method approach adopted.

In deciding to carry out qualitative research in order to explore the perceptions and opinions of informal later-life learners as to what constitutes a 'quality' learning experience, I drew on Gillhooly et al.'s (2007) study, which is just one of many that show older people perform much more positively through methods that seek to represent familiar life situations and so it was important to use a methodology that reflected this approach as far as possible. The study was embedded in the perceptions of learning of the participants themselves and that the elements to be investigated were both important to them and expressed in language they were familiar with. It was also important to be careful not to introduce my own ideas about what learning experiences should be like in later life nor judge or grade the responses of the individual later-life learners. As social phenomena are so complicated, different methods are often needed to unravel these and mixing different types of methods can strengthen a study (Greene and Caracelli, 1997; Patton, 2002).

Although my research is a case study of just one learning organisation, in one sense, all projects may be interpreted as case studies in that they take place at particular times in particular places with particular people (Robson, 2011). While some commentators see case studies as being essentially qualitative (Stake, 1995, 2005) it is now widely accepted that they can make use of both qualitative and quantitative data collection methods (Gerring, 2006; Yin, 2009). By contrast to social surveys, which collect only a relatively small amount of data from each case, a case often being an individual respondent, (Platt, 1992), case studies tend to collect relatively large amounts of information about a few cases, often just one, in considerable depth. Indeed, the central defining characteristic of a case study, according to Robson (2011), is the concentration on a particular case within the boundaries identified. In my study of informal learning in later life, involving a sample of participants in one learning organisation, a case study approach was used to capture the perceptions of the individual learners in their natural, informal learning environment.

Finally, I aligned myself with the approach taken by Stenhouse (1975, 1978) who put forward an argument for case study in education in general and the testing of pedagogical strategies in particular. In doing so, he linked it to the notion of 'teacher as researcher' which involves a 'condensed' field experience based on observation, popular in applied fields such as education, compared to immersion into a 'tribe' for a long period of time as in social anthropology from which it is derived (Stenhouse, 1982). This was a position I was comfortable with given my background in education in general, and as a teacher in particular, and my role as a participant observer in the 'classroom' situations.

The Case Study

My case study research was focused on a city-based charity that has been 'championing an Active Life for Older People for 20 years' (organisation website –

for the sake of anonymity a full reference is not supplied). It is a user-led charity providing low-cost activities (around £1.00 per hour) for people over the age of 50. It provides over 300 weekly learning and health-related groups across communities in a large urban area. At the time this research was carried out, the charity had approximately 3,000 learners enrolled and the classes were predominately informal in nature.

The learning groups ranged in size but were usually around 10 and rarely larger than 20. Tutors were part-time employees and remunerated either through the fees of the learners, the resources of the charity, or through supporting partner organisations such as the National Health Service. These tutors were experienced in the area they were leading but did not always hold a teaching qualification. This is in line with the profile of the lifelong learning workforce in the UK, which is very varied and has a focus on having the right experience not just formal qualifications (Schuller and Watson, 2009). The types of courses on offer, their structure and the pattern of their provision, were influenced by the learners through an annual, organisation-wide satisfaction survey.

Sampling

The participants in this study were all in later life (over 50 years of age), mainly women and, in general, were relatively well-educated. Almost all those invited to take part in the research volunteered to do so and the vast majority of learners were able to express their opinions lucidly and unaided. The positive response may also have been due to the positive relationships I had established with individual tutors who were also encouraging the learners to take the opportunities being presented by this research to express their opinions. I accept that there is always the issue of power relations between a researcher, perceived perhaps as a teacher, and the learners. However, qualitative enquiry itself, in general, proposes to reduce power differences and encourages disclosure and authenticity between researchers and participants (Karnieli-Miller et al., 2008). In addition, the voluntary nature of the sessions was always emphasised as was the right of individuals to withdraw.

The sampling of participants bore in mind the approach advocated by Burns (2000) that 'the key word in the sample population is representativeness' (p. 83). I sought to ensure that the sampling at each of the three fieldwork phases was representative of the learning organisation although they were not representative of any other grouping. Those participating in later-life learning are not typical of the general population given the low numbers of older adults attending classes in general (Phillipson et al., 2010; McNair, 2012). Therefore, no valid generalisations could be made to other populations as one could with a random sample (Cohen, 2000). However, the intention at the outset was to secure findings from this sample of later-life learners that could have value to aid older learners in other informal later-life learning settings.

Phase 1: Feasibility Study

The Feasibility Study took the form of a discussion held at the organisation's main office with a small number of learners (five) who had responded to the invitation by the Head of Learning to take part in research into learning in later life. They included both men and women and at the start I explained my interest in researching what made learning in later life valuable. Stressing my wish to involve the learners themselves in the study and to hear their voice to ensure the research was meaningful, I outlined how the findings would be relevant to them. In fact, they had a key role in identifying possible areas of research and the broad methodology to be adopted.

Initially discussions took place around the following four general questions about learning informally in later life. The questions sought to build on the work of Withnall (2010) who looked at the learning experiences of older learners over the course of their lives, the factors that affected whether they chose to learn in retirement and the role learning may play in their lives, as they grew older. The questions were intended to facilitate the identification of issues relating to the process of learning, which could be investigated. The questions were open-ended enough for the participants to express their views about learning and to raise any issues arising from their participation in later-life learning. Each question had been piloted with a small group of adults to test their clarity, the terminology, and their lack of ambiguity.

1 What do you think learning is?
2 What factors really help you to learn best?
3 What barriers, if any, are there to helping this to happen?
4 Why is learning important to you?

I asked the learners in the Feasibility Study to speak about their perceptions and experiences and ensured everyone had a say. The benefits of using the Feasibility Study emerged quickly with a clear focus of their attention being on what they valued in learning and why some courses were more attractive or better than others. From these discussions the research questions emerged, which were the focus for discussion during the focus group sessions.

Phase 2: Focus Groups

As the next step, I attended nine activities within the weekly learning programme and in most instances took part directly alongside the learners. Doing so enabled me to better understand the nature of the learning activities taking place and what the facilitator was expecting the participants to do or achieve during each session. It also helped me to develop a rapport with the learners and to make a connection with the tutors leading the groups. Each session began with, or was followed by, the focus groups involving the participating learners. The tutors were also able to participate if they were doing so from their own experiences as learners in informal later-life learning. The comments of all the participants were noted and transcribed.

The nine focus groups involved a total of 66 participants of whom 48 were women and 18 were men. The particular activities where I carried out focus groups, were chosen because between them they involved four key aspects:

- a range of activities,
- a variety of types of learning from physical (Tai Chi, Steady and Stable, Yoga) and creative (Art, Drama) to, academic (Art History, English) and social (Philosophy, Men's Group) classes,
- a number of different centres in different geographical areas,
- a cross-section of learners from the organisation's population.

A semi-structured approach was used with the focus groups involving key questions to ask of all the participants with specific wording and a set order for the questions. The questions asked arose from the Feasibility Study discussions where the issue of some courses being more attractive to groups of learners than others and sometimes to specific learners and not to other learners. Once again, the questions had been piloted both with a small group of adults and my tutor to test their clarity, the appropriateness of the terminology used, and their lack of ambiguity. The three questions asked were:

1 Tell me about a learning session or activity that you think was of high quality; what was it about it that was so positive, that you enjoyed and really engaged you?
2 Can you let me know anything that you have found can get in the way of making that happen; what can stop learning from being really positive and enjoyable?
3 What would you say that you do as tutors or learners to help make learning of high quality; how can you make it positive and make the learning so enjoyable too?

However, the wording was modified based on the flow of the interviews and even the order of the three questions was changed, where necessary, to follow an issue more logically. The variable nature of the groups in later-life learning, including the various effects of ageing, such as reduced hearing abilities or speed of cognition, made the need for flexibility inevitable. There was no pre-selection of participants and, in the majority of cases (in six of the nine classes) all the learners present took part. Each participant was enabled to contribute and most did during the discussions.

Transcription and thematic analysis of the focus group data were used to create the content for the questionnaire (survey) and influenced the language used. The questionnaire thus comprised a series of statements, derived from the focus group data, relating to the quality of learning experiences. I then compared the quantitative data arising from the survey to see the extent to which the participants agreed with or counteracted the general statements derived from the analysis of the qualitative data.

Analysis of Feasibility Study and Focus Group Data

My approach to the analysis of the qualitative data collected from the Feasibility Study and the focus group fieldwork involved thematic analysis. Thematic analysis differs from other analytical methods that seek to describe patterns across qualitative data (such as discourse analysis) as it is 'theoretically unbounded' and is about understanding people's everyday experiences of reality, in great detail, in order to gain an understanding of the phenomenon in question (McLeod, 2001).

Braun and Clarke (2006) describe a 'theme' as 'something important about the data in relation to the research question and represents some level of *patterned* [their italics] response or meaning within the data set' (p. 82). Furthermore, they assert, the 'keyness' of a theme is not necessarily dependent on quantifiable measures but rather on whether it captures something important in relation to the overall research question. In my approach to thematic analysis I adopted an 'inductive' or 'bottom up' approach (Frith and Gleeson, 2004) where the themes identified were strongly linked to the data themselves (Patton, 1990). In such an approach the data gathered by discussions in the focus groups, for example, may bear little relation to the specific questions that were asked of the participants and they would also not be driven by the researcher's interest in an area or a topic (Braun and Clarke, 2006).

The qualitative data gathered from the focus groups contained a total of 298 comments, each comment being one full contribution from an individual. From analysis 28 themes emerged and many comments covered more than one theme. At the same time, these themes were organised into three categories that corresponded with the three 'stakeholders' in quality learning environments, namely the tutor, the organisation and the learners themselves. Twelve themes were categorised under 'tutor' stakeholder, eight themes under 'learners' stakeholder, and a further eight themes under the 'organisation' stakeholder.

Phase 3: Survey (Questionnaire)

Each of the 28 themes emerging from the focus group references was then set out as a statement on the questionnaire, grouped under the three stakeholders as headings. The participants were invited to indicate on a five-point Likert scale, ranging from Strongly Agree (5) and Agree (4) through Neutral (3) to Disagree (2) and Strongly Disagree (1), the extent to which each theme had been characteristic of learning in sessions they perceived to be ones of 'quality'.

Finally, a qualitative open question, 'Is there anything else you can think of that makes a learning session or learning experience high "quality" for you?' was asked. Such an open question encouraged participants to identify any characteristics of quality learning which, they felt, had not been covered by the previous 28 statements and, in doing so, possibly identify new themes.

For the questionnaire, the quality themes were represented as statements that allowed learners to consider them as active characteristics of learning sessions. For example, the 'learning new things' theme was changed to 'I definitely learned new things' so that the learner could consider to what extent it was true of each of them during the 'quality' sessions they had identified. In a similar vein, quality themes associated with the role of the tutor were framed in such a way as to refer to the tutor. For example, 'asking questions' was changed to 'They let me ask questions' to be tutor-specific.

I originally tested the questionnaire informally with a small group representing adults in the later-life learners age range and other younger adults. The next stage involved a formal piloting of the questionnaire with four groups of those to be involved with the final questionnaire. This was not only to improve the simplicity, clarity, and unambiguousness of the questions but other associated aspects such as how effective my introduction and instructions were, how long the group took to complete the questionnaire *in situ* and what practical arrangements were needed for completion to be successful. The groups were chosen from across the range of courses (and learning environments) on offer and reflected the profile of learners with respect to gender, age, and ethnicity.

To improve aspects such as validity and collection rates, I decided to continue to visit each of a smaller number of groups myself rather than survey the organisation as a whole. By doing so, my reliance on the tutors or managers as overseers of this process was eradicated and I was able to provide the detailed context and instructions required. The participating learners were in later life and many were over 70 or 80 years of age. Such elderly learners required thoughtful approaches, which, within a critical geragogy framework, ensured they were engaged and involved while retaining control and feeling valued. The language used was gleaned from the focus groups, which often needed to be further adapted and used with care. I was also able to talk to the tutors of each group about learners with particular disabilities and special or other needs and take these into account.

A number of additional benefits accrued from this amendment to the survey process:

- Being present ensured that there was a consistent set of instructions, in line with the provisions set out in the research methodology, across all the participants and a consistent level of support and additional resources where needed.
- I was able to emphasise that this research was not an evaluation of the provision of their learning organisation nor was it an evaluation of themselves

as learners. I was also able to stress that they could consider learning experiences beyond Golden Gates if appropriate.

- It was possible to carry out the survey as objectively as possible and without influence. There is a natural wish for learners to support their tutors (Padgett, 1998) and questionnaires can be mistaken for satisfaction surveys so there was a need to continually stress the difference.
- The collection rate, which is often a problem of logistics as well as physical effort, was overcome. It did not rely on tutors collecting and handing them in to a third party or learners posting in scripts later having failed to complete it in the time available. Consequently there was a 100% return rate as I was able to ensure everyone present, who agreed to participate, handed in a script.
- There was also a high completion rate as I was able to check individual scripts as they were handed in and point out where questions had been missed offering encouragement to complete when necessary. This was not a perfect system as some people declined to address some of the questions, although very few, and in some larger classes, I did not get to check every aspect of every script thoroughly. Nevertheless the completion rate was very high at 99.47%,
- Direct involvement meant that I could extend my role as a participant observer during each session and make field notes of both observations and comments to aid the context and address my research questions.
- I was able to encourage the participants to consider additional characteristics of 'quality' learning in every case so that any absence of further 'indicators of quality' being raised was not due to the participants not knowing they could have put their own ideas forward.
- Finally, it was possible to stress at all times to learners that I was looking to capture their voice and to understand what they thought. The groups were, without exception, encouraged by feeling they were part of that voice and they were also motivated by knowing they were adding to the thoughts and perceptions of the focus groups making up the questionnaire.

The Quality Learning Questionnaire was then constructed with necessary changes in mind and a cohort of 28 learning groups was involved in the survey. In total, the questionnaire involved 178 women and 27 men and from all groups, 202 participants took part (representing a 98% response rate). The classes where the questionnaire was to be distributed were selected using the same criteria as for the focus groups and also in agreement with the tutors or managers of learning who acted as 'gatekeepers' to the cohorts of learners. Overall, the participating learners appeared to be a normal cross-section of learners at the organisation and each group was aware of my potential involvement with them either through a personal letter or verbally through the class tutor. The 28 group sessions took place at 10 different venues over a total of seven days. At the end of that time, all questionnaires had been securely gathered in.

Participant Observation

This element of the research took place throughout the period of the fieldwork phases. As a method of gathering information, participant observation has the advantage of directness – not having to ask people about their views, feelings, or attitudes but simply focus on what they are doing. At the same time, it is a way of getting at 'real life' *in situ* and out of the laboratory. The use of observation as a research tool is succinctly summarised by Robson (2011):

> As the actions and behaviour of people are a central aspect in virtually all real world research, a natural and obvious technique is to watch what they do, to record this in some way and to then describe, analyse and interpret what we have observed.
>
> *(p. 315)*

However, participant observation is not without its disadvantages. There is certainly an issue about the extent to which an observer's presence affects the situation under observation – a phenomenon referred to as 'reactivity'. McCall (1984) considers reactivity to be a common feature of observational studies but not a universal one. One strategy can be to ensure the observed are unaware of being observed or alternatively, the strategy I adopted, ensuring they are so comfortably accustomed to myself as the observer that they carried on essentially as if I wasn't there.

During the fieldwork phase, I participated in and observed classes during which I adopted a 'participant observer' approach. In doing so, I was able to gain a first-hand understanding of what was happening in learning sessions contemporaneously by collecting further data through discussions and the use of a questionnaire. Therefore, in this study, observation was used as a supplementary method to collect data that may validate, corroborate, or simply set in perspective the data collected by these other means.

The data and other information from direct observation, although contrasting with that from virtually all other techniques, can complement those data-gathering methods too. Interview and questionnaire responses are notorious for discrepancies between what people say that they have done, or will do, and what they actually do, or will do. Such an observational method can be classified as formal or informal observation depending upon the degree of pre-structure in the observation exercise. Unlike the formal approach, where a checklist of pre-specified aspects is chosen for attention and everything else is considered irrelevant for the purpose of the study, I adopted an informal approach so that I had a greater freedom about what information I was gathering and how it was recorded.

My participation as an observer was not one of concealing my identity but instead I adopted a participant-as-observer role. The fact that I was in this position was made clear to the group from the start and it was from this standpoint that I sought to make close relationships with members of the group. In this way, not only was I able to observe through participating in activities, I was able to ask members to explain various aspects or gather their opinions of what was going on. Dressing informally enabled me to merge into the context, with appropriate clothing for physical exercise classes, to signal equality of status with those being observed.

I also deliberately avoided 'intervention' that would get in the way of naturally occurring events and suggest a separation of status. My experience of being in educational settings, including school and college classrooms as a local authority adviser and inspector, had helped to evolve my observational techniques. For example, making notes unobtrusively while holding a 'normal' conversation and working alongside one person or group while being able to observe or 'eavesdrop' on others. By the nature of the various teaching and learning approaches evident across the learning sessions, in some focus groups, such as philosophy discussions or art classes, I was more of a 'marginal participant'. Here I was again completely open about my role and was accepted by the group as more of a 'passive' observer.

Throughout the qualitative fieldwork of the Feasibility Study and the focus groups, I stressed this position verbally to both groups and individuals and reinforced my position in the introduction to the questionnaire. Their open-minded approaches to discussions during the qualitative fieldwork phases and the positive response to the opportunity to express their views during the quantitative fieldwork phase (survey) provided evidence that the participants viewed and accepted me as a partner. The cooperation of the tutors was important in enabling access to the groups and providing a suitable research environment. This was aided by making contact with each tutor personally at the outset and sought to spend time with them to outline the nature of the research programme and our relative roles during the fieldwork sessions.

Bias

Issues of bias are present in all research involving people especially where there is a close relationship between the researcher and the setting and between the researcher and the respondents (Robson, 2011). I was conscious of using a range of strategies outlined by Padgett (1998) to deal with such threats. For example, restricting the times I was present with participants so I did not suffer from any bias to do with prolonged involvement, which may lead to positive, or negative bias. I also worked against bringing any bias from my own experience in learning to bear on the interpretation of data by regularly reflecting back on the comments and language associated with the Feasibility Study and focus groups.

Validity and Reliability

Validity, whether or not a method's findings represent the phenomenon they are intended to measure, and reliability, whether or not, if the research project's measures were repeated on the same population, it would create the same results both times (Hesse-Biber, 2010) are key features of research. In this research, reliability was not really an issue as I did not seek to develop a psychometric test and would expect things to change over time. Therefore, I am not expecting any further research in this area to necessarily replicate my findings.

However, in qualitative research, alternative terms to validity and reliability are considered. For example, Lincoln and Guba (1985) proposed two primary criteria for assessing a qualitative study – trustworthiness and authenticity – which assimilate reliability and validity into qualitative research, using alternative terms to legitimise the approach and justify the research outcomes. Trustworthiness comprises credibility (involving confirmation of findings by the participants), transferability (involving detailed descriptions as a rich database to be revisited), dependability (involving keeping and making available detailed records of the research), and confirmability (involving as far as possible avoiding subjectivity and bias).

Not everyone agrees with the irrelevance of validity and reliability to qualitative research and adopting a completely new approach and terminology and Hammersley (1992), for example, takes a position midway between the two. Defining trustworthiness and authenticity as 'balance', 'fairness', and 'completeness', Patton (2002) argued that this is achieved by the researcher's sincere commitment to understand the phenomenon as it is revealed, openly acknowledge intricacies and multiple viewpoints and be fair in exposing both affirmative and dissenting voices with regard to conclusions reached.

I do not believe that in the qualitative phases the learners told me what they thought I wanted to hear as, according to the Head of Learning, this subject had not been discussed with them previously. In addition, I did not comment on it directly at any point and, by doing so, express my own views, which may have affected the views of the participants. Therefore, it can be asserted that in discussions with the learners, the authentic perceptions of the learners were captured about what quality is in their learning experiences.

Triangulation is at the very heart of a multi-strategy approach. It is a valuable tool used to enhance the rigour of the research. My research approach involved triangulation as data were gathered through interviews (qualitative), a survey (quantitative) and observations (adopting a qualitative approach). It enabled the results of the qualitative phases of evidence gathering to be cross-checked against the results of the quantitative phase (the survey). By their very nature, survey studies cannot adequately identify the nature and meaning of individual learner's experiences (Lamb and Brady, 2005) by being unable to go into the depth of the rationale for a response given in the way an interview, for example, would be able to do.

In carrying out the survey directly myself, the validity arguably increased, firstly because I was able to personally ensure that all groups received the same guidance and input at the start and secondly because where misunderstandings arose, I was able to address these on an individual basis. When questionnaires are returned indirectly, the researcher does not truly know who completed it, if the respondents understood what they were answering, or if they completed it with appropriate levels of care and accuracy.

By overseeing the survey personally and directly, I also knew the responses were from across a range of groups representative of the charity where previously it could have been skewed depending on which participants responded from across the whole organisation. Such a response, even a large one, could have been from one type of class, one age group, or one ethnic group, depending on the guidance of the tutors or the learners' willingness to participate on any one particular day. By using the survey method chosen, a representative cross-section of learners was engaged by design and not by default.

Finally, it was possible to ensure that the responses were across the full range of individual learners in those groups so that the old, the shy, and the disabled all responded and received continual encouragement to do so. By being present, it was possible to know that every answer was an individual answer and not a group suggestion and also that the answers given were from the person allocated the script and not someone else providing answers on their behalf.

Ethical Matters

I carried out this research in accordance with British Educational Research Association (BERA) guidelines. There were two main ethical issues relevant to this research; the first was concerned with the sensitivity of measuring 'quality' where the facilitators or the organisation may have felt they were being judged or evaluated. The second was involving participants who were potentially vulnerable. In addition, there were associated ethical issues of anonymity and confidentiality that could have worried older learners so that they felt they could not comment freely. I therefore employed a series of practical steps to deal with the important issues of data protection and storage.

From the outset open-mindedness was sustained in my research in line with Dewey (1910) who advocated open-mindedness as one of the fundamental aims of education. He conceptualised it as the childlike attitude of wonder and interest in new ideas, which includes an active desire to listen to more sides than one; to give heed to facts from whatever source they come; to give full attention to alternative possibilities; and to recognise the possibility of error even in the beliefs that are dearest to us.

However, it must be acknowledged that in any cohort of older people there may be 'invisible' vulnerabilities (e.g. older people suffering from loneliness, depression, and early onset dementia which had not been brought to the attention of the organisation) and I remained alert to signs that might have indicated that any participant was not comfortable with participating in the research. Informed consent forms were used to gain and document permissions, including voice recording usage. Finally, the broad outcomes of the study were fed back to the organisation and, therefore, it is in a position to make arrangements for the findings to be shared with the participants in the study.

Summary

This chapter has presented and explained the theoretical basis for the research methodology adopted. It has also described and justified the practical steps and research methods used in order to enact it. The four features of the mixed-method approach, the Feasibility Study (Phase 1), the focus groups (Phase 2), the Quality Learning Questionnaire (Phase 3), and the Participant Observations, are each presented to outline the way they were developed, how they were used to sample perceptions and how the analysis of each set of findings was approached. Finally issues of validity and reliability together with associated ethical issues have been outlined both in theory and in practice.

These findings are unique, not just to those taking part, but in the field of informal later-life learning. Not only have the participants identified characteristics of quality for the first time, but also they are a manifestation of the thoughts, feelings, and perceptions of the later-life learners themselves. Together, they may provide an evaluative framework that could prove useful if applied across different contexts and various learning situations. The details of the findings from this research are outlined in the following chapters.

3

AGEING AND LEARNING THROUGHOUT A LONGER LIFE

The Ageing Population

The passage of time for humans is related to a number of physical and biological changes that range from the greying of hair and wrinkling of the skin to a degeneration of reproductive capacity, immune system response, and cardiovascular functioning (Morgan and Kundel, 2001). During this time, such changes differ in scope and intensity for different people so individual experiences of ageing can vary greatly (Stuart-Hamilton, 2000). These individual experiences are positioned within a current context whereby the world is experiencing declining mortality levels and general improvements in population health (World Health Organisation (WHO), 2002). These changes, together with a decline in birth rates, have led to the profile of the world's population changing too. Quite simply, the world is getting older (Jarvis, 2001; Withnall, 2010) with unprecedented numbers of older people in terms of percentages of populations as well as actual numbers (United Nations Census Bureau, 2013). In the United States, for example, individuals aged 65 or older will outnumber those under 18 by 2034 (US Census Bureau, 2018).

Global Demographic Changes

Specific population projections by the United Nations Census Bureau (2013) concerning the world's population in 2010, for example, indicated that the number of people aged 60 years and over is expected to triple over the following 40 years (up to 2050) from 737 million to two billion and to three billion by the end of the century (2100). More recent figures from the United Nations Census Bureau (2015) indicate that whereas in 2015, 12.3% of the world's population

DOI: 10.4324/9781003269892-3

was aged 60 years or over, by 2050 it is projected that this figure will rise sharply to 21.5%. For the world's population of those aged 80 years or over the rise is just as dramatic, from 1.7% of the world's population in 2015 up to 4.5% by 2050.

Developed Countries

In regional terms, developing countries will experience the steepest increases in older populations in terms of numbers but it will be in Europe where the greatest percentages of older people, as proportions of the overall population, will be found. United Nations Census Bureau (2015) statistics show that the percentage of Europe's population aged 60 years or over in 2015 was 23.9% while by 2050 it is anticipated that this figure will rise sharply to 34.2%. For those aged 80 years or over within Europe's population the rise is just as dramatic, from 4.7% of the population in 2015 up to 10.1% by 2050. At the same time, life expectancy at birth for both men and women is expected to continue to rise. In Europe, for example, overall life expectancy is anticipated to rise for 60-year-olds from 21.9 years in the period 2010–2015 up to 25.4 years by 2045–2050 (i.e. from 81.9 years to 85.4 years of age).

In the United Kingdom, changes in the elderly population mirror worldwide and European demographic changes. According to the United Nations Census Bureau (2015) the proportion of the population aged 60 years or older in 1980 was 20.0%, rose to 23.0% by 2015, and will rise to 30.7% by 2050. This trend is set to continue at a pace with the proportion of people aged 80 and above in the UK having risen from 2.7% in 1980 up to 4.7% in 2015 and is expected to further increase to 9.7% by 2050.

Implications of the Demographic Trend

Sarah Harper (2006), as Director of the Oxford Institute of Population Ageing, stated that this phenomenon, of the rapidly ageing population, is not solely the result of a short-term 'baby boomer' bulge. Rather, Harper interprets the ageing population as an example of 'demographic maturing'; a global trend that heralds long-term shifts in individual and societal behaviour. Harper (2006) goes on to predict that the social, economic, and political areas that this shift may affect include: the labour market, saving and consumption patterns, family and household structure, social interaction and networks, demand for health and welfare services, leisure and community behaviour, and even geopolitical order. According to Stuart-Hamilton (2000), for some, it will also involve making use of a variety of care services and for a large percentage of older persons, whatever their age or health, ageing will bring a decline in their independent status. These increasing numbers representing the older section of the community will rely on greater support from social or medical services putting pressure on a country's finances and workforce.

Later Life

Notwithstanding some of the characteristics of ageing that have been noted (Stuart-Hamilton, 2000), it is becoming increasingly difficult to define later life. In the past this later phase of the lifespan was often seen as the 'post-work' stage but the age at which people are actually leaving the workforce depends on a number of factors such as health status, redundancy, voluntary severance, moves to self-employment or caring duties, often for elderly parents or relatives.

Although later life is recognised as a distinct phase in the lifecycle, it has also been conceptualised as a social construction that results from public policies, services, and markets catering exclusively for the supposed needs of older adults (Guillemard, 2000). In the mid-1900s, later-life experiences, such as retirement, were equated with a loss of status and role and hence social exclusion (Cumin and Henry, 1961). However, more contemporary studies show such characteristics of retirement as being too simplistic and, as Phillipson (1993) argued, the transition into retirement can be thought of as a form of 'diverse engagement' with civil society. Findsen and Formosa (2011) summarise such engagements as '"citizenship transitions" constructed around closer involvement with family, friends and community networks, "consumer and leisure transitions" constructed around the development of more individualised lifestyles or "work transitions" constructed around new types of engagement with paid work' (p. 13).

The post-work age, for many, will be lengthy owing to increasing longevity and needs to be more clearly defined for the purposes of this research. One way of characterising older members of the population is to differentiate them as belonging to the 'Third Age' or the 'Fourth Age' – identified by Laslett (1989) as a way of separating the working [active] years of the first part of later life on one hand from frailty and decline on the other. The Third Age (3rd Age) characterises the period in later life when learning, potentially, takes an increasing role in the lives of older people who are no longer engaged in work or bringing up a family. Gilleard and Higgs (2000, 2002) suggested that the 3rd Age should be viewed not so much as a chronological age group, but as a 'cultural field', a social space marked out by the opportunities for participation in mass consumer society. Findsen and Formosa (2011) lauded the recognition of such a grouping by saying that: '... despite such debates on the correct conceptualisation of the 'third age', there is no doubt that the concept has, by definition, revolutionised the link between ageing and learning' (p. 51).

They go on to suggest this 'Third Age lifestyle' fosters, amongst older people, an experience of 'ontological insecurity', which tears down their former identity, usually based on occupational and familial experiences. The 3rd Age, then, is very much what defines the new type of retirement lifestyle that Blaikie (1999) described as moving away from sickness and physical or cognitive deficit towards the maintenance of good health and a sense of liberation. In the 3rd

Age, older people sometimes take advantage of opportunities such as learning to maintain or develop a new sense of identity. In doing so older learners have been found to build self-confidence, retain control over their lives, and continue civic engagement with other people (Reder, 2009; Duncan, 2014).

It has been argued that the majority of our increasingly aged population will not need intensive Fourth Age (4th Age) levels of care (Findsen and Formosa, 2011) but will nevertheless gradually lean more heavily on family, friends or charities as increasing numbers suffer from the onset of dementia and other ailments more prevalent in old age (Jarvis, 2001). Dementia is an overarching term used to describe any condition where a variety of different brain functions such as memory, thinking, recognition, language, planning, and personality deteriorate over time (Banks, 2006). Although one in every 90 people in the UK has dementia, it is rare below the age of 65. However, above that age, the rate is up to 1 in 20, rising to about 1 in 6 of those aged over 80 (Graham and Warner, 2009). Emerging evidence suggests that sustained engagement in learning may protect against dementia and, at the very least, enhance the quality of life for those with dementia (Boulton-Lewis, 2012; Field, 2012; BeLL Project, 2014).

The defining of the 3rd Age, for example, in terms of 'quality of life' highlights the acknowledged difficulty of attaching a chronological age to these phases (Laslett, 1989). For some, the 3rd Age begins at age 65, followed by a transition to the 4th Age at about 85 (Tesch-Römer and Wurm, 2012). For others, such as Schuller and Watson (2009), the 3rd Age is conceptualised between the ages of 50 and 75 with the 4th Age comprising those over 75.

However defined, it is expected that the increasing size and the changing composition of the cohort of those in later life, and their new forms of 3rd Age engagement, will have a significant influence on society in the future. Reports, including the *Foresight Mental Capital and Wellbeing Project* (GOScience, 2008) and *The Learning Revolution* (DIUS, 2008b), stress the benefits of older adults being strategically supported to maintain active engagement with the world at large to enhance their wellbeing. Indeed, subjective wellbeing in later life, in which learning can play a positive role, has been linked to optimal ageing (Simone and Hass, 2013).

Later-Life Learning

Within our ageing context, there is an accepted need for initiatives that support older people's wellbeing and productivity (Jamieson, 2007), encompassing strategies that are both supportive and cost-effective in helping to sustain health and wellbeing amongst our older members of the population. Learning in later life has a contribution to make within this arena and has been advocated as a means for supporting independence, developing skills, and enhancing cognitive wellbeing (Glendenning and Battersby, 1990). For example,

Botwinick (1984) indicates that there are many 'avoidable' health stressors in life that can be modified by training or education. In addition to health education, there are many specific areas of learning that have been shown to have direct benefits for older adults engaged in informal later-life learning. For example, Noice et al. (2013) examined 31 studies of participatory arts programmes for older adults including dance, expressive writing, music (singing and instrumental), theatre arts, and visual arts which revealed overwhelmingly positive cognitive and affective outcomes including improvements in memory, creativity, problem solving, everyday competence, reaction time, balance/gait, and quality of life.

The terms 'adult education', 'lifelong education', and 'lifelong learning' are used to portray the changes that adults make in skills, knowledge, aspirations, and attitudes throughout an individual life course. However, these terms are often used interchangeably with little distinction between them (Findsen and Formosa, 2011). For Wain (2009) lifelong learning and lifelong education are not the same thing; the latter, 'education', is considered to be a movement to link learning to formal adult learning facilities through deliberate policy at local, national, and global levels. By contrast, the former, 'learning', is considered the broader concept, which is both lifelong and life-wide. Lifelong learning, therefore, is in all areas of life, not just through educational establishments, and, according to Evans (1991), entails developing equal learning status across formal, informal and non-formal contexts.

Later-life learning has, therefore, forged a place in the world of lifelong learning/adult education but it has been quite a difficult journey. The notion of learning as a significant feature of the 3rd Age only started between 1962 and 1972 (Jarvis, 1990) and those in the 3rd Age have had to demonstrate, or have proven, that they can continue to learn well into very old age (Jarvis, 2001). However, it has gradually become accepted that the mind does not 'cease to function' when individuals retire from work and, indeed, there is now growing evidence that life-long learning actually helps to protect the mind against decline in cognitive functioning (Blakemore and Frith, 2005).

There is empirical evidence of the positive impact adult learning has on improving general mental health (Field, 2009) and the National Institute of Adult Continuing Education (NIACE)-funded research inquiry into the future for lifelong learning (Schuller and Watson, 2009) made a compelling case for the benefits of later-life learning by recognising that learning in later life already: '... makes a major contribution to sustaining economic and social well-being, to enabling people to understand, adapt to and shape change and to promote social justice' (p. 21).

Therefore, there is an urgent need to ensure that where older learners participate, they are engaged in truly effective learning opportunities, ones considered to be of 'quality' in order to maximise the benefits. However, changes to the way in which adult education is funded by the UK government have led to reductions in provider budgets. As a consequence, fewer courses have been available; those on offer carry higher fees and have fewer local centres to work out of. This situation was outlined clearly by the Inquiry into the Future of Lifelong Learning (IFLL) culminating in the Learning Through Life Report (Schuller and Watson, 2009). The enquiry found a system heavily weighted in favour of young, full-time students.

In raw terms, Schuller and Watson (2009) found that for every £55 spent on adult learning in the UK, approximately £47 funded learning for people aged 18–24 years and £6 funded learning for people aged 25–49. In contrast, only £1 was allocated to providing opportunities for learning for people 50–74 years old with £0.29p going towards learning for people 75 years old and older. The imbalance in both the aggregate and the per capita figures was dramatic. This relatively low level of funding to support adult learning may leave the poorer adults leaving full-time work, or other consuming obligations such as caring for children, grandchildren or older adults, without the financial means to participate.

Forms of Learning

Jarvis (1985) saw learning as taking place in three different ways – formally, non-formally, and informally. He saw formal learning as an institutionalised system, which follows a chronological and hierarchical path. Non-formal learning is characterised by being some form of systemised and organised learning activity and is not part of the formal education system. Informal learning, he attested, was simply where a person acquires knowledge and skills from his/her daily experiences. Other commentators have also used such categorisations in their work (Coombs et al., 1973; Coombs, 1985; Merriam and Bierema, 2014).

However, others such as Schuller and Watson (2009) use the term 'informal learning' for non-formal learning and informal learning is, in fact, the more commonly used term in organised groups such as the University of the Third Age (now termed simply, u3a). Therefore I have adopted the following definitions as informal learning, rather than non-formal learning, was a term also recognised and used by later-life learners in my early discussions with older learners.

Formal Learning

Formal learning, or adult education, is, by definition, the formal approach to learning where the emphasis is placed on the provider in terms of organisation, provision and structure whereas with informal learning, the focus is on learners as participants and recipients. Formal learning takes place in an educational institution, with a set curriculum, involves assessment and often leads to qualifications. According to Rogers and Horrocks (2010), formal learning is: '... organised, delivered through structured classes and run by schools, colleges, universities and other statutory and non-statutory agencies making up the educational system' (p. 11).

Informal Learning

Informal learning, which takes place outside formal educational contexts, has a strong connection to 'lifelong learning' and is further distinguished from formal learning by the activities typically being held over short periods of time, being voluntary in nature and taking place in local, easily accessible places. Informal learning has a curriculum in most instances and a tutor too although the latter can be a member of the learning group. Therefore, I define informal learning, as organised and led in some way but not necessarily as a course, not necessarily having progression routes built into the programme and where the emphasis is as much about socialising as learning. Such informal learning opportunities range from Tai Chi exercises and Zumba classes to current affairs discussions and Russian language learning and from painting with watercolours to computing.

The Learning Revolution (2008a) describes a huge variety of *planned* activities and therefore differentiates itself from incidental learning which occurs organically and simply by living, however that takes place. Embracing informal learning in this way, The Learning Revolution (DIUS, 2008b) sought both to raise its status and to promote it. This was because it was seen as important in its own right for many people and not only as an access route to other learning or employment. In describing informal learning it stated:

> Although informal learning can support the development of work related skills, this movement is made up of a kaleidoscope of part-time, non-vocational learning where the primary purpose is not to gain a qualification. People participate for enjoyment and are driven by their desire for personal fulfillment or intellectual creative and physical stimulation.
>
> (*p. 3*)

The participants in informal learning are not objectively assessed or comparatively graded, as they would typically be within formal learning contexts. The 'facilitator' of informal later-life learning may or may not be a qualified teacher and while the facilitator is often paid as a tutor, volunteers can also lead informal learning sessions (Merriam and Bierema, 2014).

If engaging in learning has the potential to foster positive benefits (GOScience, 2008; Withnall, 2010) then we might ask ourselves, what does effective 'informal' learning look like and what do the learners themselves consider are the characteristics contributing to quality learning? Arguably, learning environments where 'quality' is prioritised may be contexts where later-life learners are likely to gain the positive benefits that have been attributed to learning in later life including developing skills and competencies, supporting independence, and contributing to sustained personal fulfilment and wellbeing (Glendenning and Battersby, 1990; Dench and Regan, 2000; Field, 2011). However, the nature and characteristics of 'quality' need to be understood before such a link can be explored fully.

Incidental Learning

As mentioned previously, Jarvis (1985) defined informal learning as the process whereby every person acquires knowledge, skills, attitudes, and aptitudes from daily living. However, this does not necessarily involve the 'permanent capacity change' defined by Illeris (2004) and equates more to 'incidental learning' (Marsick and Watkins, 2001), which is where knowledge or skills are acquired in the course of carrying out an activity, a job, or an everyday task. According to Taylor (2012): 'Incidental learning happens outside the learner's conscious awareness, while informal learning involves a conscious effort on the learner's part such as learning how to play the guitar or taking a self-guided tour of the museum' (p. 14).

Illeris (2004) termed incidental learning 'everyday learning' and described it as an accidental by-product of doing something else, including everyday living, but being not highly structured and where any gains in knowledge or skills may be taken for granted. Incidental learning, therefore, might lead to permanent change but it might not – such learning might be very transient.

Participation in Informal Later-Life Learning

According to a NIACE survey (McNair, 2012), opportunities for informal learning are being taken up by a significant proportion of the older population in the UK. Surveying those aged 50 years or older, McNair reported that one older person in five indicated that they were involved in some form of learning. However, this also indicates that 80% of older people did not perceive themselves to be involved. It is also of interest that half of those 80% of older people 'not learning' said that nothing would have made learning more attractive to them and this position rose to three-quarters for those aged over 75 years of age.

It is notable that the NIACE survey did not investigate the features that would make learning more relevant to those in later life and, in particular, did not explore the factors that would contribute to a quality learning experience. An example of this inattention to, or indifference of, the 'quality' of informal later-life learning can be found in the operation of u3a (formerly The University of the Third Age).

u3a is an international movement of learning cooperatives of older people, which enables members to share many educational, creative, and leisure activities. Membership has increased considerably in recent years and such organisations have increased provision for those wishing to learn in later life, helping to counter the financial constraints placed on many local authorities and universities who have been compelled to cut their non-vocational education provision for adults in response (Withnall, 2016).

The Third Age Trust (as of July 2023) has some 430,000 members in the UK alone. It is a self-help organisation for people no longer in full-time employment, providing educational opportunities in a 'friendly environment' – very often the homes of members. Across the UK, the Third Age Trust consists of over 1,000 local u3as (July 2023), each a charity in its own right, run entirely by volunteers with around 50 new u3as being established each year (http://www.u3a.org.uk). Local u3as are learning cooperatives, which draw upon the knowledge, experience, and skills of their own members to organise and provide self-interest. Between them, u3as offer the chance to study well over 300 different subjects in fields such as art, languages, music, life sciences, computing, crafts, and photography with walking, history, and 'going out' the most popular activities (Withnall, 2016). Overall, the u3a approach is about learning for pleasure (Midwinter, 2003).

However, while being commended for meeting various social needs of older people, the u3a movement has also been critiqued. Formosa (2007), for example, elaborated on how the u3a institutions 'form part of a large microcosm of symbolic institutions that reproduce subtly existing power relations' (p. 3). For example, the large imbalance of women in u3as leaves many older men not wishing to be involved in the organisation (Williamson, 2000) and most u3a programmes do not meet the needs of all older participants but only financially secure people from an 'elite background' (Formosa, 2002).

Furthermore, while much is known about the range, cost, and accessibility of provision from providers such as the u3a, there has been no discernible research into the 'quality' of such provision and especially how later-life learning opportunities meet the needs and expectations of those learning within it. All those setting up u3a groups have to sign up to agree to a mission statement and a set of principles and objectives (Appendix A) none of which focus on features related to learning or the learning environment. Investigating the u3a in Malta, Formosa (1999) critically analysed why the membership of such providers was closely linked to gender, class, and previous exposure to education and concluded that such programmes could no longer be assumed to be examples of good practice. He added that it was not viable to claim that 'any education per se' empowers older learners (Formosa, 2002).

Findsen and Formosa (2011) identified a number of rationales for later-life learning including: the *functional rationale* of learning to aid older persons' adjustment to retirement; the *moral rationale*, which supports access to lifelong learning opportunities as a right; learning as a means of self-fulfilment and personal growth, defined as a *humanistic rationale*; and finally a *critical rationale*, concerned with empowerment and transformation. Learning in later life, therefore, may be viewed from a number of diverse perspectives with regards to how it may positively affect the lives of older people. It has further been argued that participation in later-life learning can enhance both the cognitive and emotional capital of the participants including protecting against cognitive decline and such conditions as depression and anxiety (GOScience, 2008). Indeed, lifelong learning has been promoted as a way of empowering older individuals and supporting their independence and therefore contributing positively to their wellbeing (Dench and Regan, 2000; Withnall, 2010).

Some researchers have theorised and investigated the conditions that support effective learning for adults. Wlodkowski (2008), for example, cites four intersecting motivational conditions that are essential to attend to when teaching adults and being culturally responsive. Alongside enjoyment, he asserts that 'establishing inclusion', 'developing attitude', 'enhancing meaning', and 'engendering confidence' also need to be met if learners are to be fully engaged in the learning process. Indeed, it is the act of 'learning' that has been shown to have positive effects on the lives of older people (Findsen and Formosa, 2011).

However, this does not mean that learning for older adults is without its challenges. For example, Baringer et al. (2004) recognised the challenge to independence and control posed by returning to learning. Individuals grow to be independent in life, but as adults returning to the classroom, they may be influenced by the educational experiences of their youth. Therefore many adults opt for informal learning with its lack of formality, structure, and assessment with some railing against their negative memories of schooling and even its 'reliance for discipline on adult violence' (Withnall, 2010, p. 47). Nevertheless, according to Kolland (2013), for many older adults:

> Lifelong learning in the post-retirement phase can be taken as a statement against the deficit model of ageing, against a solely work-related view of learning and as a statement for a self-determined way of living.
>
> *(p. 117)*

Motivation for Informal Learning in Later Life

The population of later-life learners is very diverse but it may be still possible to identify some characteristics that would appear to apply to most of the group and to those in the 3rd Age in particular. The most obvious element amongst older adult learners in informal learning is that they voluntarily choose to undertake learning; the second element is that they bring a range of experiences and knowledge with them. Houle (1961) characterised the motivations to undertake adult learning along a continuum of three 'orientations to learning' related to their present pattern of life. This continuum of orientations ranged from those who wish to undertake it to gain some form of accreditation (goal orientated) at one end to those who come for social or personal reasons (activity orientated) at the other. These learner states are summarised as:

a goal-orientated learners whose intention is the achievement of some end product or the solving of some problem,
b learning-orientated learners whose intention is simply to pursue an interest in a subject,
c activity-orientated learners whose intention is to satisfy social or personal growth needs.

Individually, of course, later-life learners have many and varied personal reasons for undertaking some form of study (Withnall, 2010). For some learners, it may well be the satisfying of particular needs that underpin both their motivation and their continuing engagement (Boshier, 1991). However, as Rogers and Horrocks (2010) highlight, the implications for the 'teacher' of the differing intentions of each of these three orientations are considerable, as the responses of each kind of learner to the demands of the learning programme will vary.

Personal Needs

According to Merriam and Bierema (2014), the most potent motivators for adults to learn are internal rather than external and include enhanced self-esteem, improved quality of life, and personal fulfilment. In adults who are internally motivated, the goal of learning, for Maslow (1970), is self-actualisation, which he describes as 'the desire to become more and more what one is, to become everything that one is capable of becoming' (Maslow, 1954, p. 92). Rogers (1969) also felt learning needed to be self-initiated and the goal was to develop a 'fully-functioning' person.

On such assertions, a range of 'motivation' theories were developed (Ahl, 2006) including a theory by Baltes (1997), which was focused specifically on older people. Baltes was interested in the reasons behind cognitive decline in old age and discovered the connection between the declines in sensory and cognitive functioning. Successful ageing, as successful development in general, he asserted, was defined as the maximisation and attainment of desired outcomes and the minimisation and avoidance of undesired outcomes. He created a general framework for the understanding of developmental change and resilience across the lifespan (Baltes, 1997). His framework builds on the assumption that throughout the entire lifespan, people encounter certain opportunity structures, such as education, as well as limitations in resources such as illnesses, that can be mastered adaptively by an orchestration of three components: selection, optimisation, and compensation (SOC) (Freund and Baltes, 1998).

Selection involves accepting the limitation of resources such as time and energy inherent to human existence, especially as people get older. Ageing necessitates the selection of goals because not all opportunities can be pursued (Carstensen et al., 1995). Optimisation is defined as the allocation and refinement of internal or external resources as a means of achieving higher-level goals (Freund and Baltes, 1998). Finally, compensation, when used to confront the loss of resources or the decline of goal-relevant means in a selected goal, refers to substitutive processes needed to maintain a given level of functioning in the targeted goal (Baltes, 1997).

However, Ahl (2006) challenges the assumption that motivation is a phenomenon existing within the individual learner because it suggests a deficit when it is perceived as not being present. Instead Ahl (2006) contends that motivation lies in the relationship between the learners and those providing learning opportunities that have their own motives. Her critical assessment of adult learning motivation literature (Ahl, 2006) reveals that motivation theories often 'stigmatize' people as 'unmotivated' because problems in motivation are only attributed to the individual. This assertion, concerning the sharing of responsibility for motivation between the learner and those providing the learning, offers an important counter-narrative to the dominant discourse about 'unmotivated' learners.

To address the challenges to facilitate learning for later-life learners, there is an imperative to understand, and take steps to address, their needs both as individuals and as older learners. For example, Jones and Bayen (1998) suggest that tutors provide more time and encouragement for learner questions as research has demonstrated, for example, that older adults are four times more likely to request assistance than younger adults (Elias et al., 1987). Daines et al. (1993) suggest that older adults, involved in formal adult education, learn best when they feel secure, they can try things out in safety and their needs are being met in ways that they can see are relevant and appropriate.

According to Daines et al. (1993), older learners need to know what they are required to do; especially where they have been involved in setting their own goals and so are actively involved and engaged. Indeed, having autonomy and control is one of three factors leading to a model of self-perceived wellbeing in older people (Creech et al., 2014a) alongside a sense of purpose (having opportunities, feeling positive) in life and social affirmation (the need for affection, behavioural confirmation, and status).

Barriers to Later-Life Learning

For many older adults, certain 'barriers' can inhibit their participation in later-life learning and may even act in tandem, thus compounding the difficulty for individuals. In preventing many older people from taking part, these barriers also prevent them from gaining the benefits that learning can bring and, perhaps, being more engaged with, or participating in, later life at all. Darkenwald and Merriam (1982) provide a useful categorisation of elements that prevent people from undertaking learning in later life, classifying them as:

- Situational – barriers related to the circumstances experienced by a person at a particular time such as a life crisis.
- Institutional – barriers (unintentionally) erected by learning organisations that function to exclude certain groups.
- Informational – barriers arising from the failure of an agency to properly communicate the learning opportunities it has to offer.
- Psychosocial – barriers, which are disproportional or attitudinal beliefs, perceptions or values that inhibit a person's participation.

Therefore, although this research is not concerned with barriers to learning as such, if there are barriers to engagement, they could be due to factors in the learning environment leading to a learning opportunity being limited in its 'quality'. Research has shown those more likely to access later-life learning have relatively high prior qualifications, are female and are in good health (Aldridge and Tuckett, 2010; Jenkins and Mostafa, 2012). McNair (2012) suggested that there might be additional factors that act as barriers to participation amongst these groups such as lower levels of confidence or the lack of the funding necessary to join in informal learning opportunities.

A Theoretical Framework for Learning in Later Life

According to Schuller and Watson (2009), learning is arguably what humans do best. They go on to say:

> Individuals cannot survive without learning, nor can societies. Not all learning is good. There are many habits and practices, which are repeatedly learned – even systematically taught – that are unpleasant or even evil. But without learning in almost all its diversity we would literally not be human. (p. 7)

Interestingly, Ozuah (2005) reminds us that 'all the great teachers of ancient times were teachers of adults not children' (p. 84).

Through the last half of the twentieth century, one major theoretical framework perspective in the later-life learning field emerged in the form of critical geragogy (Battersby and Glendenning, 1992; Battersby, 1993). Arising out of the overview of learning theory in general, and adult learning theory in particular, it is this perspective of the coming together of critical theory and geragogy that frames my study. The following sections discuss the emergence of critical geragogy and its relationship to critical pedagogy, critical educational gerontology (CEG), and geragogy.

Critical Pedagogy

Critical pedagogy is a philosophy of education and social movement that has developed and applied concepts from critical theory and related traditions to the field of education (Kincheloe and Steinburg, 1997). Such advocates reject the neutrality of knowledge and insist that issues of social justice and democracy itself are not distinct from acts of teaching and learning.

The concept of critical pedagogy can be traced back to Freire (1970) who aimed to examine issues of relational power in the education of adults and workers with the goal of creating not only a better learning environment but also a better world. In doing so Freire endorsed students' ability to think critically about their education situation to allow them to 'recognize connections between their individual problems and experiences and the social contexts in which they are embedded'. For Burbules and Burk (1999), in critical pedagogy everything is open to critical reflection except the premises and categories of critical pedagogy itself. In further developing this philosophy, Giroux (2010a) espoused that Freire believed that 'all education in the broadest sense was part of a project of freedom, and eminently political because it offered students the conditions for self-reflection, a self-managed life, and particular notions of critical agency' (p. 716).

(Critical) Educational Gerontology

Peterson (1976) first defined 'educational gerontology' as the integration of the institutions and processes of education with the knowledge of human ageing and the needs of older people. For Findsen and Formosa (2011), educational gerontology can be considered to be: '... instrumental and expressive, formal and informal, for and about older people, a study and a practice, remedial and preventative. However, it is always designed as a positive approach to helping people better understand and assist themselves' (p. 54).

CEG has a direct connection with critical pedagogy – the philosophy of education and social movement that combines education with critical theory (first described by Paulo Freire (1970, 1973)) described previously. As Freire heavily endorsed students' ability to think critically about their education situation, guided by passion and principle, to help them develop consciousness of freedom, recognise authoritarian tendencies, and connect knowledge to power and the ability to take constructive action (Giroux, 1994).

The decade following the establishment of the theory of critical pedagogy, the 1980s, was characterised by a growing awareness of increasing age discrimination and the powerlessness of retirees (Formosa, 2002). This led to the development of a critical approach within educational gerontology. By focusing attention on three interlocking components – knowledge, power and control – CEG asks questions such as why we teach, who controls the learning process, and whose interests are being served? (Findsen and Formosa, 2011).

Nevertheless, CEG arose as a new theoretical perspective concerning the 'emancipation' of adult learners. It has been credited to Phillipson (1983) who argued that the aim of education should be to illuminate the social and political rights of old age. Glendenning and Battersby (1990) also challenged the notion, of educational gerontology as the prevailing conventional wisdom about learning in old age, in six areas:

1 The tendency to regard older people as a relatively homogeneous group.
2 The tendency to base programmes for older people on the concept of need, thereby legitimising the psychological deficit model of older adults' learning abilities.
3 The assumption that education can be an effective intervention strategy for ensuring older people's wellbeing.
4 The lack of philosophical debate as to why older people should be educated.
5 The belief that education, in whatever mode, is a neutral enterprise and is inherently good for older people.
6 In view of the marginalisation of older people in society, whether the amount of effort spent lobbying for greater access to resources could be justified given that later-life education was not on the political agenda.

This overt patronisation highlighted by Glendenning and Battersby (1990) came about in part, through prevalent thinking about learning in old age as a deficit model as Formosa (2011) indicates:

> The critical epistemology in ageing studies emerged as a reaction to the dominant 'decline and loss' paradigm that views ageing as a series of decrements to which both older adults and society need to adjust (Havinghurst, 1953). This paradigm stresses the need for older adults to find new roles following the end of work and independence of their children by either re-engaging in earlier roles or taking on new responsibilities.
>
> *(p. 325)*

Percy (1990), however, put forward an alternative 'humanistic' viewpoint suggesting that the aims and purposes of education and learning for older people should, in fact, be no different from those of people of any age group. He viewed those in old age as equally capable of being the teachers themselves, facilitating learning with their peers and acting as 'educational resources' for each other – an idea that underpins the U3A ethos. Where both approaches (educational gerontology and CEG) agree, however, is that learning has a role to play in retaining the independence of adults into later life and supporting their continued participation in decision-making about themselves.

Therefore, CEG, as a theoretical framework, is not itself concerned with whether older people can be taught or can learn or indeed how this should take place. Instead, it is concerned with the political structures and powers that underpin such learning and the role of the older people themselves to shape the social system in which it is established. Indeed, the work of King et al. (1984) described this role as embracing 'criticality', arguing that in older age, learners show a gradual movement from accepting knowledge presented by known authorities to a more relativist attitude where solutions need to be evaluated in context. In this way, older people become empowered, are able to live independently and engage in active ageing.

Geragogy

Almost contemporaneously, Lebel (1978) argued that older adults are sufficiently different to warrant a separate educational theory. In doing so he coined the term 'geragogy' which sought to identify the teaching styles most suited to the oldest section of society rather than adults per se. However such a position received some criticism; according to Peterson (1983): 'Although some would argue that older people are so distinctive that a special methodology should be created for them ... it is neither practice nor necessary to separate older learners too completely from middle-age learners' (p. 149).

Although accepting this position, that learning is a lifelong activity and older adults are not so distinctive to merit a special methodology, Findsen and Formosa (2011) assert that older adults do inhabit a physical, psychic and social realm that is, to some extent, different from that experienced by middle-aged adults. From their perspective, there is a need to fine-tune adult teaching and learning to aid the learning experiences of older adults. As such, where adults are generally post-work and post-family, and sometimes frail or with intellectual limitations, instructors are required to become sensitive to the unique characteristics of older learners and to tailor their instructional plans accordingly.

Wlodkowski (1999), for example, suggests older adults thrive in learning experiences embedded in respectful relationships and a culture of inclusion. Peterson (1983) suggested course material should be presented in a way, which reflects the world rather than abstract components. Although the term 'geragogy' was coined to identify the teaching styles most suited to the oldest section of society (Lebel, 1978) as opposed to adults more generally, it embraces many of the features associated with teaching younger adult learners.

Critical Geragogy

The concept of 'geragogy', referring to the management of teaching and learning for older adults (Formosa, 2002) as outlined previously, contrasted with the work of John (1983, 1988) who, in further developing the notion of geragogy, identified teaching strategies and learning activities that were designed simply to stimulate older adults. This view of pedagogy as a top-down, teacher-directed activity promoted the idea of older learners as a homogeneous group and fed a deficit view of dependent older people.

This notion was successfully challenged (Battersby, 1987; Findsen and Formosa, 2011) through the advocating of a critical geragogy framework, which challenges beliefs and practices related to ageing and embraces the securing of individual freedoms and the retention of control by older adults into later life. Critical geragogy challenges the assumptions of old age as a time of 'deficit' and older learners being dependent. Instead it promotes the idea that learning in later life can lead older people to greater personal control and autonomy by being 'critical' and able to challenge the beliefs that can determine how they live their lives (Glendenning and Battersby, 1990). In proposing a set of principles for the practice of critical geragogy, Formosa (2002) invokes the concept of where learning also includes reflection by older learners, through learning, about themselves and their roles in 'ageist societal structures'. Indeed, such 'transformational' learning 'shapes people; they are different afterwards in ways both they and others can recognize' (Clark, 1993, p. 47).

Transformational Education

Transformational education is considered to be a form of learning engaged in by adults that 'has brought a new and exciting identify to the field of adult education' (Cranston and Taylor, 2012). For Mezirow (2000) transformative learning is:

> ... a process by which we transform our taken-for-granted frames of reference (meaning schemes, habits of mind, mindsets) to make them more inclusive, discriminating, open, emotionally capable of change and reflective so that they may generate beliefs and opinions that will prove more true or justified to guide actions.
>
> *(p. 8)*

Such 'transformational 'learning' has been defined in many forms. Illeris (2004) offers a synthesized model, drawing on a number of learning theories under his three general dimensions of learning – cognitive, psychodynamic (emotional), and social-societal. In surveying this field, Illeris (2007) defined learning as: '... any process that in living organisms leads to *permanent capacity change* and which is not solely due to biological maturation or ageing' (p. 3).

Illeris (2009) considered learning to be not only a matter of the nature of the learning process itself, as previous theories have done, but all the conditions that influence, and are influenced by, the process of learning. These include all the psychological, biological, and social conditions, which underpin his three dimensions of learning (cognitive, psychodynamic, social), which, he proposes, are omnipresent. In any given context, there may be dominance of any of these dimensions.

This recognition of the factors other than the 'cognitive' influencing the learning process resonates with the dynamic model of adult learning proposed by Yang (2003). Drawing on the transformative nature of human existence, Yang postulated that learning is powerfully influenced by feelings and emotions. Yang (2003) proposed that each of his three facets – conceptual knowledge, perceptual knowledge, and affectual knowledge – needs the other facets to make sense of human learning. Conceptual knowledge (information), he suggested, would be of little relevance without being connected to what a person has already learned through experience (perceptual knowledge) and how motivated a person is to know that information (affectual knowledge).

My own research is underpinned by an understanding of learning as a range of processes within the three dimensions of learning (cognitive, psychodynamic, and social) outlined by Illeris (2007). As he attests that they are always present, and for all groups of learners in any learning, they exist in the informal later-life learning environment too. This includes the great variety of contexts later-life learning takes place in, the great diversity of such a heterogeneous group (Glendenning and Battersby, 1990), and the great diversity in 'biological and environmental factors influencing lifelong learning' (Baltes et al., 1980).

Although acknowledging that emotions, intuition, contact, and relationships play a role in the transformational learning process, Baumgartner (2012) states that they are still secondary to the critical cognitive aspects. However, this adult learning theory is not without its critics. Newman (2012) questioned the very existence of such a theory as being 'all things to all people' (p. 49) and instead talks about 'good learning'. One of his main reasons for doubting its existence is that 'transformation can only be verified by the learners themselves' (p. 39) and that in telling their stories of transformation their 'stories' can 'contain invention as well as record' (p. 40). Therefore, according to Merriam and Bierema (2014), the issue is not belief in transformative learning, with its power to change the way people see the world and perhaps change for the better, but how to facilitate this kind of learning in adults and then to evaluate its outcomes.

The Quality Cirque (Part 1)

Figure 3.1 summarises key elements of the framework of critical geragogy for learning in later life as one component in a Quality Cirque. This is a diagrammatic representation of four key ingredients contributing to quality informal later-life learning arising out of this research. They are presented as a small circle (a cirque) as one component is linked to the next. Continually paying appropriate attention to each component can contribute to constantly increasing the quality of learning taking place. This first quarter identifies critical geragogy,

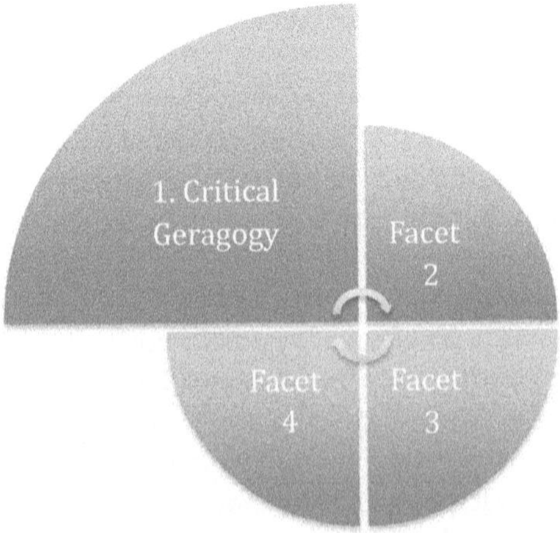

Facet 1	Critical Geragogy

- The *empowerment* of learners to make decisions about their learning
- The *independence* of learners taking control over when and how they learn
- The *transformation* of learners through acquiring knowledge and skills
- The *engagement* of learners through motivation and being active learners

FIGURE 3.1 The quality cirque for informal later-life learning (part 1).

which involves empowering those in later life to retain or take control of their lives and remain independent of thought and actions as long as possible.

This occurs through the 'transformation' that learning can bring about, involving both 'cognitive' change and emotional change through participation and reflection. This involves the engagement of those in later-life learning from decision-making about context to learning strategies to evaluation of progress. The other three components in the 'quality cirque', which together 'unpack' the constituents underpinning quality informal later-life learning, will be identified as the thesis unfolds.

The Learner Voice

The learner voice is aligned with a critical geragogy perspective by enabling later-life learners to articulate for themselves the features they value in learning and in doing so reinforcing their power to effect change through active participation. I argued in Chapter 2 that the methodological paradigm used in this study is a logical way of embracing this underpinning theoretical framework for later-life learning.

Withnall and Percy (1994) suggested that the role of facilitators of older learners is to discover what participants wish to achieve and to provide an enabling physical and psychosocial environment that meets those goals. However, it is evident that the needs of the older adult section of the community are often not known or, if known, are not heeded. This was recognised, in the UK, at a national level in 2008 when it was announced that Dame Joan Bakewell, a television personality and writer, was engaged by the UK government to act as the Voice of Older People at the age of 76 and represent the views of older people on matters of concern.

The importance of listening to, and capturing the authentic voice of, older learners was reinforced through the major investments the UK research councils made in the New Dynamics of Ageing (NDA) Programme, which, as the earlier Growing Older Programme from 1999 to 2004, broke new ground in its time by commissioning 24 projects all focusing on aspects of quality of life in old age and contributing to policy and practice in the field (NDA, 2013). One of the distinguishing features of the NDA Programme was that older people were involved directly not just as objects of study but also as participants in the whole research programme through an Older People's Reference Group. This group met throughout the lifetime of the programme and, through making their voice heard, made an active contribution to local, national, and international events.

In accordance with the principles of critical geragogy, and the moves towards prioritising the voices of older people, I gathered the views and accounts of personal learning experiences amongst later-life learners. The methodology I adopted included discussions with individuals and groups of later-life learners. In particular, I used focus groups because this was a forum where groups of learners could collectively construct their accounts of 'quality'. Focus groups were particularly important as a space where older people could be 'heard', not discriminating against those with low levels of literacy and encouraging participation from those who may be reticent or lack confidence in one-on-one interview situations (Kitzinger, 1995).

Summary

This chapter has outlined the changing democratic profile leading to the increased numbers, actual and relative, of older people in society and the need to research how society can best adjust to their needs, especially in the field of learning. The parameters of the participants have been outlined and the benefits of engagement of the learner voice, finding out what the older learners themselves think, have been raised. It is with this focus on listening directly to what the learners say that the methodological approach used in this study was adopted.

Although there are increasing numbers of people living in an active later-life period, the 3rd Age, factors such as diminishing accessibility, higher costs and less external support have helped to staunch any increase in the percentage actively learning (McNair, 2012). Therefore, large numbers of older people, and especially the oldest old (post-75 years of age), are potentially not gaining the benefits of learning in later life identified through research. At the same time, not enough is known about what makes the process of learning most effective; in particular, what factors in the learning environment can support sustained activity and cognitive and emotional wellbeing amongst the learners.

This chapter has also clarified the types of learning taking place in later life and outlined both how 'informal' learning is being defined for the purposes of this study and the nature of it. It also outlines how older adults differ from younger learners and how a more appropriate teaching and learning approach (geragogy) might be adapted to take into account both their learning needs and their personal needs.

The 'transformation' associated with critical geragogy embraces the focus on cognitive change identified by Illeris (2007) and the emotional involvement invoked by Yang (2003) through critical reflection. Such an approach may well help to overcome some of the barriers to participation outlined and lead to the identification of how greater numbers of learners, especially the disadvantaged and less educated, can benefit from learning in the future. A rationale for my research is that such benefits may be more readily accessed and gained if the learning was of the 'quality' that later-life learners say they value. The benefits that later-life learning can bring and the quality of such learning are explored in more detail in the following chapter.

4

THE BENEFITS OF LATER-LIFE LEARNING

Introduction

In this chapter, I summarise the wider benefits that are associated with later-life learning and examine the key messages from literature with regard to the contexts within which such beneficial learning has been found to take place. I approached my research with a broad interest in what was valued in the later-life learners' experiences of learning. Following the initial Feasibility Study, I focused more specifically on the idea of what was perceived as quality in informal later-life learning. My rationale for discussing the wider benefits identified in later-life learning (Dench and Regan, 2000; Field, 2011) is that it is important to understand just what those wider benefits might be in order for those understandings to inform notions of quality in learning experiences. Here, I present the reported gains from later-life learning under the headings of cognitive, health, social, and psychological benefits. In the final section, I discuss how research has offered key messages about the environmental context in which such benefits occur.

Research into the Benefits of Later-Life Learning

There has been a growing body of evidence since the late 1990s concerning the benefits of later-life learning (Glendenning and Battersby, 1990; Rowe and Kahn, 1999; GOScience, 2008; Withnall, 2010). One strand of research drew upon the rich data available in longitudinal birth cohort studies (Schuller et al., 2004), identifying adult learning as a positive influence on life satisfaction and wellbeing, the increased retention of mental processes, and the absence of chronic diseases (Merriam, 2001). However, there has been relatively

DOI: 10.4324/9781003269892-4

limited research that has focused on the teaching strategies and environmental factors that maximise those benefits, especially in informal learning, and very little that accounts for the learners' perspective.

Lifelong learning in the 1990s was the basis for a new international debate about the role of education and training in relation to the perceived need for economic competitiveness in the face of globalisation, especially within the European Union (Brine, 2006). However, research began to identify other beneficial outcomes apart from the economic (Schuller and Field, 1998) and since the late 1990s, there has been a growing body of work on the wider, non-economic benefits of learning (Blunden et al., 2010; Jenkins, 2011). Rowe and Kahn (1999), for example, asserted that education is guaranteed to help in the development of coping skills and strategies for solving problems which, in turn, help to offset the cognitive effects of normal ageing and delay the clinical symptoms associated with dementia. Duncan (2015) identified a 'breadth' to the range of benefits from learning: '... from mental health to community participation, from making "close friends" to "getting out of the house", from relaxation to skill development and from increased "confidence to greater awareness of other cultures"' (p. 6).

While no one can stop the ageing process, there are some factors that have been associated with increased retention of mental processes: namely education, exercise, absence of chronic diseases and illnesses, and involvement in activities to stimulate the brain (Merriam, 2001). While it is evident that some older adults are not as quick to learn new things as younger people (Cozolino and Sprokay, 2006), neuroscientific research has now identified that older people can often compensate for this reduced processing speed through a wealth of experiences that tend to support superior reasoning and judgement abilities if given time to think and reflect on the learning activity (Strauch, 2010).

However, longitudinal studies, although providing some important contributions, are based on a narrow range of data sources (Field, 2011) and reveal very little about the pathways and processes through which such contributions were made (Jenkins and Mustafa, 2013).

A Rationale for Later-Life Learning – the Benefits

Although my discussion of the link between later-life learning and benefits is organised under cognitive, health, social and psychological sub-headings they are, however, not totally distinctive just as the benefits arising from later-life learning are not always associated with just one field of research.

Cognitive Benefits

The human brain is made up of billions of nerve cells (neurons) with a highly complex web of connections between them transmitting messages through electrical impulses and the movement of chemicals across minute gaps known as synapses (Gibb, 2012). According to Blakemore and Frith (2005): 'Thirty years ago, scientists believed that the structure of the brain develops in childhood and once organization of the brain has emerged, there is very little room for changes and for plastic alterations' (p. 123).

More recent research has shown, however, that the brain can, when stimulated, continue to grow new cells (neurogenesis) and connections and, in addition, that existing connections can also be strengthened throughout life (Perry, 2006).

Research into brain function in older adults too has moved on significantly over the last 15 years benefitting from brain-imaging techniques such as Functional Magnetic Resonance Imaging (fMRI) and Positron Emission Tomography (PET). According to Blackmore and Frith (2005), such work has shown that the adult brain, in certain regions at least, is almost as pliable as a child's brain and that such brain 'plasticity' enables the nervous system to continually adapt to changing circumstances that happen, for example, when we learn something new.

According to Blakemore and Frith (2005), with every new experience the human brain slightly rewires its physical structure and learning provides opportunities for this to happen. A stronger brain with many connections does not only function better but when conditions such as dementia, or diseases such as Alzheimer's, occur stronger brains are both in a better position to resist these degenerative diseases and better able to compensate for their effects by using other, unaffected parts of the brain (Wilson, 2002; Graham and Warner, 2009).

Linking Neuroscience and Education

In addition to the body of research supporting learning as a way of maintaining or developing cognitive functions in later life (Dench and Regan, 2000; Field, 2011), Schuller and Watson (2009) argue that learning provides opportunities for the maintenance of independence and 'active ageing'. Such positive effects of learning are in addition to the many benefits of learning as reported by leading researchers in the field from improved cognitive performance (Hultsch et al., 1993), enhanced wellbeing (Field, 2009) and improved self-confidence and levels of social engagement (McNair, 2012). Research by Brayne et al. (2010) reported that although more education did not protect individuals from developing neurodegenerative and vascular neuropathology per se, by the time they died, it did appear to mitigate the impact of pathology on the clinical expression of dementia before death. Put simply by Marmot (2004), 'the higher the education, the longer people are likely to live and the better their health is likely to be' (p. 15).

Cognitive Reserve

Kandel (2006) asserted that while a sensory neuron has, on average, 1300 connections to around 25 other cells, only about 40% of these connections are active. If the sensory neuron is continually stimulated these will increase to 2,700 connections with 60% active (which is more than 300% activation). Conversely, if these connections are not used, they will shrink (Kandel, 2006). However, they may remain physically intact and so can activate again quickly if needed. Therefore, the old and simple phrase 'use it or lose it' has gained a new meaning in the age of cellular neural plasticity.

Furthermore, recent research has added credence to the notion of education being one of the most prominent producers of this extra 'brain power'. For example, an MRI study amongst adult military recruits in Sweden showed that learning a foreign language caused the brain to increase in size (Mårtensson et al., 2012) and researchers at Edinburgh University identified that the bilingual benefits of learning a second language hold true no matter when in life you learn it (Bak et al., 2014). Therefore, it appears people are not just born with cognitive reserve; it is a malleable element of the brain and we can boost reserve even when we are older – and do so by learning. The importance of reaping such a 'boost' to our cognitive reserve is brought into stark relief by the research of Bonsang et al. (2010) who found the very act of 'retirement' starts a decrease in an individual's cognitive capacity. Therefore, maintaining the so-called 'cognitive reserve' via intellectual occupations, engagement in leisure and social activities as well as on-going educational activities is important throughout adult life (Sauter et al., 2019; Peeters et al., 2020).

Health Benefits

Much has been written on the health benefits of learning in later life and some examples are provided here. It is now established that learning of any kind contributes strongly to mental and physical health and wellbeing (Robotham et al., 2011). However, it is a complex area, needs further research and can best be described as a 'dialectic' relationship – one in which it is difficult to establish a definitive cause and effect (Findsen and Formosa, 2011).

Health and Later-Life Learning

The relationship between learning (education) and health can also be described as a two-way process: increased knowledge through learning leads to better health (Field, 2009) while healthy older adults are more likely to reap the benefits to be gleaned from learning by being able to attend regularly, be less likely to suffer from the debilitating effects of stress on learning (Perry, 2006) and benefit from a healthy blood flow to the brain (Banks, 2006).

Education is a major component of psychotherapy for psychological trauma where individuals learn reflective skills and develop insights into their inner world (Ross, 2006). Transformative learning (Mezirow et al., 1990, 2000) discusses these same techniques, challenging assumptions and restructuring belief systems. According to Ross (2006) 'we know from brain imaging that these techniques of psychotherapy change and repair the brain' (p. 31).

Articulating the benefits to health from increased learning, Feinstein and Hammond (2004) recognised improvements in health brought about by improvements in health knowledge. For example, learning about good health through health promotions advocating a healthy diet, less smoking, and regular exercise would improve the chances of older adults making choices that would benefit their health greatly. Aldridge and Lavender (2000) indicated that the benefits of learning also included more direct improvements in physical health.

Informal learning embraces a range of courses, many of which involve physical exercise in classes such as Tai Chi and dancing and through outdoor activities such as rambling. Steady aerobic exercise, over months and years, produces dramatic improvements in a person's circulatory system, which, according to Crowley and Lodge (2007) 'is one way [that] exercise saves your life' (p. 100). Improved blood flow around the body provides the steady flow of oxygen that a healthy active brain requires while during exercise the brain releases chemicals such as endorphins, known as 'feel good' hormones. These secretions are important in regulating pain perception as well as regulating emotion including helping to prevent depression (Banks, 2006). Thus, participation in informal learning that involves physical activity may have particularly salient health benefits.

Finally, adult education has been shown to increase social capital, for example, in terms of people's engagement with community activities and voting behaviours and these increased levels of social capital are in turn associated with better health (Feinstein et al., 2003). The benefits of enhanced social capital are discussed in the next section as part of the social benefits of learning. The value of social capital is stressed by Hafford-Letchfield (2009) who suggests that 'lifelong learning impacts upon a range of health and social care outcomes such as wellbeing, recovery from mental-ill health, the capacity to cope with stress inducing circumstances and the onset and progression of chronic illness and disability' (p. 3).

Social Benefits

Through her research amongst older adults, Berkman (2000) highlighted that social engagement challenges individuals to communicate and to participate in exchanges that stimulate cognitive capacities. There is significant evidence of the benefits of social interaction and social networks to stimulate and enhance learning (Dawson and Baller, 1972; Chène, 1994; Mangrum and Mangrum,

1995). Informal later-life learning is a social activity and across several countries and cultures, older people who participate in social activities have been found to benefit from access to socio-emotional support and a reduced risk of social isolation and loneliness (Betts Adams et al., 2011).

Specific examples of the social benefits from collaborative learning can be drawn from subjects such as music (Hallam et al., 2011). For example, VanderArk et al. (1983) investigated the relationship between wellbeing and music-making in a residential nursing home. In this study, 20 participants aged 60 to 95 were assigned to the experimental group, while a further 23, matched for age, were assigned to a control group where there was no music-making, simply social discussion. Significant improvements amongst the experimental group were reported, including more positive life satisfaction. Such benefits did not arise in the control group identifying that learning together as a social activity is different, and more beneficial, that just being together in a group. In such learning, according to Dench and Regan (2000), teachers of all stages, ages, and subjects must be ambitious for, and expert in, developing their student's abilities in speaking and listening, giving them time to use speech to unpack and share their thoughts with one another.

Social Capital

Lifelong learning has been analysed as instrumental in the creation of social capital (Coleman, 1988; Schuller et al., 2000). The view that there may be a link between lifelong learning and social capital has now been supported through brain analysis, using fMRI scans, showing the direct positive impact of social engagement on the brain. According to Cozolino and Sprokay (2006), writing on neuroscience and adult learning:

> It is becoming more evident that through emotional facial expressions, physical contact and eye gaze ... people are in constant, if often unconscious, two-way communication with those around them. It is in the matrix of this contact that brains are sculpted, balanced and made healthy.
>
> *(p. 13)*

They go on to say that among the many possible implications of this finding for the adult educational environment is that a caring, aware mentor may support the plasticity that leads to better, more meaningful learning. Participation in learning also tends to enhance social capital by helping develop social competences, extend social networks, and promote shared norms and the tolerance of others (Schuller et al., 2004). According to Rowe and Kahn's (1999) model of successful ageing, such active engagement with life is an essential ingredient to growing older in a positive, healthy manner.

Psychological Benefits

There has been a great deal of interest over recent years in the concept of psychological wellbeing and numerous attempts both to define and quantify it. Indeed, there have been attempts at definitions by bodies such as the Organisation for Economic Co-operation and Development (OECD), the European Commission, and the UK Office for National Statistics among others (Vanhoutte, 2012). There is also an increasing body of evidence arising from academic research focusing on the factors that influence psychological wellbeing, including the positive effects of learning (Field, 2009).

Mental Health

In a review of community learning, McGivney (1999) reported that participation in learning had positive consequences for mental health and in a further study by Cooper et al. (2010), learning was shown to lead to increased wellbeing and to be associated with better health as well as higher levels of social and civic engagement.

It has also been argued that before learning can occur, a basic requirement is the feeling of safety and inclusion (Strange and Banning, 2001). According to Perry (2006), the learner needs to be 'right for learning' as, if stressed, the mind focuses only on what is the threat at the time rather than exploring new things. In stressful instances, the learner becomes disinterested and overwhelmed by new things and novelty (Perry, 2006). Conversely, when we feel safe in the world around us, we crave novelty although if this novelty is 'too new' then we crave familiarity – things that are comforting, safe and secure in order that we get the most from the learning experience (Daloz, 1999). In such cases, by accurately attending to the learner's internal state, an effective educator can identify where the learner is on the 'alarm-arousal continuum'. Perry (2006) goes on to say: 'A creative and respectful educator can create safety by making the learning environment more familiar, structured and predictable. Predictability in turn, is created by consistent behaviour' (p. 27).

However, the reduction of stress does not necessitate the elimination of 'risk'. According to Lightfoot (1997) risk-taking within the context of learning is defined as: '... a way of framing the world, where it is imaginative, inventive, uncertain, and goes beyond the ordinary and predictable in ways that can titillate, excite, and very often frighten ... oriented toward some uncertain and wished-for future' (p. 1).

Risk is also seen as being a vital part of learning (Asen, 2004; Biesta, 2007) exerting positive influences on learning and development in individual, organisational, and societal contexts (Reio, 2007).

Wellbeing

The government report of the Office of the Chief Scientist into Mental Capital and Wellbeing, the *Foresight Report* (GOScience, 2008) concluded that individual wellbeing is enhanced if individuals do five simple things: connecting, being active, taking notice, giving and, significantly for this research, learning. The latter proposal was supplemented with the advice:

> Try something new. Rediscover an old interest. Sign up for that course. Take on a different responsibility at work. Fix a bike. Learn to play an instrument or how to cook your favourite food. Set a challenge you enjoy achieving.
>
> *(GOScience, 2008, p. 23)*

The background papers to the Foresight Report, it says, provide evidence to show that learning can help to promote wellbeing, as well as protecting against normal age-related cognitive decline. Importantly, it goes on to say that when learning takes place in social settings, it can promote wellbeing indirectly through social networking. However, although quantitative analysis cannot yet yield precise estimates of the size of the positive effect of learning on wellbeing, research continues to identify positive effects of learning such as the simple use of Information and Communication Technology (ICT) contributing significantly to older adults' wellbeing (Damant et al., 2017).

Finally, although research does not measure wellbeing directly, it does identify factors that could be seen to be causal or are perceived to be so. As later life is increasing in length for most people, and providing increased opportunities within an enhanced life course, the impact of learning in later life is becoming, according to Schuller and Watson (2009), 'increasingly interesting and important'. This increasing evidence of the extent of the benefits of learning in later life has also led to increased interest in research in this area.

The Learning Environment for Later-Life Learning

This chapter has, thus far, identified the reported benefits of learning in later life from enhanced life satisfaction (Schuller et al., 2004) and improved coping skills (Rowe and Kahn, 1999) to improved cognitive performance (Hultsch et al., 1993) and offsetting the likelihood of dementia (Graham and Warner, 2009). At the same time, it has also offered key messages about the context in which such benefits occur such as learning together (social learning) (McNair, 2012) and learning in stress-free environments (Perry, 2006).

Informal later-life learning, however, takes place in a variety of settings, many of which are not designed for that purpose. The 'physical' context represents a learning environment that Hiemstra (1991) defines as 'all of the physical surroundings, psychological or emotional conditions, and social or cultural influences affecting the growth and development of an adult engaged in an educational enterprise'. It may be possible that the wider benefits of learning would be more fully experienced if the learning context were to be structured in such a way as to be meaningful and supportive to older learners themselves. According to Caine and Caine (1991) too, in supportive learning environments, whatever is learned is embedded in the context in which it is learned.

For example, research literature concerned with life-long learning suggests that where the tutor enables the learners to increase their knowledge (Feinstein and Symons, 1999), to learn something new (Blackmore and Frith, 2005), and to be challenged to learn new things such as a foreign language (Bialystok et al., 2012), those benefits such as improved cognitive performance (Hultsch et al., 1993) could be gained. At the same time, research would suggest that such benefits would also be gained if learners took time to reflect on their learning (Strauch, 2010), engaged in social activity (Berkman, 2000), practised (Gembris, 2008) and communicated with each other (Cozolino and Sprokay, 2006).

Finally, research suggests that where the learning enables the learners to engage in physical activity (Praag et al., 1999), engage in collaborative learning (Hallam et al., 2011) and do so in a stress-free environment (Perry, 2006) benefits would be accrued too. However, there is a gap in the existing body of research concerned with the learning environment and how it relates to the perceptions of older learners with regard to the characteristics of 'quality' in their learning. In the following sections, I discuss the research identifying features of the teaching and learning environment that may underpin high-quality, effective adult or later-life learning under the headings of cognitive, physical, interpersonal, and intrapersonal factors.

Cognitive Factors

According to Zull (2006), adult learning in general, and learning new things in particular, causes 'cognitive dissonance' arising from new memories being formed and as such may function as a way of strengthening the brain's capacity and enhancing cognitive function. For Wlodkowski and Ginsberg (1995), evaluation of an individual's progress in learning can only be provided following activities that permit the learner to test out such new behaviour and that depends on the skill of the tutor too.

Involving adults in clarifying their own idiosyncratic needs and in defining clear learning objectives is acknowledged as an important aspect of adult learning (Knowles, 1990). However, according to MacKeracher (2004), most adults have little experience in verbalising their own needs, let alone turning them into learning objectives. Therefore, it is, perhaps, the facilitator's responsibility to create the inclusive learning environments that account for, and meet, diverse needs. It has been suggested that one role for facilitators of later-life learning may be to spend some time during the first few learning sessions deliberately lowering anxiety to a manageable level (Wlodkowski and Ginsberg, 1995). Adults who are getting too much or too little information for their current learning task may, in fact, not be learning at all (Hart, 1975).

According to Brown et al. (1989), adult learners learn most productively when they observe and interact with others using such role behaviour in normal daily activities and where they have a safe environment in which to test it out. Challenge to expand knowledge and skills to new zones can also come in the form of physical activity, which, when used alternatively with mental activity, enhances learning by providing the brain with time out to process ideas and experiences (MacKeracher, 2004). Learners, who take part in only one type of activity whether creative, cognitive or physical for example, would therefore benefit from the enhanced learning that new ideas and experiences bring.

However, many 'teachers' are untrained in identifying and applying such effective strategies to underpin learning. Hiemstra and Sisco (1990) point out that instructors can unknowingly create surplus 'load' for learners by assuming a traditional authoritarian stance and not respecting learners' opinions or experiences. Following good adult education practice, that honours and respects the learner, is important for giving learners more power to engage in educational activities. It has been reported that, for many, if they could not attend later-life learning classes in safe and accessible environments, then they would not attend at all (Withnall, 2010).

Hebb (1972) pointed out that although adults and children both experience emotions, stress, and anxiety arousal processes, the level, strength, and duration of the reaction increases with intellectual capacity and with age. From this perspective, adults are thought to need a supportive and encouraging learning environment that does not threaten them (Kidd, 1973; Rogers and Roethlisberger, 1991). Feeling safe, and not threatened, can be associated with features such as the size of the adult learning group; if it is large and deemed impersonal, large groups may impair the abilities of the learners to act in ways they wish to do and feel comfortable doing.

Physical Factors

The physical learning environment is important with parameters such as size of the room, adequate lighting and the lack of distracting background noise all helping to provide supportive learning context. Other features, such as cleanliness, are universal but important and even the finer points such as the temperature of the room can have an effect on learning (Dunn and Dunn, 1978). There are clear issues relating to contexts for participation being 'senior friendly spaces' (Manheimer, 2009) and in addition to physical barriers, specific places may be associated with social values, power structures or particular memories that might inhibit participation (Armstrong, 2012).

Indeed, manipulating the physical shape of the group, such as where and how participants sit, can have an enormous influence on how they behave (Rogers, 2003). In addition, the physical or technical equipment used to support and enhance the learning experience needs to work and aid learning. Facilitators, or tutors, also need to understand the drawbacks of using technology as well as the benefits. Burge (2000) stressed that technology that appeals to some adult learners is not likely to appeal to all.

There are additional features of learning in later life, which can be affected by the physical environment for learning. With increasing age, the acuity of the sensory receptors for vision and hearing declines very slowly. Some individuals remain unaware of such changes while, for others, these declines can be corrected. However, such declines affect learning by reducing the quantity and quality of the information input to the learning process. Adults experiencing such declines typically develop coping behaviours to compensate and even use information from past experiences to replace unseen or unheard material (Hiemstra and Sisco, 1990; Novak, 1993).

Interpersonal Factors

Research has shown that establishing inclusion, including the creation of an atmosphere promoting a learning community so everyone feels respected and connected (Wlodkowski, 2008), reduces the levels of stress in learners and that this lack of stress makes for more effective learning. Learners need to feel comfortable in the environment in which they are learning and, in part, this comes from the shared respect of fellow learners. For MacKeracher (2004), such respect comes from being treated as an equal. She says:

> When interaction in learning is effective, participation is based on equality, co-operation, collaboration and shared power and control. Both facilitator and learner must understand that such characteristics are not based on some altruistic process in which one 'gives' control and power to the other.
> *(p. 196)*

Shared respect can also come about by enabling learners to ask questions, which may be to further their understanding of something new or it may be a question borne out of an individual's experience, which requires airing and sharing. Wlodkowski (2008) supported such a notion by saying: 'By making the learners' goals, interests and cultural perspectives the context of challenging and engaging learning experiences, instructors can secure their continuous participation' (p. 109).

He goes on to recommend addressing this condition throughout the lesson with strategies such as providing frequent opportunities for adult learners to respond to the content through a range of strategies specifically including question and answers.

Adults who value their own experience as a rich resource for further learning, or whose experiences are valued by other people, have been described as better learners (Combs, 1974; Thibodeau, 1979). Similarly, a positive rapport between teacher and learner provides a feeling of social inclusion that generates much motivation and enthusiasm and, consequently, a sense of community. In such situations, where learning experiences are embedded in respectful relationships, older adults thrive (Wlodkowski, 1999).

Intrapersonal Factors

Personal motivation to learn is as important in later-life learning as in other stages of life. Deciding to participate in learning at all, when it is not statutory, is an expression of self-motivation as is continuing to attend learning classes. Kidd (1973) describes motivation in learning as being either a drive to reduce uncertainty and meet unmet needs or a drive towards positive growth through exploring the unknown. He suggests that adults who attend learning experiences on the basis of personal growth tend to be relaxed, do not require much structure or direction from facilitators and are able to negotiate and plan their own structure, directions, feedback and reinforcement with minimal assistance. Ahl (2006) interprets motivation as a way for later-life learners to express a strong sense of direction and maintain social control over their lives. In the context of later-life learning, promotion of motivation is thus bound up with the learning environment (i.e. environments where self-direction is promoted would, in theory, support motivation), rather than being a disposition within the individual.

According to Bjorklund (2011), as people age they appear to become less efficient at processing information into long-term memory, and retrieving information from long-term memory storage. Although this research is by no means conclusive, he says, he goes on to stress that many factors such as personal interest and good instructional techniques may well mitigate any memory and aging deficits. This internal motivation for learning, for Rogers (1983), is always present and support for it follows active participation. She goes on to say that: 'Even when the impetus or stimulus comes from outside, the sense of discovery, of reaching out, of grasping and comprehending, comes from within' (p. 20).

However, external factors to ensure active participation in learning are important too: firstly providing the opportunity to get involved and secondly to motivate involvement from outside. Wlodkowski (2008), in answering the question concerning what do tutors need to do to gain learners' attention, addresses both factors. For the latter he espouses that though learners may feel included and have a positive attitude, their involvement will diminish if they cannot find learning meaningful; while for the former, he suggested engaging in activities such as role-play and shared problem solving.

Such shared learning in informal groups, especially where they have been in place for some time, are often seen as good examples of learning communities or communities of learning (Wenger, 1998; Wenger and Snyder, 2000). According to Wenger (1998), a community of practice becomes a learning community when learning is not only a matter of course in the history of the group's practices but is at the very core of its enterprise. He views communities of practice as being made up of learners who have different levels of knowledge, behaviours, attitudes, and norms of the group. It is the sharing of this expertise through positive behaviours and support, which makes for this 'quality' experience.

One way of engaging learners is to make learning interesting to them. In this vein, learning that is new, not boring and repetitive, can be actively engaging rather than being one-dimensional such as when espoused by a 'lecturer'. Again engagement is 'in the eye of the beholder' and knowing the background of the individual learners and understanding their specific learning needs, would enhance the chances of the learning opportunities being relevant to, and of interest to, each learner. One further way to make learning interesting is to present information or tasks according to a particular learner's 'learning style' – the way in which they prefer to learn (Messick, 1976) and includes cognitive as well as affective, social, and physiological ways of responding to learning tasks. However, there appears to be no clear-cut way to categorise learning styles as Adey et al. (1999) stated: 'Research on learning styles and strategies is full of uncertainties and controversies, and therefore impossible to reach unequivocal conclusions' (p. 1).

However Adey et al. (1999) go on to say that learning 'strategies' are easier to define as they are deliberate actions that can be applied to a situation to memorise and manage times and emotions. They include techniques such as mind-mapping, mnemonics, keeping learning logs or even listening to background music. Individual later-life learners may have a penchant for learning through some strategies more than others.

The tutor or facilitator also has a direct part to play in external 'motivation' (Wlodkowski, 2008) and such external motivation is seen to establish inclusion amongst adult learners, develop positive attitudes towards learning, enhance the meaning of learning, engender competence and deal with ethical considerations – all important parts of a tutor's role in motivating learners (Brophy, 2004).

Individual learners, Rogers (2001) contested, were seeking first enjoyment, pleasure, and enrichment in a social atmosphere as knowledge itself could be accumulated from a range of other sources. Facilitators can use the power of emotions to affect learning and retention positively. By intensifying the learners' emotional state, they may enhance both meaning and memory (Wolfe, 2006). Csikszentmihályi (1990) describes pleasure differently in writing about pleasure in the context of 'flow' – a state of self-forgetfulness and goal-directed activity, which includes keeping thoughts and emotions integrated. He sees 'fun' not as 'hedonistic' pleasure but 'eudaimonic' which is related to overcoming challenges and gaining self-fulfilment.

As noted earlier in the chapter, some researchers have debated whether older people learn as quickly as younger people, and studies have explored compensatory processes (Cozolino and Sprokay, 2006). It has been suggested that there may be benefits to be gained from contact with learning tasks or materials in the days between weekly learning sessions. Encouragement is also a factor associated with the learning environment itself and actively involving learners in the session enables the tutor to provide an environment in which learners can find their voice in a supportive and safe atmosphere (Tisdell, 2000). As Immordino-Yang and Damasio (2007) suggested when concluding their research on the role of emotions in learning: 'Our hope is that a better understanding of the neurological relationships between these constructs [cognition and emotions] will provide a new basis for innovation in the design of learning environments' (p. 3).

The Quality Cirque (Part 2)

Figure 4.1 illustrates the place of 'benefits' within the Quality Cirque. Adopting a critical geragogical approach to later-life learning will enable access to the benefits such learning can bring. This is aided by the engagement of learners in the whole teaching and learning process and the creation and provision of environments allowing the benefits, presented here, to be maximised.

Summary

In presenting the benefits of later-life learning in this chapter, I classified them into four groups: cognitive, health, social, and psychological benefits. The cognitive benefits included improved cognitive performance (Hultsch et al., 1993) and offsetting dementia (Graham and Warner, 2009) while the health benefits included reducing the incidences of chronic diseases (Merriam, 2001) and improved personal health choices (Feinstein and Hammond, 2004). The social benefits included improved levels of social engagement (McNair, 2012) and improved coping skills (Rowe and Kahn, 1999) while psychological benefits included improved mental health (Cooper et al., 2010) and enhanced wellbeing (Field, 2011). They are, however, not totally distinctive just as the benefits arising from learning in later life are not always associated with just

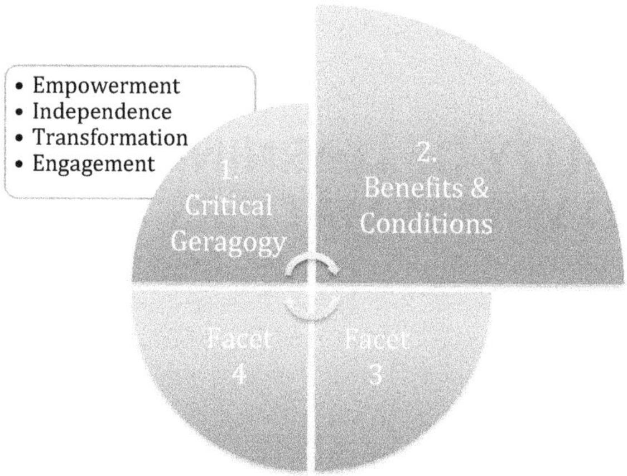

Facet 2 **Benefits and Environmental Conditions**

- ***Cognitive benefits*** **such as cognitive dexterity and offsetting dementia**
- ***Health benefits*** **including reducing instances of chronic disease**
- ***Social benefits*** **including levels of social engagement and social skills**
- ***Psychological benefits*** **including improved mental health and well-being**
- ***Environmental conditions*** **which support the needs of the learners as older people and establish conditions under which learning may thrive**

FIGURE 4.1 The quality cirque for informal later-life learning (part 2).

one field of research. Nevertheless, it is a useful way of segmenting a large and growing body of evidence.

Where research has been done in context, it has often been focused on formal learning, such as in adult education colleges, rather than informal learning which is the focus of this enquiry. For learning to be engaging and of maximum value to later-life learners, it is possible that learning opportunities should embody what the learners themselves perceive quality to be. In doing so it may embody some or many of the environmental factors that research has suggested have the most positive influence with regard to beneficial learning experiences.

5

THE QUALITY OF LEARNING IN LATER LIFE AND WHY IT MATTERS

Introduction

In the previous chapters, I have outlined the nature and the context of later-life learning and indicated the wider benefits that are possible. I have framed this within a critical geragogy framework where I considered what really effective later-life learning, learning which empowers older people and may even be transformative in some respects, might comprise.

Here I investigate the range of issues related to both the understanding and application of the concept of quality to learning in general and informal later-life learning in particular. In doing so I explore the notion of standards and measurement and consider whether, from a critical geragogy perspective, quality can ever really be 'evaluated' and become a feature of an evaluative framework. In my research, I did not seek to measure quality but rather sought to explore what the later-life learners considered quality might be and, through participant observation, explored whether those characteristics of quality were obviously discernible in their learning activities.

While a substantial amount has been written about quality in education (West-Burnham, 1992; Sallis, 2002; Cheng, 2011), there is a comparatively small amount of the literature that is specifically focused on adult education and the needs of those learning in later life (Mark, 2004). At the same time, the complexity of the notion of quality, and the challenges in conceptualising it, apply equally to the later-life learning sector. As Jarvis (1995) noted at the onset of the quality movement in education in the UK: '... whilst the language of quality is appearing in adult and continuing education, the definition of the concept is much more problematic' (p. 226).

DOI: 10.4324/9781003269892-5

The Complexity of Quality

Quality is an elusive concept and one that is difficult to define, even being described as 'slippery' (Pfeffer and Coote, 1991). Quality has a variety of meanings and the word implies different things to different people (Sallis, 2002). Ambiguous and contradictory meanings arise because quality can be used as both an 'absolute' and a 'relative' concept. People use quality as an *absolute* term freely when describing a variety of things from expensive restaurants to luxury cars. It is an ideal from which there is no compromise and things that exhibit quality, as an *absolute*, are of the highest possible standards that cannot be surpassed (Sallis, 2002).

The *relative* definition views quality not as an attribute of a product or service but as something that is ascribed to it (Sallis, 2002). Quality in this sense is about being measured against criteria. It is not an end in itself but a means by which the end product is judged as being up to, or not up to, standard. While the *absolute* notion can be considered 'elitist', the *relative* notion is potentially 'egalitarian' (Sallis, 2002). For example, the *elitist* notion is described by Pfeffer and Coote (1991) as something 'most of us admire, many of us want but few of us can have' because the notion is synonymous with 'high quality' or 'top quality'. This raises two problems for the application of 'quality' as an absolute notion in education: first of all it is ill-defined and therefore can be different things (standards) to different people and, secondly, it makes the assumption that the majority of learning institutions, or indeed practices, cannot be of 'quality' because only a 'top few' can.

Total Quality Management (TQM)

Any discussion about the nature of quality, from either an absolute or a relative perspective, requires a clear idea of who is ascribing the notion of quality. For example, TQM is a methodology whereby organisations apply an understanding of quality to all principles and practices across their operations with the premise that 'customer satisfaction is everything' (Peters and Waterman, 1982). Organisations that follow the TQM path regard quality as being defined by the 'customer' and this placing of the individual as an instrument in defining quality is central to the TQM approach (Lomax, 1996; Sallis, 2002).

This approach puts the 'customer' as the evaluator of quality rather than an externally driven framework and, indeed, my own study looked to the learners themselves to identify the principles by which the quality of informal learning in later life could be understood. However, in applying the TQM approach to education, it is important to define exactly what is the product and who is the customer. As Gray (1992), in comparing education to the output of factory or the service in a retail outlet, put it: 'Human beings are notoriously non-standard, and they bring into educational situations a range of experiences, emotions and opinions, which cannot be kept in the background of the operation' (p. 19).

Therefore it may be more helpful to regard education as a service rather than a production line (Sallis, 2002) as services usually involve direct contact between the provider (the facilitator or the organisation) and the customer (the learner). This is a close relationship and the service cannot be separated from the person delivering it and the person receiving it.

This perspective both accords with, and is at odds with, the critical geragogy framework. The agreement arises because the views of the learner, the 'consumer' of the learning process, are important and the processes of teaching and learning may lead to empowerment and emancipation for the individual customer or learner promoted by critical geragogy (Formosa, 2011). As older learners are not a homogeneous group (Withnall, 2010), it is the individuals' *absolute* notions of quality that are valued.

The TQM model is also at odds with the critical geragogy framework as in TQM the views and opinions of the learners as 'customers' would be used to shape the future provision of products and services while with informal learning experiences, that is not the case. The reshaping in TQM takes place within a competitive environment that seeks to make one provision more attractive than another when, in the reality of informal later-life learning, there is not a market containing a wide range of local and accessible provisions that prospective learners could choose from.

However, as critical geragogy is about engagement, transformation, and empowerment through learning (Formosa, 2002) the idea of a 'process' of learning being the central objective, as implied by the explanation of TQM, rather than a product is appropriate. It means feedback from the learners, as customers, could be used to significantly affect the 'quality' of the service being provided for them. This could be carried out at an individual level but there may also be value in the collation of individual views to identify common values and shared expectations.

The relative notion – with its focus on measurement against a set of criteria and a judgement of quality ascribed to it, could also have a place within a critical geragogy framework. In applying an absolute value, individuals are using internal criteria by which to form a judgement and their internal scale to perceive whether something reaches the threshold of quality or not. Critical pragmatism, as advocated by Brookfield (1986), involves 'context dependent pedagogical orientations that focus on collaboration and creative practice as well as allowing space for self-directed learning and reflection on accumulated life experience' (p. 360). In this way, the collection and sharing of absolute qualities could lead to a set of criteria useful in measuring quality 'relatively'. The reflection on, and sharing of, personal perceptions of quality is also in line with the critical geragogy framework, which Battersby (1987) espoused as a 'liberating and transforming notion which endorses principles of collectivity and dialogue central to teaching and learning' (p. 7). According to Formosa (2002), the adoption of such a communal approach would aid the transformation of ageist social structures and this would include a new and shared understanding of quality.

Qualia and Quality

In the absence of objective criteria and agreed formal standards in informal later-life learning, the personalised view of quality in the later-life learning environment has links with the concept of 'qualia'. Qualia enable individuals to define their own unique 'experiences' of quality learning and embody the emotional and intangible elements making up feelings as well as any practical experiences (Wright, 2008).

'Qualia' is a term used in philosophy to refer to individual instances of subjective, sensory experience (Chumley and Harkness, 2013). Deriving from the Latin adverb 'quails', meaning 'what sort' or 'what kind', it embodies aspects such as the pain of a toothache, the taste of oranges or the perceived redness of a glass of wine. Dennett (1988) wrote that *qualia* is 'an unfamiliar term for something that could not be more familiar to each of us: the ways things *seem* to us'. The perceptions of the learners may be the coming together of more tangible aspects such as the 'brightness' of the room with intangible aspects such as their feelings of safety merging into the perceptions that together make for quality in informal later-life learning. As Scarlett and Winner (1995) said: 'Who else (but the individual learner) can tell us whether a learning experience has qualitatively changed their life for the better?' (p. 61).

Emotion may also be related to perceptions of quality, and it has been argued that emotion plays a greater role in learning for those in later life (Hebb, 1972) than at any other time in the life course. Boud et al. (1993) remind us that 'learning must involve the whole person and not just the intellect'. Later work by Lawrence and Nohria (2001) stresses the interrelationship between emotions and reasoning, stating that reasoning does not work very well without affective signals to provide goals, intentions and ultimate motives, which 'contradicts the conventional wisdom that emotions lead to impulsive and irrational behaviour that usually get humans into trouble' (p. 154).

The Properties of Qualia

The definitions of qualia suggest that qualia may be understood as having 'absolute' features that perhaps arise from individual understandings of phenomena such as learning. Dennett (1988) sought to define qualia in more detail and in doing so identified four properties that are commonly ascribed to qualia: they are *ineffable*, they are *intrinsic,* they are *private* and they are *directly or immediately apprehensible in consciousness.*

Qualia are *ineffable* and arise from direct experience. Applied to the context of learning, qualia might thus be understood as residing in the experiences of individual learners within the learning environment and not a hoped-for, hypothetical learning situation. For example, Duay and Bryan (2008) sought to identify what seniors (aged 65 to 88) wanted from learning experiences through direct discussion. The researchers chose this method of enquiry, as they believed 'qualitative studies involving in-depth interviews offer a strategy for gaining a deeper insight into what learning means to the individual learner and what he or she considers helpful and hindering in learning situations' (p. 2). In doing so the individuals were describing their own feelings, not passing on, or communicating, those feelings to others so they could feel the same.

Qualia are *intrinsic* and have non-relational properties, which do not change depending on the experience's relation to other things. For individual adult learners, qualia evoke personal responses and lead to tacit or intuitive knowledge, which is acquired but rarely articulated (Merriam and Bierema, 2014). Lawrence (2012) defines such 'embodied knowing' as an intuitive process, which is 'spontaneous, heart centred, free, adventurous, playful, non-sequential and non-linear'. However, in Chapter 3 in general, and The Learning Environment section in particular, I outlined research that has identified how the context of informal later-life learning can influence the perceptions and experiences of quality. Therefore, I believe, 'quality' might be understood differently from one context to another, and that environmental conditions might influence perceptions of quality with the idea of absolute qualia sustainable in each individual context of learning.

For later-life learners, a range of factors in the learning environment can affect cognitive, social, and psychological responses in the learners (Schuller and Field, 1998). Each response is non-relational in that it is felt uniquely, and is not relative to other learners. However, quality, as expressed by the learners, can be viewed as being relational in the sense as changing for that one individual person as the learning environment and context change with learners able to articulate how they felt some learning experiences met their perceptions of quality while others did not.

Qualia are *private* and, according to Dennett (1998) 'all interpersonal comparisons of qualia are systematically impossible'. Therefore, any simple linking of individual qualia for comparison purposes, such as a survey, can be meaningless. The use of surveys to try to capture personal perceptions was critiqued by Lamb and Brady (2005); they asserted that, by their very nature, survey studies couldn't adequately address the nature and meaning of the individual's learning experience. However, the collation of individual responses for other purposes does not necessarily diminish the private nature of each response.

What it does do is offer the opportunity to consider a body of evidence against which to reflect and qualia can be used 'relatively' in this way as outlined later.

Finally, Dennett (1988), in defining the fourth qualia characteristic, says they are *directly or immediately apprehensible in consciousness* so to experience a quale is to know all there is to know about that quale. In support of this Dirkx (2001) points out that emotions are present in any learning experience and rather than analysing and dissecting these emotions we 'imaginatively elaborate their meaning in our lives' (p. 69). He is careful to point out that such emotions should not replace more analytic, reflective, and rational processes but rather are intended to provide a more 'holistic and integrated way of framing the meaning-making that occurs in contemporary contexts for adult learning' (p. 127).

Interpreted within a critical geragogy framework, where the emphasis is on high-quality learning being learning that supports personal control, autonomy, and capacity to effect change (Glendenning and Battersby, 1990), the principles of qualia may be understood as privileging the individual experience within learning contexts. Exploring quality through the perceptions of individual learners draws on what Withnall (2010) called the 'resources' of the older learners including 'experience, knowledge, skills, self-confidence and a sense of solidarity' (p. 35). In identifying new, personalised and unique perceptions of quality in learning, the participants endorse the view of later life, not as a period of deficit and decline but as a period of profound creativity (Hickson and Housley, 1997). Therefore, in setting out the idea of qualia, I am arguing that the principles of qualia may be critiqued in the context of learning in terms of the emphasis on the 'absolute' and unchanging nature of qualia. The very notion of qualia suggests that in seeking to understand quality in later-life learning, it is the experience of individuals that must be privileged.

The Quality Context

In order to fully understand some of the complexities in defining quality in educational contexts, it is necessary to have a way of conceiving the variables involved in the field of education and of organising and interpreting studies of the relationships between these variables. One useful context to help the capture and organising of individual perceptions of quality in later-life learning is the Biggs '3P' model (Biggs, 1993) of 'presage', 'process', and 'product'. This model helps to categorise the variables that interact with each other affecting the learners' perceptions about the quality of the education on offer. Although predicated in the context of higher education, the 3P model is relevant to the context of later-life learning because, as argued by a number of researchers (Withnall, 2010; Findsen and Formosa, 2011), a panoply of influences before, during, and after the learning sessions influence older learners' responses. For example, access to learning, the attitude of the learners and the approach

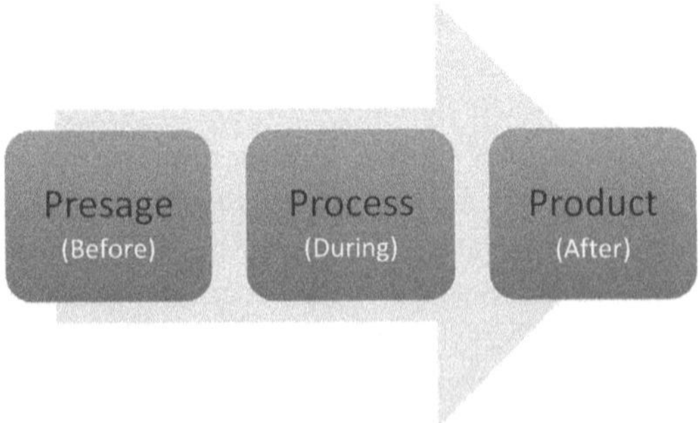

FIGURE 5.1 A flowchart outlining the Biggs '3P' model.

of the learning institution all influence the experience of learning (Withnall, 2010). The 3P model does not limit the variables to any one part of the learning journey and in that way the learners' perceptions of quality may be determined by contextual variables that surround the whole learning experience and not just what happens in the class itself (process variables).

Presage variables simply define the context before learners start learning, process variables describe what goes on as the learners learn, and product variables relate to the outcomes of that learning (Biggs, 1989) (Figure 5.1).

Presage and Quality

Presage, or input, variables such as the costs of the course, the resources available, and the selection of students or staff may at first appear irrelevant to informal later-life learning compared to competitive education environments. However, they can still affect the learning environment. For example, the selection of staff is important and the criteria used in the selection may not be those that the learners themselves value in their facilitators such as the ability to motivate learners (Wlodkowski, 2008). Research by Dunn and Dunn (1978) also identified how the physical learning environment, a presage variable, can be relevant to the motivations for engaging in the processes of learning informally in later life while Jacobi and Stokols (1983) go further and refer to the 'social imageability of the physical environment – the capacity of places to evoke vivid, widely held social meanings among their occupants' (p. 159).

Process and Quality

Although attention has increasingly been given worldwide to the process of teaching and learning (Biggs, 2003; Gibbs, 2010), it has been argued that the concept of quality needs to be developed more closely linking it to such conceptions of teaching and learning. Such a model, articulating clear links between teaching and learning practices and quality, could facilitate the understanding and measurement of quality in a way that reflects pedagogic practice (Cheng, 2011). With these links between pedagogy and quality in mind, I focused on enabling participant learners to outline their perceptions of quality related to process; what goes on in the teaching and learning environment that positively (or negatively) affects learning, in line with the assertion of Gibbs (2010), albeit associated with higher education, who says:

> What best predicts educational gain is measures of educational process: what institutions do with their resources to make the most of the students they have. The process variables … concern a small range of fairly well-understood pedagogical practices that engender student engagement. (p. 2)

Effective practices in the learning environment for later-life learners were outlined in Chapter 4 and, in particular, I highlighted the central role of the relationship between the facilitator and the later-life learners (Brown et al., 1989). That is not to say that the features of presage and product are absent as the categorisation of variables into presage, process or product is not always straightforward. One strength of the 3P model is that it recognises that what happens before the learning and after the learning can also influence the process of learning. A second is that it acknowledges that few relationships between a single dimension of quality and a single measure of either educational performance or educational gain can be interpreted with confidence because dimensions interact in complex ways (Gibbs, 2010).

Product and Quality

Product in educational terms often relates to measures of what has been learned and is most often judged against a set of standards. As Green (1994) outlined: 'Where quality is a measure of one thing against another or something in relation to what it has been on a previous occasion then the notion of 'standards' is introduced' (p. 12).

The use of standards in this way enables the comparing of learners or institutions through, for example, examination results or league tables. However, in informal later-life learning there are, typically, no set objective assessments of outcomes and neither are there formal recorded measures of what has been learned against prescribed sets of criteria. This is in line with the qualia framework as learning experiences, from the qualia perspective, are *intrinsic* and *private* (Dennett, 1988), they are unique to that person, at that time and in that context rather than being comparable to other entities or even themselves. There are no externally set standards that the learners are aiming to achieve or examinations or other assessments to 'pass'. However, that does not weaken the value of 'learning for pleasure' to gain the benefits from doing so and nor does it mean that there should not be gains arising from that learning for any one individual (Bissland, 2013). The learners, however, define those gains, and 'records', for them, may be as varied as a painting produced or a new exercise learned.

Assuring Quality

Assuring the quality of presage, process and product may be interpreted as a form of evaluation, the purpose of which, according to Robson (2011) is: '... to assess the effects and effectiveness of something, typically some innovation, intervention, policy practice or service' (p. 176).

If a critical geragogy framework for later-life learning involves challenging beliefs, practices, and structures (Formosa, 2002) then evaluation has a role to play. However, within a critical geragogy approach, it is important to ask who is responsible for evaluating, what is being evaluated, and for what purpose. The critical geragogy framework would put the learners at the centre of the evaluation, (who), in order to glean their perceptions of quality across the '3P' categories and for the purpose of challenging (improving) practices (Formosa, 2002) and potentially effecting social change (Formosa, 2012). According to Patton (1982), evaluation is often concerned not only with assessing worth, or value, but also in seeking to assist in the improvement of whatever is being evaluated against. Patton (1982) considered that:

> ... the practice of evaluation involves the systematic collection of information about the activities, characteristics and outcomes of programs, personnel and products for use by specific people to reduce uncertainties, improve effectiveness, and make decisions with regard to what those programs, personnel, or products are doing and effecting. (p. 15)

The Process of Evaluation

The process of evaluation can support the purpose of evaluation, which can be, for example, the maintenance of, or improvement in, the quality of later-life learning. In TQM, for example, the purpose is underpinned by four imperatives: the 'competitive imperative', the 'accountability imperative', the 'professional imperative' and the 'moral imperative' (Sallis, 2002). Each is discussed here, identifying their relevance to informal later-life learning.

The *competitive imperative* is concerned with 'attracting customers'; quality is seen to be an important factor in attracting learners and focusing on the needs of the 'customers' is an effective way of facing competition and surviving (West-Burnham, 1992). In informal later-life learning, the rationales for older adult learning, such as the functionalist relating to meeting the 'needs' of older learners (Findsen and Formosa, 2011), highlight that there is limited, if any, discourse around the idea of competition.

The *accountability imperative* is where institutions must meet the demands for openness and demonstrate high standards to an external party or parties. Part of this imperative involves value-for-money and failure to provide 'quality' can jeopardise institutional wellbeing and even survival (Sallis, 2002). There is no external funding body involved directly in informal later-life learning in the UK but there are often sponsors, such as charities, and local authorities whose grants subsidise the costs of courses. However, the lack of oversight of the 'quality' of informal later-learning suggests it has a lower standing than its formal counterpart and the benefits that are said to be obtained through inspection processes are therefore not available to the informal later-life learning community.

The *professional imperative* implies a commitment to the needs of the learners and the obligation to meet their needs by employing the most appropriate pedagogic, or perhaps geragogic, practices. This professional duty is aligned to the professionalism of both 'teachers' and managers within the learning organisation. Some problematic issues, in practice, limit the extent to which engagement with evaluation is possible. For example, many informal learning providers in the UK are charitable organisations characterised by a kind of intellectual democracy in which there is no distinction between teachers and taught (Findsen and Formosa, 2011) and where external tutors, when used, are employed as individual consultants with their own approach to teaching and learning and, indeed, professionalism.

According to West-Burnham (1992), the *moral imperative* is the most appropriate purpose underpinning any drive towards quality in teaching and learning in informal later-life provision. He attests that learners 'deserve' the best possible quality of teaching and learning and asserts, applying the moral imperative to schools, that:

> It is difficult to conceptualise a situation where anything less than total quality is perceived as being important or acceptable for children's education.
>
> *(p. 6)*

Findsen and Formosa (2011) point out that it is generally argued that older persons have already 'paid their way' in the economy and deserve a decent [quality] return on their lifelong investment of work and taxes. The moral imperative is also concerned with both optimising the opportunity for learners to achieve what they wish to achieve and maximising the opportunities to gain the emerging benefits from doing so. This is more likely to occur in informal later-life learning settings that embrace their perceptions of what a quality-learning environment should be. Elmore (1999) advocated access to both instrumental education and expressive education on the basis of social justice using the notions of fair equality and equal citizenship.

Forms of Evaluation

Ensuring the quality of provision through evaluation can be carried out internally within the learning organisation or by a body external to it. In either case the evaluators, typically, determine the criteria for quality and then use them to make 'appropriate judgements' accordingly (Sallis, 2002). However, the question arises as to how, from a critical geragogy perspective, external or internal evaluators can make 'appropriate' judgements if the criteria they are using have been determined by themselves. McKen (in Lomax, 1996) argued that if evaluation is to be a feature of quality improvement in later-life learning, it is the learner who should be at the heart of the decision-making.

Internal Evaluation

Internal evaluation is often known as quality assurance and it is a key ingredient in many effective education and training programmes (Rogers and Horrocks, 2010). The introduction of quality assurance mechanisms requires an investment in the training of those concerned internally, whether administrators, facilitators or learners themselves, with the expectation that their application of shared expectations on the nature of the learning environment would lead to findings which could, potentially, then lead to an increase in the quality of the learning experience provided (Mark, 2004). Cross and Steadman (1996) argue the assessment of learning is based on: '... the fundamental notion that learning can and should be monitored and that feedback from assessment should lead to more effective instruction, with the ultimate goal of improved learning' (p. 7).

In considering how evaluation by the organisation should take place, Rogers (2001) points out that 'evaluation' in adult education is an integral part of any learning process and in adult education, evaluation is achieved for the benefit of three partners in the learning process – the learners the organisation and the tutors – that are also present in informal later-life learning. The first (a) the learners, for example, will want to know that quality assurance will lead to improvements in the quality of provision and any concerns they have will be addressed; the second (b) the organisation, will want to know the level of quality that is being achieved for the resources available; and thirdly (c) the tutors, through quality assurance, can gauge how they are performing against their own or others' expectations (Rogers and Horrocks, 2010) including those of the later-life learners themselves. These three partners, interacting in the learning environment have an impact on quality at the three stages of presage, process and product.

Evaluation through the learners can be done informally by asking people what they are doing, what are they learning, what they think about the quality of the event, looking at the outcomes of any activity undertaken or even observing who is happy or unhappy for example. On the other hand, it can be done more formally through any organisational self-evaluation scheme, which may include the instruments outlined above but carried out in a more objective and systematic manner (Rogers, 2001). In either case, informally or formally, a critical geragogy approach would expect the empowerment of the learners themselves through their direct involvement.

Such 'inclusive' evaluation could also have a valuable role in identifying the 'progress' of individuals compared to shared learning objectives but these need to be expressed at the outset and, once again, at an individual and personal level. This approach is in line with the position of West-Burnham (1992), who indicated that it is up to the learner to say what quality is, and is not, for them and whether they have experienced it or not.

As outlined earlier when commentating on the TQM approach, the notion of the customer determining specification, presents a problem in education. Firstly, the notion of 'customer' in education is itself a tricky, indeed contentious, conception. For example, is the customer the service user (the student) or those who pay for the service (the government, the employers)? In informal later-life learning, learners in the UK pay for themselves and are more likely to fall into the category of 'customer' while in other countries, such as Singapore and Taiwan (Findsen and Formosa, 2016), local or national governments fund learning.

Secondly, the student as the customer, for example, is not always able, nor necessarily in a position to, specify what is required (Elton, 1992). This may involve a very restricted choice owing to, for example, entry requirements, lack of available places on courses or lack of knowledge about the full range of courses. In later-life learning, there are no entry requirements (only age and some financial wherewithal) but restricted facilities or resources do curtail the range of learning opportunities available. However, unlike formal education, learners in informal learning often get asked to provide feedback on the quality of their learning and, in doing so, help to shape the content of courses and approaches in the future.

Therefore, in informal later-life learning in the UK, the notion of customer is less clear. Such learners can be thought of as customers because they pay for the opportunity to engage in some learning but the model of 'customer' breaks down because older learners may not be able to specify in advance what their expectations are. Nevertheless, the learners are at the centre of the learning process and any 'internal evaluation' must capture their 'voice' either individually (absolute quality) or through a collation of their individual perceptions that can be used as an evaluative framework (relative quality). Such a collaborative approach would correspond closely to the principles of critical geragogy and may be described as 'learner-centred' with the support of autonomous, self-directed learning as a core principle (Heron, 1999).

External Evaluation

Schwandt (2000) saw evaluation as another way of measuring quality that is outside the perceptions of the learners themselves. He defined evaluation as: '… the act of interpreting the value (merit, worth, significance) of some activity, object, decision, program, policy, idea' (p. 553).

and noted that evaluation of quality can be special knowledge delivered by an impartial, third-party expert or action-orientated self-understanding. However, the question arises how does the idea of external evaluation and its practices align with the notion of 'absolute quality' in general and the notion of 'qualia' in particular? If external evaluation has value in assessing and improving 'quality' then, from a critical geragogy perspective, it may be that the criteria used in any evaluation framework are those arising from the individual perceptions of learners, based on their qualia in absolute terms but applicable in relative terms across a variety of later-life learning contexts.

According to Mark (2004) this process of evaluation, undertaken by a specialist assessing the value of a programme, practice or policy against an approved set of criteria, is unaffected by the subjective preferences and feelings of those involved in the activity. External evaluation can take place in a variety of ways. In education, it can involve an international or national body setting the standards for quality and the employment of personnel, external to the provision, to monitor and evaluate its quality. For example the United Nations Children's Emergency Fund (UNICEF), is predicated on setting in place international policy while in England a government-supported inspection system, the Office for Standards in Education (OfSTED), measures the quality of education establishments from nurseries to universities.

The Voice of the Learners as Evaluators

If the 'qualia' of later-life learners are to be captured and used to measure, maintain, or improve the quality of provision how can this be done? The linking of qualia to quality in this way is often achieved through evaluation and, in the process, aesthetic judgements regarding individual sensuous experiences come to be aligned with moral judgements about social personae (Chumley, 2013). It is through discourses generated in contexts such as discussions or focus groups, that any associations between individual perceptions of quality can be discovered as participants are empowered by having their subjective evaluations valued. In focus groups, for example, individual learners are able to make comments in their own words while being stimulated by thoughts and comments of others in the group (Robson, 2011).

Later-life learning in the 3rd Age involves the three 'partners' identified by Merriam and Bierema (2014) in adult learning in general – namely the tutors, the learners and administrators from the learning organisation. Quality, therefore, could be understood as being related to the values or standards that have been agreed upon by these partners. However, in most informal learning, the three partners each have their own values or standards and may not formally share them. According to Wlodkowski (2008) the teacher has a role to collaborate with learners and in doing so foster a sense of community and social inclusion.

The engagement and perceptions of all parties are important but the perceptions of the learners in helping to define quality, as captured through their voice, is paramount. The notion of the perceptions of the learner as being important (Sallis, 2002), of the idiosyncratic nature of qualia (Dennett, 1988) and the context before, during and after learning all having an influence (Biggs, 1993) all highlight the importance of using the learner voice to discover the perceptions of quality of later-life learners.

Gathering the perceptions of older learners about what constitutes quality is an example of finding out what they want (a desire, a wish to be satisfied) rather than what they need (a lack of something that requires fulfilment). The benefit of asking them directly is that what they want can vary significantly from what others think they need (Findsen and Formosa, 2011). As Peterson (1983) pointed out: 'Educational programs for older persons often fail to consider the desires of their prospective clientele, assuming that these are equivalent to their needs' (p. 74).

However, using satisfaction surveys does not necessarily equate to identifying 'quality'. In higher education institutions, students have very little information on which to make quality comparisons and, in practice, do not draw direct links between satisfaction and quality (Roberts and Higgins, 1992). In fulfilling the requirements it sets itself, the course or institution mediates students' expectations and affects the satisfaction accordingly (Lloyd, 1992).

Golden Gates itself uses an Evaluation Form (Appendix B), which is, in essence, a satisfaction survey. It encourages the participant later-life learners to rate the 'Quality of [Learning] Sessions' as excellent, good, satisfactory or poor without identifying any criteria by which such judgements could or should be made. In addition, learners, therefore, may be able to identify their short-term needs, but may not have enough knowledge and experience to know what they need in the long term. In commenting on the needs of students in higher education, Marchese (1991) stated that satisfying students' needs is not the same as satisfying their wants and satisfaction surveys still leave control of the product or service in the hands of the providers. As Sallis and

Hingley (1991) assert: '… educational institutions need to be careful that they base their quality standards upon an analysis of customer wants and needs and not just upon their own [the institutions'] definitions' (p. 3).

By asking the learners directly, using an exploratory and open-minded approach, they will be more likely to identify the characteristics of quality learning appropriate to them rather than choosing from an externally produced set of features against which they are to judge and rate but have not been involved in creating.

The Quality Cirque (Part 3)

Figure 5.2 illustrates the third component involved in the Quality Cirque. Adopting an approach to quality that deals with qualia, the whole person and the expression of their feelings as well as knowledge and understanding will

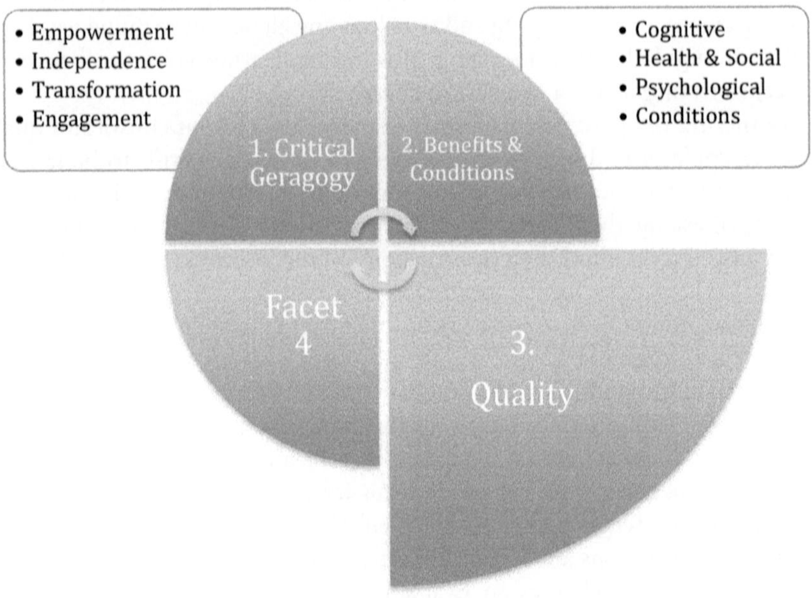

Facet 3 Quality

- ***Qualia*** **– using the emotional perceptions of learners alongside their knowledge and understanding to determine 'quality' in later-life learning**
- ***Context*** **– considering quality across the stages of learning including aspects before (presage), during (process) and afterwards (product)**
- ***Evaluation*** **– valuing the role of evaluation in determining the 'quality' of learning and privileging the internal 'voice' of the learners themselves**

FIGURE 5.2 The quality cirque for informal later-life learning (part 3).

garner a fuller understanding of their abilities and needs. This should apply to the whole 'context' of later-life learning involving the processes before (presage), during (process) and after (product) the learning sessions. To understand the progress individuals have made, including transformation, appropriate evaluation processes need to be in place including involving the learners themselves if the benefits from learning are to be secured and understood.

Summary

The notion of quality is complex and I have used the two ideas of absolute and relative interpretations of quality as a starting point. I then reflected on the approach of TQM, which embraces the idea that quality is to be defined by the 'customer' and its relationship to the critical geragogy framework. Qualia describe learning as being perceived as a subjective experience and brings together the emotions and feelings associated with learning arising from direct involvement in the process of learning. In adopting the framework of qualia, these determinations are personal, they are unique and value the role of emotions in creating perceptions, especially in those in later life. The 3P model was introduced as a way of categorising the elements within the learning environment over which the notion of quality could be asserted as the features relating to perceptions of quality can occur before (presage) or after (product) learning as well as within the learning sessions themselves (process).

A form of evaluation or quality assurance can be carried out internally by those directly involved whether the tutor, learners or the organisation. Such evaluation can also be carried out by a body external to the process of learning but this approach, where the criteria for judging quality are devised by people other than the learners and outside the learning context, is at odds with a critical geragogical approach. It also requires resources not normally associated with informal later-life learning. Instead providers opt for simpler 'satisfaction surveys'. Although such an instrument does provide an opportunity for learners to 'participate' and have a say in their learning, they are unlikely to get at the heart of 'geragogical' processes and certainly not the 'quality' of them.

The voice of the learners is the most important one in evaluating quality and is heard by giving them the time and the opportunity to express their perceptions and provide evidence on which they are predicated. In doing so they can produce a rich source of information on which all those involved can ensure the wishes of the older people, as later-life learners, are being both valued and being met.

6

THE CHARACTERISTICS OF QUALITY LEARNING

Introduction

The findings from the three fieldwork phases (Figure 6.1) are presented in the chronological order the fieldwork took place within the overall mixed-methods approach as each activity had a direct and cumulative relationship to the one following. Therefore, this chapter presents the analysis of the Feasibility Study data and the findings from the analysis of the outcomes of the main study, which includes focus groups. The following chapter (Chapter 7) outlines the outcomes from the analysis of the Quality Learning Questionnaire survey.

Phase 1: The Feasibility Study

The purpose of the Feasibility Study was to start to explore features of informal later-life learning that were valued by the participants. The feature of 'quality' emerged from the session and the later-life learners input, therefore, helped to formulate my research questions:

What are older learners' perceptions of quality, in informal later-life learning?

a What are the learners' perceptions of the environmental factors that underpin quality learning experiences?
b How does informal learning reflect the principles of quality as defined by the participants themselves?

I stressed my intention was to involve later-life learners directly in the study from the outset, to hear their voices first-hand and to ensure the research I

DOI: 10.4324/9781003269892-6

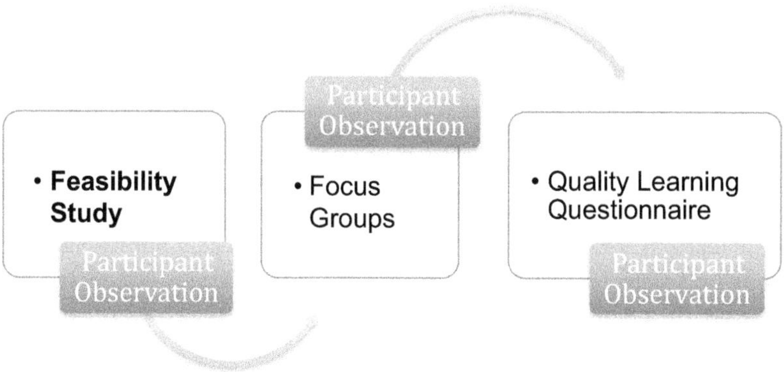

FIGURE 6.1 The feasibility study within the mixed-method approach.

undertook was meaningful to them. The identification of a key issue of 'quality' in informal later-life learning formed the basis of subsequent discussions with the focus groups.

Five participants, all volunteers, took part and I was able to articulate that I was there (researching) because I felt they had an important contribution to make to an under-researched area (Maxwell, 2005). All of the learners became actively involved, began to talk about themselves and their lives, and gradually began to comment as learners. Learning was a significant part of their daily routine, especially after the 'shock' of retirement when lives were left 'unstructured' and without routine. Using semi-structured, I asked four questions to focus discussions on learning and learning contexts. All comments made by the participants were noted and are outlined in the following sections. Those that I was not able to attribute to an individual are presented in quotation marks and where the comments are attributable to an individual participant, they are also presented in italics. In this way, all comments contributing to the voice of the learners were noted and together led to the identification of key themes emerging from these initial discussions.

Question 1 – What Do You Think Learning Is?

Learning, or training, at work was seen to be task-focused and, consequently, retirement was seen to be a time to 'follow your interests' both formally (e.g. at college) and informally (e.g. at Golden Gates). Volunteering was also seen to be a significant way both to learn and for 'passing on what we have learned' to younger people in a generative way (Newman et al., 1997).

There was quite a variance in the perceptions of the learners about just what learning is from 'acquiring information' to simply 'doing something you love'. Although there was no direct outlining of a 'list' of factors making it up, there was some allusion to factors contributing to it, with notions of 'developing', 'updating', or 'experiencing' often identified as being related to learning too. Some participants were not clear whether learning took place just through the classes they attended (informal learning) or was a natural part of everyday living (incidental learning). Therefore, there was a need to probe further if aspects related to 'learning' rather than just 'living' were to be uncovered. In terms described by Jarvis (1990), although the participants attended informal later-life learning classes in a wide range of subjects to gain knowledge, understanding and skills (educational gerontology) they did not attend any classes to increase their knowledge about ageing and how to age more successfully (gerontological education).

Question 2 – What Factors Really Help You to Learn Best?

Throughout these discussions, there was a continual reference back to the times the learners spent at school – the members of the group being universally positive about their primary school experiences and almost universally critical of their time at secondary school. In alluding to such experiences, stressed that the role and personality of the 'teacher' was just as important in older-age settings.

The participants were surprisingly open about teachers in classes they had attended as later-life learners who were not perceived as being supportive of them; some teachers, it was reported, had even been critical of the learners, which had acted as a disincentive to succeeding or attending altogether. Such a dichotomy of approach is against the suggestion of Wlodkowski (2008), who states that all 'instructors' involved in the learning of adults should announce a 'cooperative intention to help' (p. 138) to create an inclusive and partnership approach. One participant said such teachers '***did not understand us***' and other learners agreed, describing both the needs they had as older people and their individual needs as later-life learners. In articulating how they had felt on such occasions, when they received neither the respect nor the support they needed, they described themselves as being 'vulnerable'. Through body language, including a watering of their eyes, two of the learners became quite emotional about this important issue.

In teasing out factors that could help them in their learning, the participants had identified three key features – the organisation of the learning environment, the characteristics of the tutor or teacher leading them, and the approach of the learners themselves. In addition, it became evident that the quality of the relationships the learners had, not only with each other but also with the tutor and the organisation, was a factor in their learning. Within the 'approach of the learners', the social side of learning in later life was mentioned regularly and was also more thoroughly probed and expanded upon.

Question 3 – What Barriers, If Any, Are There to Helping This [Effective Learning] to Happen?

In discussions, participants were very clear about what had discouraged them from learning. The organisational or environmental factors identified were very wide ranging and the learners continued to reference back to their school days and the negative impression they had left in most cases.

It was felt that many teachers of their informal learning classes often did not get to know the later-life learners as individuals (excused as there were 'lots of people in the class') and specifically where learners had difficulties arising from old age such as deteriorating hearing or sight. It was reported that often such needs were not known by the tutors and so were not taken into account to aid learning. Learners felt that where classes were not enjoyable, they simply did not learn but that having 'friends' in the class (not just other learners) was helpful. These comments resonate with the work of Wilson (1993) who describes adult learning as 'situated learning' being always social and relational because it occurs with other people and is always active in nature because the doing and the knowing are never separated in the learning experience.

The learners felt that 'mixed ages' and 'mixed ability classes' were not a good idea (although they did not expand on these terms) when talking about 'formal learning' and especially at local colleges. They did not enjoy learning at 'night school' as the young or middle-aged learners were very different from them. They made references to different social characteristics (chatty, noisy, fast-talking) as well as different reasons for learning (for qualifications, as a requirement from their place of work). They felt the classes worked best when they were graded according to ability not according to age and that all older people are 'not the same' and should not be 'clumped together'.

The learners, in identifying a number of emotional and psychological barriers to participating in learning, elucidated some of the existing research concerned with why the majority of people in later life do not participate in learning (McNair, 2012). It was apparent that the nature of formal education with its relatively large-sized classes, mixed-ability formats, and associated assessment (judgement) was less attractive than informal learning. This supports the work of Duay and Bryan (2008) who identified such factors as 'pressures' associated with traditional education. Therefore, informal education may provide a more pertinent approach to learning in later life by providing a more 'comfortable' learning experience.

Question 4 – Why Is Learning Important to You?

All the participants agreed that learning can help to develop a person's personal qualities and help to retain a 'sense of worth' into later life that may have been lost through retirement or other significant life changes or simply by ageing.

They took great satisfaction both in participating (in dance and art classes) and in succeeding (language and computer classes) in learning. It made their lives richer and they could not envisage a life without learning. The majority referenced how they enjoyed watching other learners 'doing it' and not just the teacher as they felt it easier to follow their peers and consequently learn from them. The learners, in turn, went on to talk about how they enjoyed teaching other people, passing on their knowledge and skills and, in a quite touching way, especially 'to those older than us'.

These learners demonstrated a need to continue to be accepted by their peers in their social group; learning was seen to be a way of 'keeping up' with them and being able to communicate with them so as not to be excluded through a demonstration of their ignorance in some form. They saw 'success' in old age as being able to 'play a part in society' and not feel left behind to 'wither away'. Their expressed wishes, through learning, to be 'kept up-to-date' and 'not be left behind' resonated with the assertion of Ahl (2006) who argues forcibly that the concept of motivation in adult learning should be seen as a euphemism for direction and control rather than a particular disposition residing in the individual.

Summary

The Feasibility Study provided a significant insight into the experiences and perceptions of learning as articulated by this group of informal later-life learners. A number of overarching topic areas emerged. The most striking theme was the emphasis on the central importance of the social and interpersonal dynamics in general and the interaction amongst the learners themselves in particular. In addition, the importance of the actions of the tutors and the value of their aptitudes and approaches, the role of learners themselves and what they contributed to the learning process and the influence of the environment or organisational arrangements. All these features were valued by the later-life learners and affected the 'quality' of learning, both positively and negatively.

Many comments were made about the factors that helped later-life learners to learn best, to make the learning experience of the 'quality' they would hope for and these covered a range of issues. As the participants were already later-life learners, they had overcome many of the barriers that were mentioned and I was interested in such barriers only to the extent they may stop people from attending informal learning once they had already started to attend. In other words, the 'quality' of their learning experience – the factors that made learning important and accessible and productive once older people were there – became central to my research. My research questions arose from these Feasibility Study discussions and the next research phase provided an opportunity to explore the nature of the learning experience with some focus groups. I set out the findings from that phase of the research fieldwork here.

Phase 2: The Focus Groups

Introduction

The second phase of the fieldwork took the form of discussions using focus groups (Figure 6.2). Nine focus groups took place involving 66 participants (Table 6.1).

Eight participants were also tutors all aged over 50 (all of whom participated as informal later-life learners themselves). Group size ranged from four to twelve with a mean number of seven participants. All groups, excluding the Men's Group, were predominately female and across the focus groups, the participants welcomed the opportunity to engage in discussions about their learning and to lend their voices to the emerging dialogue about what constitutes 'quality' in informal later-life learning.

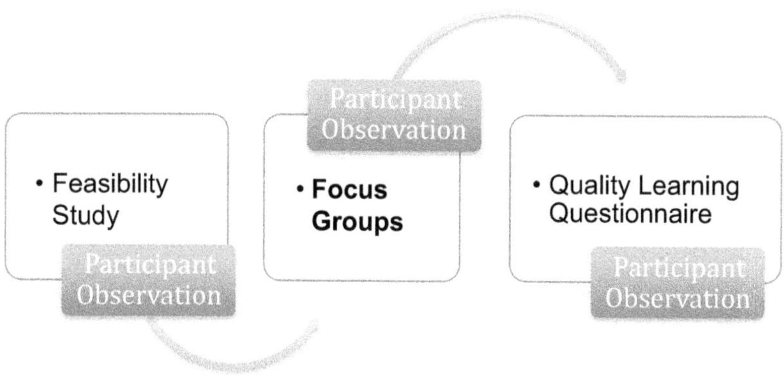

FIGURE 6.2 Focus groups within the mixed-method approach adopted.

TABLE 6.1 Description of the focus groups

Focus Group	*Activity*	*Venue No*.*	*Learner No.*	*Female / Male*	*Type of Learning*	*Time of Day*
FG1	Tai Chi	1	7	6 / 1	Physical	Afternoon
FG2	Art History	1	6	4 / 2	Humanity	Afternoon
FG3	Philosophy	1	8	4 / 4	Humanity	Morning
FG4	Steady & Stable	2	12	9 / 3	Physical	Afternoon
FG5	Art for All	3	10	7 / 3	Creative	Afternoon
FG6	Yoga	4	5	5 / 0	Physical	Morning
FG7	English Literature	4	7	6 / 1	Literature	Morning
FG8	Drama	4	7	6 / 1	Creative	Afternoon
FG9	Men's Group	5	4	0 / 4	Social	Morning
Total			66	47 / 19		
%				71% / 29%		

It was important to involve participants who were as representative of the organisation as possible. Therefore attention was paid to:

a Involving both genders of learners.
b Using both morning and afternoon learning sessions.
c Targeting a wide variety of types of activity (learning).
d Involving a range of venues attended by learners.

Focus Group Questions

This phase of the fieldwork was characterised by a semi-structured approach with the same three open-ended questions being asked of each group. At all times, respondents were encouraged to explain the reasons for their answers and also not to confine their experiences of learning in later life to those that were current, or most recent. However, they were reminded that they were to draw on their experiences as later-life learners (over 50 year olds) not as adult learners *per se* and that they should focus on their involvement in 'informal' learning not any 'formal' learning they had been, or were, involved in. They were also asked to consider experiences and perceptions of informal later-life learning classes that were not held at Golden Gates too.

Phase 2: Focus Groups (Part 1): Stakeholders in Quality Learning.

The analysis of the discussions with participants of the Feasibility Study had indicated that they identified the learners, the tutor, and the organisation as three distinct but associated stakeholders involved in later-life learning and especially where learning went well. Therefore in analysing the findings from the responses of the focus groups, these three categories were used as an initial framework (Figure 6.3).

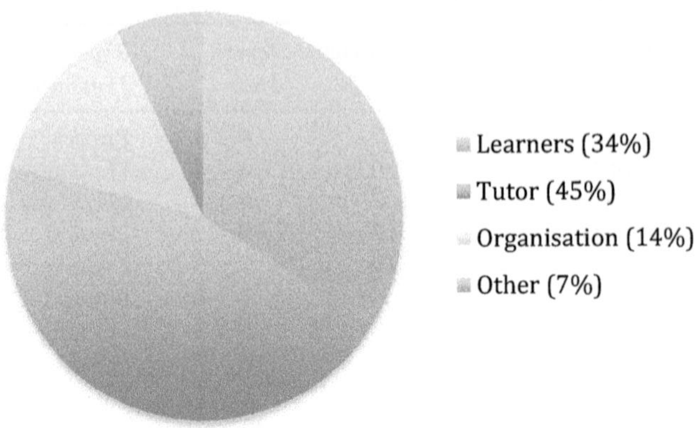

FIGURE 6.3 The stakeholders in quality informal later-life learning identified by qualitative categorical analysis of the comments made by the focus groups.

The Stakeholders – The Learners, the Tutor, and the Organisation

The numbers of comments associated with the three stakeholders – learners, tutor, and organisation – are summarised in the following paragraphs. exemplified through specific examples. The relative numbers of comments in the charts illustrate the comparative strengths of the focus on each 'stakeholder' in response to each question.

Question 1: The Relative Contributions of the Learners, the Tutor, and the Organisation to Quality

Q: Tell me about a learning session or activity that you think was of high quality; what was it about it that was so positive, that you enjoyed and really engaged you?

In answer to this question, the majority of comments were concerned with the tutor including:

> *The teacher has to be enthusiastic about what they are doing.*
> *A good tutor, someone that engages you, that takes a keen interest in you.*

A number of learners identified that they themselves, as learners, contributed to ensuring a quality learning session. Here 38 comments were coded as being concerned with the learner, and included:

> *That's what makes the class, the people.*
> *Motivation that makes you want to go along and be willing to do everything.*

Finally the organisation was seen as a stakeholder that helped to ensure such learning sessions are ones of quality. A further ten comments alluded to this including:

> *The equipment. We have now got the screen and the computer thing [projector].*

Question 2: The Ways in Which the Learners, Tutor, and Organisation Act as Barriers to Quality

Q: Can you let me know anything that you have found can get in the way of making that happen; what can stop learning being really positive and enjoyable?

In answer to Question Two, concerned with barriers getting in the way of quality learning, the comments were spread more evenly across the categories. The organisation, as well as the learners themselves, was seen as being able to pose barriers but once again, the majority of comments were coded as being concerned with the tutor. In some instances the responses to this question could be seen as the reverse of question one – in other words the absence of key indicators supporting quality learning act as a barrier to quality learning taking place. The tutor was said to cause problems in a number of ways and comments indicating the perceptions of the focus group participants included:

> *Some of the people who dropped off probably knew as much as you [the tutor] do and so they stopped coming.*
>
> *If the teacher doesn't really care, she's got this thing to do and whether you learn or not, it is very obvious she will do it and doesn't care.*
>
> *Also the personality of the tutor – they must be interested in the subject.*

It was also thought that the participants themselves could produce barriers as learners:

> *I think this does happen sometimes in classes when people are chatting when the tutor is trying to tell you something.*
>
> *[In one class] I found a lot of animosity between two students and caused great friction.... There was an incredibly unhelpful atmosphere while he was there.*

The organisation was also the subject of comments associated with barriers to quality learning. These included:

> *I don't like the chopping and changing of tutors. If I like a tutor I want that tutor all the time.*
>
> *[If you have to] pay a full term's fees for the term. It is a lot of money and if you had to do so [pay up front] you may not go.*

Question 3: The Relative Positive Contributions of the Learners, the Tutor, and the Organisation

Q: *What would you say that you do as tutors or learners to help to make learning of high quality; how can you make it positive and make the learning so enjoyable too?*

In answer to Question Three, concerned with the relative positive contributions of the learners, the tutor, and the organisation in enhancing the quality of learning sessions, once again the majority of comments were concerned with the tutor. However, there were almost as many comments associated with the learners.

With regards to the role of the tutor, the learners stated that:

> *The tutor needs a certain amount of preparation, I think, to make it interesting.*
>
> *The tutors need to be able to get it [information] across and be good at communication.*

At the same time, the participants recognised that they, as learners, also had a role to play if the informal later-life learning sessions they were participating in were to be ones perceived to be of quality. One participant said:

> *I think if we support the tutor rather than coming in with a poor attitude that helps ... but if we came in with a negative attitude, saying we don't fancy doing that today, that wouldn't help.* and another participant suggested that:
> *You've got to listen, pay attention, otherwise it's not a good experience.*

Nevertheless the organisation, as a third stakeholder in informal learning, was thought to have a part to play too. One participant learner suggested that:

> *It helps when we have the equipment and it's not always the tutor's fault. We have been given more equipment now.*

Types of Learning

Across all of the topic areas the greatest number of comments were associated with the tutor in every type of learning investigated, which was in line with the overall finding. The greatest percentages of comments in support of the role of the tutor in quality leaning were in the social sessions and the physical exercise type classes. The significant role of the learners, as a stakeholder grouping, was again supported by participants across all types of learning through having the second most references after the tutor. For those responding from classes deemed as ones that are 'creative', the role of the learners and the approach they bring to the learning was almost as important as that of the tutor. Those involved in both literature and in humanities classes, involving a great deal of discussion, strongly associated characteristics of the organisation as being of importance.

Summary of Phase 2 – Part 1 Analysis

The three stakeholders in learning – the learners, the tutor, and the organisation – being important in the provision of quality informal later-life learning, has been illustrated both by the number of comments associated with them and also by the nature of the comments made by the participants.

The next stage of the Phase 2 fieldwork analysis involved a thematic analysis of the comments made during the focus groups to identify any specific characteristics of quality that were articulated by the focus group participants and to explore the degree to which any specific characteristics were supported as important facets of quality learning experiences.

Phase 2: Focus Groups (Part 2): Characteristics of Quality Learning

This second part of the analysis took the form of a thematic analysis using the computer software (NVivo). The aim of this step of the analysis was to identify any specific characteristics associated with each of the three stakeholders as well as provide more contextual detail.

The 298 comments made by the participants, identified through the initial categorical analysis described previously, revealed a number of themes, labelled as characteristics, that the participants considered to contribute to quality in their learning environment. From the thematic analysis of the text associated with each of the stakeholders (learner, tutor, and organisation) 28 characteristics emerged associated with quality learning. In doing so, the relative numbers of 'characteristics of quality', associated with the learners, the tutor, and the organisation respectively, were revealed.

Figure 6.4 identifies the relative numbers of characteristics of quality in learning associated with each of the three stakeholders (learner, tutor, and organisation).

Part A: About the Learners

Table 6.2 sets out the findings from my thematic analysis under the stakeholder category 'learner'. The analysis revealed eight distinct themes, each

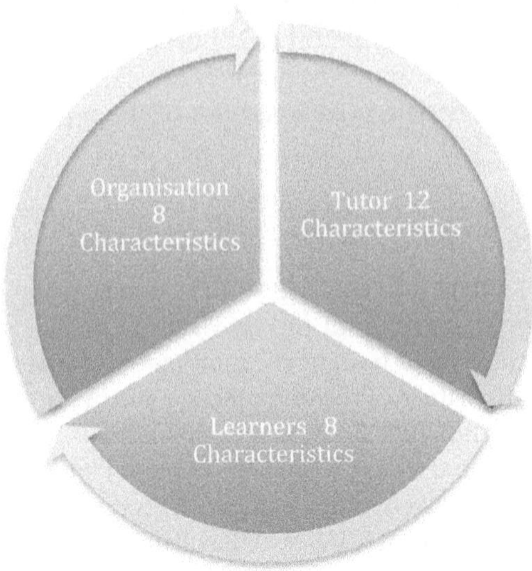

FIGURE 6.4 Numbers of characteristics of quality in informal later-life learning associated with each of the three stakeholders.

TABLE 6.2 Relative strength of the characteristics of quality in informal later-life learning associated with the 'learner' aspect

Characteristic Number	*Characteristics of Quality*	*Number of Coded References*
4	Have their individual learning needs met	51
6	Are motivated to learn	37
1	Learn new things	23
2	Find the group or class friendly	22
7	Take part in the learning activities	16
8	Encourage others to learn too	12
3	Are challenged in their learning	9
3	Are treated with respect by others	7
	Number of the 479 total references coded as themes relating to the Learners,	177
	Percentage of coded references about	37%

interpreted as a 'characteristic of quality' concerned with the learner's role in quality experiences of informal later-life learning.

Over one third (37%) of references (177) were aligned with a perception on the part of the learners of the significant part they considered themselves to play in quality learning. Of these characteristics, 'having their learning needs met' was the characteristic receiving the most references together with being 'motivated to learn'.

Each of the eight characteristics of quality identified through thematic analysis is discussed here in characteristic order as they appeared on the later questionnaire rather than the number of references associated with each one. The relative strength of support of a particular characteristic can be gleaned from the number of references associated with it.

Learn New Things

In 'quality' learning there was an expectation from the participants that they, as learners, would learn something 'new' whether it was gaining knowledge, improving their understanding or developing a skill.

This was illustrated by the general comment from a member of the Tai Chi group about her singing class:

> *I want more, I want to learn, I don't just want to go and, you know, sing a couple of bars of songs. It's the quality of what is being given that is important.*

Comments from a member of the English Literature class articulated what the new learning was that they had undertaken:

> *I am definitely improving my writing style and accumulating more vocabulary.*

The learners articulated the perceived gains to be made from learning new things irrespective of what the components are. One participant in the philosophy class said that she was not looking to learn something specific:

> *But I go away and think, well, I've learned something today that's beneficial.*

This comment was given more depth by a fellow learner who said, for him, attending learning classes of all types was:

> *To be enthused to gain something whether its knowledge or a physical activity such as Tai Chi, to come away feeling much better physically after what I have just done and I want to go back again.*

The wish, by the learners, to learn something new raised the issue of the responsibility of the learner letting the tutor know what they already knew or could do, so that there was time for the tutor to provide the opportunity for new learning. One member of the yoga group made this point with some vigour by saying:

> *The tutor needs to know what the person has done in the past and the tutor must know how to 'run' the class.*

Finally, learners became more animated about the characteristic of quality learning concerned with 'learning new things' with their language shifting from 'hoping' to learn something new to 'expecting' to do so with the volume of their voices rising accordingly as they sought to ensure their point was recognised. They said that they had 'made the effort to attend' for that purpose. One participant in the yoga group offered:

> *I think there should be an expected result, myself. People come to the exercise class to see an improvement and I expect a result.*

Find the Group or Class Friendly

The friendliness of the group, and the associated comfort the learners feel in such a group, was said to have a significant effect on the quality of learning. There was a recognition of the role they, as participants, had to play in making their learning groups friendly.

At the outset of the discussions, a number of participants outlined the value of learning together and getting to know fellow learners. One said:

You become friends with people in the class and they are encouraging too.

For one learner, and others who agreed with her, the social side was a prerequisite of learning and was as important, if not more so, than the learning itself as illustrated by her comment:

It's the social side, being with older people, not so much the quality. Yes, you would like or want a good teacher but it's the social things really.

Once again, the role the learners themselves have in creating a situation, where the friendliness of the class was a helpful feature of their learning, was stressed and revealed through comments such as:

You [the learners] need the ability to create an environment that is positive and encouraging for people. If you have one difficult person that can make you feel bad.

Are Challenged in Their Learning

Learning 'new things' is one characteristic but being challenged is not only a separate indicator but also one that was expected in a quality learning session. This takes many forms because of the different starting points and backgrounds of the learners as well as their different learning styles (Kolb, 1984). In such sessions, the learners are not afraid to be 'challenged' as they tackle something new. This is important if 'change' is to take place in learning (Illeris, 2007) and if the mind is to be used more extensively.

First and foremost, this challenge is about learners as individuals, revealing to themselves, or others, what they can do and cannot do and also what they would like to try to know, understand or do – to be challenged both in what you learn and how you learn it. As one participant commented:

The tutor needs a certain amount of preparation, I think, to make it interesting especially in this sort of session but in the other session [of art] where we are actually drawing, you are sort of challenging yourself, learning new stuff and the tutor will just make some observations really.

What constituted 'challenge' was unique to each person but through dialogue with the tutor, challenge could be provided as one learner said:

Looking at our group we are functioning at different levels yet [the tutor] acknowledges that and challenges all of us within a sort of flexible way.

One participant reinforced the key role they, as learners, in general played in identifying what constituted 'challenge' for them, by saying that:

> *It is very important that expectations are high and that you learn to learn. We old people think we know everything and we don't so you have to keep your mind open, the tutor cannot do everything for you.*

Have Their Individual Learning Needs Met

Through discussions it was stressed that a quality learning experience was one where the learners understood what their learning needs were and were engaged in a learning experience to enable them to be met. Such learning needs can relate to the ability of the person, their specific learning style or their expectations.

The participants said that they, as learners, had a part to play in revealing their learning needs at the outset. One participant put it:

> *We have to be realistic as we are different age groups within our older age and have different kinds of physical and emotional abilities and needs.*

It is seen as a two-way process with the tutor as outlined by the comment of one member of the Tai Chi group:

> *A lot of teachers just do it in front of the class and don't actually get in there and look at each individual person. You can know each person and not only make eye contact but personally address what they are going through and meet their personal needs.*

Such dialogue could, it was suggested, involve the whole class not just individuals where they share the same learning needs. As outlined by an Art History member:

> *Not high quality learning because of what she has learned … we did not want that. More casual, like the pictures we are interested in rather than learning about the artists' history so she modified [her approach].*

It was also reported that when individual learning needs are not being met, attention and attendance could drop off. One learner said:

> *I used to do ballet and jazz here and the teacher was absolutely great. It was fun and everything came together. The suddenly she left and another teacher came. I came for just one class and I was so bored that I did not go back. I was not making any progress – I only stayed for one class.*

One member of the drama group felt the lack of differentiation in teaching and learning penalised the more able:

> *At some classes, I felt the focus is always on the lowest denominator, and not on the others. The focus is always on the lowest.*

Are Treated with Respect by Others

The 'respect' discussed here was that shown from the learners themselves to one another recognising that they, as individuals and as a group, had to enable learning to happen within a supportive environment. This manifested itself is aspects such as not talking over each other, not belittling the answers or suggestions of other learners and including everyone in activities, perhaps where sharing equipment or materials was necessary. The participants in the focus groups emphasised that respect for each other involved an inclusive culture where individuals did not feel excluded. One said:

> *If there is a clique in the class and are different and the teacher does not deal with the clique, then I feel that when I have gone to certain sessions that what I am doesn't matter and what I want to learn has not happened and I cannot join in. The clique has, like, put a wall around themselves and I stopped going.*

On occasions the disrespect was evident but could be unintentional as one member of the drama group said:

> *Sometimes participation is too much however. I went to learn in one class and one of the students from the group would hold forth for a very long time and the teacher just lets them.*

One female participant felt it was obvious to her, and to other women, that the male participants in one class, which focused on the discussion of current affairs, were disrespectful to the women as learners. She said:

> *You don't have to get up [to speak] but you can do. The men are there with their Telegraphs holding forth and us women are not given a chance. When we say something, they [the men] rustle their papers like this.*

Are Motivated to Learn

Once again, the participants in the focus groups emphasised that quality was evident in later-life learning where the learners themselves were motivated to learn. This was not external motivation from tutors or even fellow learners. Motivation, on the part of learners, was manifested prior to arriving at learning sessions through a willingness to take part and play a full role in activities. One participant in the yoga class, speaking for her fellow learners, summed this up by saying:

> *They [the learners] need to attend regularly and be ready to learn.*

For many learners, it was clear that to get the most out of learning, learners had to contribute too. One such participant commented:

> *We are adults not children. We are expected to come and be responsible and we should provide some input.*

This motivation often manifested itself through overt interest which one learner articulated as:

> *There needs to be some enthusiasm from the participants.*

In showing such enthusiasm, the learners not only motivated themselves but their motivation was thought to help the tutor and other learners too. One learner said:

> *Well, we have to enthuse the tutor because if the tutor feels that she is not getting anywhere with us it's like good and bad teachers, if they feel 'oh they are not taking this in, then I will not bother too much'.*

Another learner reflected back on an experience involving compulsory learning to illustrate this point further. She said:

> *In the early days, the 1980s, when I had a go with some adults at computers, another tutor said 'your students are very enthusiastic' but others who were sent to learn computers by their firm were not interested. They didn't want to be there, they didn't learn very well even though they were younger.*

This last comment also reflected on the discussions at the Feasibility Study gathering where the 'fear of failing' was seen as a demotivating factor working against good learning experiences. As a consequence, learners became involved in informal learning to avoid the 'pressure' and 'stress' associated with formal learning.

Take Part in the Learning Activities

Allied to motivation is action. Quality learning, it was said, took place where the participants understood their role as learners, followed the instructions of the tutors and participated fully. This could be from joining in discussions to working collaboratively with others.

One older learner expressed the need to participate by saying:

We are mature, mature, mature (laugh) so we have a part to play. It has to be two-way and we should not be totally dependent on the teacher, what we can contribute as part of that group is important too. The teacher is important but can we not contribute to make it better quality?

Another learner from the philosophy group saw it as the 'duty' of the learners:

First of all we have the responsibility to attend, to listen, to participate, all the things we have mentioned, to take a part, show interest.

Learning together, according to a further participant, was of great benefit and was a contributing factor to quality learning. She said that for her, learning was:

... to be involved, to be engaged, to extend my knowledge and be in a group.

Encourage Others to Learn Too

Through comments from the participants in the focus groups, it became evident that in quality learning experiences, there is an atmosphere of cooperation and altruism where members of the group give their expertise to help others in the group. Sometimes this was during a practical task, such as threading a sewing machine or simply encouragement through praise.

For one participant, the spirit of cooperation within a learning experience, not just being friendly, was of fundamental importance. She said:

They are also a very supportive group and that makes a really great difference.

More specifically, working in partnership to learn by taking in new knowledge or practising a skill had a positive impact as one learner articulated:

You worked with your partners, you talked to your partners, you transmitted the knowledge in each other.

Such partnerships did not necessarily have to be of equals as one learner said:

If you are brighter, or you are willing to wait for a slower member of the group, then the group become part of the teaching experience.

The learners confirmed that this encouragement and support was something that they provided for each other and was not something they relied on the tutor to provide. One expressed this by saying:

> *It was a confidence thing and a support mechanism and, despite what level you were at, someone supported you in your learning.*

Part B: About the Tutor

Table 6.3 sets out the findings of the thematic analysis, which revealed 12 distinct characteristics; each is referred as a 'characteristic of quality' and was identified as underpinning the role of the tutor within a quality informal later-life learning experience. These characteristics, identified in the focus groups, were seen as being both important and the responsibility of the tutor.

The majority of the references, 219, were aligned with the tutor and, being almost half of the total number of coded references overall (46%), illustrates the very significant part the tutor plays in older learners' perceptions of quality learning. Once again, each of the 12 tutor characteristics is discussed below and is illustrated by direct references from the learners involved.

The relative strength of support of a particular characteristic can be gleaned from the relative number of references associated with it made by the participating learners. In this second section, four characteristics of quality were

TABLE 6.3 Relative strength of the characteristics of quality in informal later-life learning associated with the 'tutor' aspect

Characteristic Number	*Themes: Characteristics of Quality*	*Number of Coded References*
9	Make learning interesting	26
11	Motivate learners to want to learn	26
12	Make learning fun	26
17	Provide challenge to learners – to learn new things	26
16	Involve the learners in their learning	24
13	Treat the learners with respect	21
15	Are experienced in what they are teaching	20
18	Ask for the opinions of the learners	15
14	Are qualified as a teacher	12
20	Encourage learners to keep on learning	10
19	Give learners confidence	9
10	Let the reamers ask questions	4
	Number of the 479 total references coded as themes relating to the Tutor.	219
	Percentage of coded references about the Tutor	46%

equally supported: 'making learning interesting', 'providing challenge to learners to learn new things', 'motivating learners to want to learn', and 'making learning fun'.

Make Learning Interesting

The references associated with this characteristic suggest that the later-life learners required learning to be interesting in order for the experience to be considered one of quality. Some tutors drew on the experiences of members of the group, which made it not just more interesting for that individual but for the rest of the group too. However, whatever teaching techniques they employed, the tutor had a clear role to play in engaging the learners with enthusiasm to make the subject interesting.

One participant characterised this by saying:

> *The teacher has to be enthusiastic about what they are doing. They have to be very enthusiastic about the subject and want to share their knowledge not 'well I'm being paid so much to do this' and that - it kills any class.*

The tutor's positive approach was considered to be central to a quality learning experience according to a member of the Art History class who said:

> *The enthusiasm of the teacher is vital.*

Further comment indicated some of the features of that enthusiasm as part of an interesting learning experience. One learner said that, for her, quality learning required:

> *A good tutor, someone that engages you, that takes a keen interest in you.*

A second learner felt it was not any one specific activity that made learning interesting but a range. He said:

> *Variety and accessibility [are important]. We have lots of different things locally and there are lots of things and variety of choices that you have not tried that are accessible and local.]*

Conversely, the participants felt that if learning is not interesting it will not encourage future learning. One expressed this by saying learning would not be of a high quality if:

> *... it's boring - you want to be stimulated and want to keep coming back.*

Lets the Learners Ask Questions

Many tutors ask questions of their class – it is a common pedagogical tool helping to involve learners as well as assessing need or understanding. However, not all tutors might enable the learners themselves to ask questions. This too has to be a deliberate strategy and one the later-life learners considered to be part of a quality experience. It is, perhaps, more important with older learners where it is taken as a sign of respect for them as people and also for their experience and expertise.

For one learner it was the key to quality learning when she said:

> *The main thing for me is the tutor and it's the chance to be able to participate, ask questions etcetera.*

For others being able to ask questions had a positive effect on the whole group. One expressed this by saying:

> *I think a lot has to do with the feeling of the whole group, so that you feel you can get up and ask a question without getting any negative judgment from anyone in the group, certainly not from the tutor. Where you feel confident in yourself.*

For another it was an integral part of the learning experience when she said:

> *For me it is really important that if I do not understand something that I can ask the instructor if not during the class then after the class.*

Motivates Learners to Want to Learn

Acknowledging their own part in being motivated, the learners stated clearly that the tutor also has a role in motivating them to learn. Not just by making the work accessible or interesting, but on an individual level through praise and encouragement. It also has something to do with their demeanour and the learning environment that they create at the outset. The participants wanted the learning not only to be interesting but the tutor to encourage them to learn either through their actions or the opportunities they provided. When asked what was important about the tutor in a quality learning experience a learner from the Tai Chi class said:

> *They [the tutor] are praising and encouraging.*

One learner contrasted their present, encouraging teacher of the Steady and Stable group with a second class she attended when she said:

> *It is up to the tutor. I go to another class apart from this one, We do the exercises, sometimes to music, but sometimes the tutor just says do it 15 times or 20 times and you are left to your own devices. You do it but there is not the same interest.*

In such cases learners are not just motivated to learn specific knowledge or develop a specific skill but are encouraged as learners *per se*. One learner supported this by saying:

> *The tutor is number one [importance in determining quality] with the right characteristics and that sort of thing – they must extend you to use your talents, make you want to do more.*

Make Learning Fun

There is a great deal of research, which highlights the benefits of having fun in learning which enables learning to take place readily. It also feeds back into other quality characteristics such as motivation (Characteristic 6) and taking part in learning activities (Characteristic 7). A number of learners stressed that, for them, later-life learning was for the sheer enjoyment of learning and valued classes where this sense of fun was reciprocated.

One learner from the Drama Group stated that quality arose from:

> *A tutor [who] allows and encourages a sense of humour. It must be very open and very relaxed to make it a good experience.*

A member of the Men's Group said that the quality of learning:

> *... depends on who is in charge. Number one, they must have a sense of humour.*

This characteristic of fun was also associated with the lack of pressure or stress, which they felt was associated with formal learning in general and learning at school in their past in particular. The lack of assessment and associated judgement characterising their experience of informal learning provided them with what they needed. One learner spoke for many others in the focus group when he said:

> *At the end of the day you don't want a lot of pressure – for the majority of people – it's just for fun.*

For one learner, this quality characteristic was more important than the 'challenge' provided during quality learning sessions when she said of Art History:

> *We take in what information we can whereas in art classes we are happy with what we are doing and get on with it and [are] not challenged too much.*

Treat the Learners with Respect

This was a powerful characteristic within quality learning. Faced with a class of learners with widely different backgrounds and needs, tutors in a quality learning experience respected both the expertise and experience the learners brought.

According to the participants, the issue of respect can manifest itself in many ways from how the tutor speaks to the learners to how they organise their learning. It is also linked to characteristics such as letting the learners ask questions (Characteristic 2) and being challenged (Characteristic 3) rather than just receiving what the tutor has decided to deliver.

Straight away one participant, speaking about quality learning, said that:

> *It has to be non-threatening. The teacher is encouraging, clear, never condemns you or makes you feel small.*

The Feasibility Study group identified adult education classes as places where they felt a lack of respect and in the focus groups the learners valued being respected too. One learner described the balance needed between encouragement and respect in this way:

> *Here we also have the chance, if we want to say something we can but there are times when one might feel there is nothing I really want to say, nothing I can add. If that happens you are normally made to feel guilty by not joining in the discussion but you might just want to listen to the discussion and take it in.*

Disrespect can also come from a lack of appreciation for what the learners already know, understand and can do as one experienced learner said:

> *I think you need a challenge. I have found everything here at a challenging level. I'm not talked down to.*

In one class, where quality learning was not evident, the tutor was considered to be quite disrespectful through harsh criticism of the learners. One learner said:

> *I did drop out of one class. I wasn't alone in this. We were not free to give our opinions especially if it was a criticism of what we were doing.*

Are Qualified as a Teacher

Although not expressed through a large number of comments, the expectation that tutors should be qualified was expressed with strong feelings when it was raised and was underpinned by comments learners made alluding to the ability of tutors. They often used 'experienced' meaning 'experienced teacher' suggesting that the person was qualified as a teacher. It does not necessarily mean school teacher or graduate, but trained in the aspects they were delivering – not just knowing about things but knowing how to teach it to others and understanding how those others may learn it best.

Of course, this is no guarantee that the best 'teaching' was by qualified teachers or that being qualified to teach in schools (pedagogy) or further education colleges (andragogy) enabled such professionals to be an expert in teaching those in later life (geragogy). Nevertheless for some learners this characteristic was important.

One learner said that a quality learning session would only be one:

> *If the teacher is highly qualified and experienced in what they are teaching.*

Another learner supported this position by stating that for him of all the characteristics associated with quality learning:

> *Top of the list is that they should be qualified.*

Some learners felt that qualifications were important but were unsure just what those qualifications should be. For example, one said that:

> *The tutors should be qualified but not necessarily in the same way [as schools].*

While another learner felt the tutors should be qualified specifically to teach older learners. She said:

> *It is different for over fifties education and the need to develop the skills of the students learning – the teacher needs qualifications.*

One learner cautioned against assuming being qualified was enough, as this, for him, did not equate to being a 'good' teacher. He said:

> *In my observations at the computer class, the people in charge are very good at getting from the beginning to the top but not very good at teaching. They have passed all the paperwork so they are qualified. It does help but it has to be a 'professional' to be able to communicate the subject.*

Are Experienced in What They Are Teaching

For later-life learners in this study, tutor experience was important. This view was partly linked to their respect for that person and partly influenced by their belief that experienced tutors were able to embellish their teaching with practical everyday examples that later-life learners appreciated and could relate to.

In some cases qualifications and experience were intertwined as with the comment from the learner in the previous section:

> *If the teacher is highly qualified and experienced in whatever they are teaching.*

For one learner, experience was actually more important. He said:

> *They must have a bit of experience, not just paperwork.*

For another learner, experience could take the place of qualifications. He said:

> *We don't worry about qualifications [of the tutor]. If you have been at something for a very long time you sort of learn it.*

For some learners, having experience rather than qualifications was a feature of teaching and learning in informal education. Their expectations were lowered as a result. One learner said:

> *But as this is non-statutory education, we are doing it for our own benefits. It is not statutory education where we need to get a qualification – we are just doing this to draw on our physical or mental interests.*

Involve Learners in Their Learning

According to the participants, tutors who involved learners in the learning and did not just treat them as passive learners were seen to be contributing to quality learning. They appreciated being active learners and they also found learning from their peers could be as valuable as learning from the tutor. The focus group participants suggested that tutors should involve learners at all stages in the learning process. For example, one participant, talking about the tutor in a quality learning experience, stressed straight away that:

> *They must give you a chance to get involved and to join in.*

A second learner, reflecting on learning other than at Golden Gates said:

> *I think, it has not happened here, but the number one [factor] is having a tutor who involves you and makes you want to join in and do as good as you can.*

One learner in the Art History class was honest enough to admit that the tutor getting her involved was important if she was to learn anything. She said:

> *Personally, if I was left on my own I would probably sit and just chat to people.*

For another learner, it was important to have a tutor who:

> *... involves everyone whatever their ability.*

In fact, learning where the tutor involves the learners can have a very positive effect on both the tutor and the learner as one participant explained:

> *Sometimes, someone cannot do something a certain way and it is up to the teacher to adapt it a certain way. One of the exercises I have been told by my teacher, I had difficulty doing it due to my back and hip problems and he [the tutor] adapted it for me. We both learned something by that.*

However, the opportunity to become involved in their learning needs to be presented in the right way to suit those who are learning. One way of ensuring this is to ask the learners how they wish to be involved. As one learner put it:

> *There is always that choice to think about what we are doing. It belongs to the people who do these sessions, it is a cooperative process and they must have an input.*

A fellow learner said it helped her to develop her skills in public speaking:

> *In The News is a very big class but you are expected to read in front of others. I particularly joined that class just so I could speak as I had been very inhibited to say anything before and in that class you have to participate and comment and get up and say what you know.*

Provide Challenge to the Learners – to Learn New Things

This characteristic was partly linked to Characteristic 1 about learning new things and also Characteristic 3 where the learners were willing to be challenged in their learning. However 'providing challenge to learners' was also about the tutor themselves finding out what their individual learners understood and could do and devising a way in which their individual needs were met (Characteristic 4). To challenge learners to learn new things or in new ways, tutors must be aware of an individual's current expertise and experience and also their learning requirements.

For one participant, such challenge happened in quality learning. She said:

> *... Looking at our group we are functioning at different levels yet [the tutor] acknowledges that and challenges all of us within a sort of flexible way.*

For another learner, providing challenge was seen as a key component of the tutor's role in quality informal later-life learning:

> *As a student you are there to absorb. Yes, you can have a part, but there is a paid person at the class and it is up to the teacher to accept whatever is going on and either to leave them to it or push them and challenge them if it is necessary depending where you are on that particular day.*

A further learner from the same focus group said that in such sessions:

> *It is your chance to try something you have not tried before and your chance to try something new.*

While another later-life learner described the challenge provided in quality learning in terms of being 'extended' by saying:

> *The tutor is number one [importance in determining quality] with the right characteristics and that sort of thing - they must extend you to use your talents, make you want to do more. All the tutors do and you are broadening your horizons too.*

By contrast, one member of the Sewing Group said she become disillusioned in one class where such challenge simply was not there. She said:

> *I went to a knitting session, a knitting class and the [tutor], well I taught her how to knit, what to do.*

Ask for the Opinions of the Learners

Asking for the opinions of learners was thought to be very important and was not the same as 'letting me ask questions' (Characteristic 10). Asking for opinions was more allied to respect for the learners (Characteristic 13) as being experienced and expert, not just within a sphere of learning or work but also from life itself. It was about relationships where the tutor empowers the learners to contribute to the learning experience.

One learner, in describing quality learning, said that:

> *Also with this class we are involved in [deciding] the topics. We have free will and can make decisions.*

One learner was able to describe how garnering the opinions of learners led to a positive atmosphere in the classes he attended:

We normally start each term asking what do you want to talk about during the term. Sometimes something will come up that day or if there is anything on someone's mind.

However, other factors can affect the giving of opinions even where the tutor is actively supporting this strategy. One learner mentioned that:

Having a small group like this is more intimate than a huge lecture hall or something like that. You have more confidence to ask and give your own opinion where if you have a big class you might not.

For some learners, an approach where the opinions of the learners are valued extends to where the tutor enables learners to give advice to each other too:

We all have our opinions on other people's work and that helps us to really want to come back and get down to it and get everyone else's opinion, which can help you.

Give Learners Confidence

According to the participants, taking an active part in learning activities was thought to be important (Characteristic 7) and so was motivation (Characteristic 11). In addition, older learners sometimes spoke of having to overcome barriers to learning that were not faced by pupils or young students. Barriers included a lack of confidence having often endured poor experiences of learning at school and being concerned that on returning to learning that they would not be able to cope with the demand it made on them.

In the opinion of one learner, asked about quality learning, simply said:

It gives you confidence.

Confidence can be gained through direct encouragement and support from the tutor as one learner said:

It was a confidence thing and a support mechanism and despite what level you were at someone supported you in your learning

Confidence may also come about through relieving the stress that otherwise negatively affects confidence as another learner said:

Stress can be a barrier to learning. No one is telling us 'I don't like what you have done'.

Encourage the Learners to Keep on Learning

According to the later-life learners, this characteristic often takes the form of praise for a specific subject where the feedback to individuals is not just on what they have done, but on what they should do next. It is about implicitly or explicitly setting goals, which are as much about the learner's ability to learn as they are about the knowledge or skill they are addressing.

In quality learning, one learner said of the tutor that:

> *They are praising and encouraging and that you are with a group of friends.*

A second learner said that this goes with a positive approach involving respect too:

> *It has to be non-threatening. The teacher is encouraging, clear, never condemns you or makes you feel small.*

Part C: About the Organisation

Table 6.4 indicates that, through thematic analysis, eight distinct characteristics were identified as underpinning the role of the learning organisation within a quality learning experience. These characteristics were, once again, viewed by the participants in the focus groups as being both important and the responsibility of the provider itself. Although the assigned statements are

TABLE 6.4 Relative strength of the characteristics of quality in informal later-life learning associated with the 'organisation' aspect

Characteristic Number	*Themes: Characteristics of Quality*	*Number of Coded References*
25	The group had a friendly feeling to it	26
22	The atmosphere was safe/non-threatening	17
21	The accommodation was suitable for the purpose	12
24	The group was not too large	8
26	The organisation listens to complaints	7
28	The room was organised – everyone could see and hear	6
23	The equipment used in the class worked well	5
27	The tutors were selected with care by the organisation	2
	Number of the 479 total references coded as thernes relating to the Organisation.	83
	Percentage of coded references about the Organisation	17%

less voluminous than the other two stakeholders, corresponding to just 17%, the organisation is nevertheless viewed as being very important in providing or supporting quality learning. The organisation was seen as responsible for ensuring learning 'had a friendly feeling to it' and the 'atmosphere was safe and non-threatening' in particular.

Each of the eight 'organisation' characteristics is now discussed and is also illustrated through appropriate references made by the participants. The relative strength of support of a particular characteristic can be gleaned, once again, from the relative number of references associated with it made by the participating learners. In this third section, 'the group having a friendly feel to it' was the most strongly supported characteristic of quality.

The Accommodation Was Suitable for Purpose

The physical learning environment can matter whether you are in a school or a university and especially, perhaps, in the kind of utilitarian settings in which much later-life learning takes place. A quality learning experience often happens because the accommodation used is appropriate to meet the needs of the learners. It does not have to be a purpose-built educational facility but does enable the learners to thrive and learn.

One learner said that for quality learning to happen, the place you are having the class in must be 'suitable'. She went on to describe the benefits that had been gained from moving to more appropriate accommodation. She said:

> *... We are in the big hall for Tai Chi [now] and that is fine but originally we used to use this [class]room and that [large] number of people doing exercise when they need room, everyone is falling over each other. So depending on what type of class it is, the surroundings can make a difference.*

It was important, members of the Tai Chi class said, not just to do certain actions but also to make learners feel better and feel like learning. One said:

> *... if you have something that is bright, airy, clean and welcoming and someone has put a bit of effort into it, then you think 'I would like to go to that space' so you grade the space in line with your learning first and it makes it much more enjoyable for you to go there.*

One learner felt that the quality of the accommodation available for learning was also a reflection of the quality of provision by saying that, in her opinion:

> *If you have a school that is run down and decrepit looking, then it says that education is not really of any value and only rubbish people go there.*

For another learner, however, accommodation, although an important element in learning, was not the over-riding factor in deciding the quality of that learning and said:

> *It's not the room. It's nice and cosy here but it doesn't matter where you are.*

The Atmosphere Was Safe/Non-threatening

It was surprising to hear how a significant number of older learners had experienced some stressful learning situations they described as 'threatening'. These manifested themselves, for example, where individuals 'took over' the class and the teacher was not able to control their outbursts or where a class was 'ruled' by a smaller group within it and other learners did not feel able to ask questions or play a part.

When simply asked what makes quality learning one learner said:

> *It has to be non-threatening.*

A fellow learner then reflected back on learning earlier in her life when not feeling safe negatively affected her ability to learn and said:

> *In school there can be a really disruptive element within the class and you wanted to learn but you couldn't. Now there is an atmosphere in this class where other people let you learn.*

One learner went further and said:

> *I think sometimes you can get a person in the class who is very dominant and if the tutor cannot control that sort of [behaviour] that can be extremely irritating.*

One participant readily shared her own experience by saying:

> *In psychology the tutor lost control of the class and there were too many [students] and they kept coming in and out, on the 'phone and the teacher did not take control.*

The Equipment Used in the Class Worked Well

In quality learning, where equipment is being used, it needs to work as it is deigned to in order to support effective learning. As much older age learning takes place in non-educational settings, much equipment is portable and, subject to disturbance, may not work. There is often no technical support. This aspect is not just focused on more sophisticated learning equipment, such as power-point projectors, it can be controlling heating or ventilation to enable the physical environment to be conducive to learning.

Asked to identify factors positively affecting quality learning one learner readily volunteered:

> *The equipment. We have now got the screen and the 'computer thing'. It is very visual and all an aid, a tool, to learning.*

However, an example where the equipment does not have to be technical or expensive, just fit for purpose, was given by one learner who, while praising the learning he had just been involved in, went on to say:

> *It has been difficult for me to comprehend everything and I should have brought a pad and a pen and tried to write it down. But I cannot listen and write at the same time.*

Another learner also alluded to the importance of equipment, albeit simple materials, by saying that, for them, quality learning involves:

> *Someone who has a passion for the subject and also that the facilities are good, like there are handouts, summaries of what the session is about or sometimes there is a nice presentation with a power point.*

The Group Was Not Too Large

This characteristic, identified by the focus groups is, of course, subjective but matters in later-life learning. In the infant stage of primary schools in England there is a 'cap' to restrict classes to 30 children, which indicates the extent to which the government sees large numbers as getting in the way of effective teaching and learning. In larger classes, it is maintained, the facilitator is not able to give the individual learners the attention and support they require. This could be considered to be just as important in later life, if not more so, where the learning groups have not been homogenised though factors such as age (year cohorts), sex (by school or by grouping), or ability (by streaming or setting) and therefore participants are less likely to progress in learning at the same rate. One learner stated that:

> *I left the psychology class because the class got too large, people just kept coming in and out and the tutor couldn't cope, it just wasn't enjoyable.*

Another learner said that quality learning cannot take place:

> *... if the class gets too big or if there is an influx of new people. It always changes the atmosphere irrespective of who is teaching you*

More specifically some learners identified how the increase in size affected the quality of learning in general, as one learner said that:

It depends on the subject but with large numbers of students in a class [you fail to learn] when you don't get any attention.

The Group Had a Friendly Feeling to It

The organisation is clearly seen to have a role in ensuring the learning environments under their auspices are learner-friendly. It is about shared expectations and how people are introduced and supported during their learning programmes. Satisfaction surveys provide some feedback but they only ask the people who have stayed, not necessarily those that have left and so do not provide a rounded picture. One such example came from discussions in an Advanced French class where it was stated that some learners had left because they found it 'too hard' but neither the tutor nor the learners knew what had happened to them.

Golden Gates was seen to provide the right provision for one learner by ensuring the classes provided had a friendly feeling to them:

All of the classes I have been to with [Golden Gates], except one at [venue], they are very friendly people and they will include you all the time. Straight away you know everybody. Okay, you cannot remember everybody's names but if they have anything you can contribute to you, as you are new to it, not used to it, they will help you.

A fellow learner, new to Golden Gates, supported this by saying:

Although I have only been coming here a couple of weeks, the people here have made me feel very welcome, showing certain useful things and helping me.

Another learner said that, by way of contrast:

One of the places I went to I felt not so included, naming no names, but I went one day and realised this is not for me. Where I draw now the first day I came I felt welcome but the other place was not welcoming or inclusive – it was a poor place.

The Organisation Listens to Complaints

This was a second characteristic that was not strongly supported by large numbers of comments but was very vocally stressed on a number of occasions. A quality learning experience was influenced by the extent to which the learning organisation was willing to listen to complaints. This was about encouraging such dialogue and then acting on the issues raised. One example of the latter point was raised in discussions in a language class that involved intense conversation. It was suffering from being held each week in a communal and noisy canteen. Despite a number of complaints, it still is.

For many, it was an important but a theoretical consideration:

I think we feel able to go to the Head [of Golden Gates] and say, look, this course isn't what we expected and I think, although I have never done that, that channel is open.

Another learner articulated how complaints should be handled by saying:

Of course if they [the students] are unhappy with the teaching they must deal with it in some diplomatic way.

Some were strong in their approach to dealing with complaints by saying:

It's our responsibility to keep up the standards. If you are not being stimulated or learning anything, or the communication is poor and it's the view of your fellow students, you need to do something about it.

While another received support from fellow learners' body language and said:

But who would want to do that – most people would just leave. Most people would not want to get the tutor into trouble.

The Tutors Were Selected with Care by the Organisation

This characteristic of quality revealed an implicit, and sometimes explicit, perception that the learning organisation selected the tutors with care – that the people in front of them in the classrooms were appropriate both in their qualifications and experience, perhaps, but also in the personal qualities they brought to the classroom. This is not always the case in later-life learning where there can be significant difficulties in the recruitment of tutors in the UK. Working against such employment are rates of remuneration, which are relatively small, and work that is temporary in nature.

Discussions around this topic revealed an implicit set of expectations that the good characteristics of tutors have been identified through careful selection and those with the unwanted characteristics have not been employed. As such this 'careful selection' was seen to be characteristic of quality learning.

One learner said that only 'good' tutors should be employed and went on to say:

Some instructors may be well qualified but do not create the right environment in the schoolroom. It doesn't make you want to learn.

Another alluded to the fact that older learners have specific needs which tutors are employed to match:

It is different if you're doing a degree or finishing high school, whatever, we want to enjoy it. We will tolerate less and it must be better quality in a way because if you are teaching at a university and someone has to take your course, they just have to take your course.

The Room Was Organised – Everyone Could See and Hear

What would seem a very basic requirement looms large in making up a quality learning experience. In schools, for example, the learning abilities of individuals are often very similar and any differences are carefully catalogued, advertised and monitored. In later-life learning this is less likely to be the case with the diverse nature of the groups and the often, through not being revealed, lack of information on personal needs. Where it is good, those with seeing or hearing needs are catered for by, for example, being sat nearer the front of the class.

One learner said that being able to hear made learning sessions one of quality and that he had experienced the opposite at times. He said:

If you are asking what gets in the way, sometimes I cannot hear the teacher or their voice, the tone of their voice is not able to project and you are not able to hear at the back of the class and for me that is important.

Not being able to hear can happen for a number of reasons such as poor sound equipment, inadequate acoustics, or even noise from other learners. One learner targeted the latter by saying:

I think it [not being able to hear] does happen sometimes in classes when people are chatting when the tutor is trying to tell you something

At the same time, learning cannot be of the quality expected where the learner cannot see what they need to see to learn. One participant commented:

Other people talk about seeing and some classes I have been to, not this one, where they will be doing exercises in the class and you cannot actually see them [the tutor]. You spend your time juwst trying to see what they are doing in the activity class and the tutor is not engaging as they are just doing their own thing. [FG1Q2–4P]

Summary

Table 6.5 provides a summary outlining the nature of the characteristics of quality associated across all three stakeholders of learning: the learner, the tutor, and the organisation. It also highlights the number of references in support of each characteristic following qualitative thematic analysis.

TABLE 6.5 Overall numbers of coded references associated with individual characteristics of quality in informal later-life learning

Characteristic Number	*Characteristics of Quality*	*Number of Coded References*
	About You	
4	I had my individual learning needs met	51
6	I was, myself, motivated to learn	37
1	I definitely learned new things	23
2	I found the group friendly	22
7	I took part in the learning activities	16
8	I encouraged others to learn too	12
3	I was challenged in my learning	9
5	I was treated with respect	7
	Sub-total of coded references for **About You**	177
	About the Tutor	
9	They made the learning interesting	26
11	They motivated me to want to learn	26
12	They made learning fun	26
17	They challenged me to learn new things	26
16	They involved learners in their learning	24
13	They treated me with respect	21
15	They are experienced in what they are teaching	20
18	They asked for my opinions	15
14	They were qualified as a teacher	12
20	They encouraged me to keep on learning	10
19	They gave me confidence	9
10	They let me ask questions	4
	Sub-total of coded references for **About the Tutor**	219
	About the Organisation	
25	The group had a friendly feeling	26
22	The atmosphere was safe and non-threatening	17
21	The accommodation was suitable for our needs	12
24	The group was not too large	8
26	The Organisation would listen to complaints	7
28	The room was Organised for everyone to see and hear	6
23	The equipment worked well	5
27	The Organisation selected the tutors with care	2
	Sub-total of coded references for **About the Organisation**	83
	Total Number of coded references from Analysis	479

7

THE DIMENSIONS AND PARAMETERS OF QUALITY LATER-LIFE LEARNING

Introduction

The 28 characteristics of quality learning in later life, identified through the focus groups, were strongly associated with informal learning environments that the participants considered to be of 'quality'. The characteristics have so far been organised and presented under the three key stakeholders of learners, tutor, and organisation and the relative involvement, indeed importance, of each stakeholder has been identified through the number of associated characteristics.

However, further thematic analysis looking for commonality amongst the themes, revealed that characteristics associated with one stakeholder often had similarities with characteristics of another stakeholder. For example, 'learning new things' under the 'learners' aspect is associated with the changes in cognitive processes outlined in the literature review chapters as is 'being challenged in their learning' under the 'tutors' aspect. At the same time the 'they made learning fun' characteristic is a feature of the 'attitude' of the tutor to the learning process and to the learners, which may be said to correspond with 'the organisation listens to complaints' indicator, which highlights a positive attitude shown under the 'organisation' aspect.

Therefore, the themes were grouped under four dimensions associated with the characteristics of quality informal later-life learning. These dimensions, attitudinal, physical, social, and cognitive, are displayed in Figure 7.1.

Attitudinal (Ten Characteristics)

These were characteristics that were associated with the attitude of those involved in learning.

DOI: 10.4324/9781003269892-7

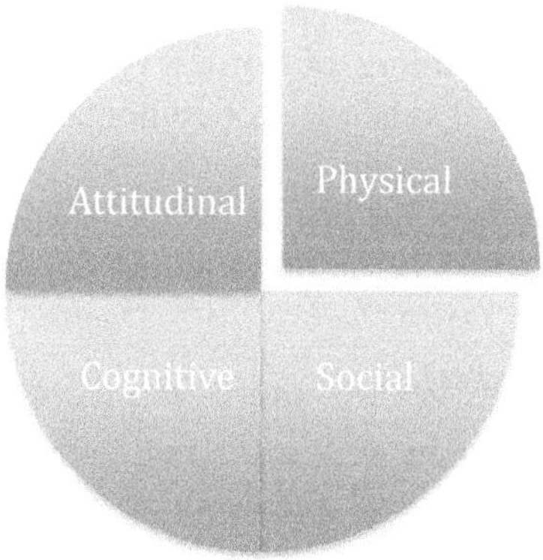

FIGURE 7.1 Chart outlining the four dimensions associated with the characteristics of quality in informal later-life learning.

For the learner, it included characteristics such as 'I was, myself, motivated to learn' and 'I encouraged others to learn too'. These were qualities of the learner which revealed their attitude to learning – were they motivated, were they encouraging?

For the tutor, it included characteristics such as 'making learning interesting' and 'giving learners' confidence' which are characteristic of the positive attitude of tutors in quality learning sessions.

For the organisation, characteristics such as 'listening to complaints' and 'selecting tutors with care' are features of an organisation that has a positive attitude towards enabling quality learning to take place.

Physical (Four Characteristics)

These were characteristics that were associated with the physical environment identified with quality learning sessions.

For the learner and the tutor, none of the characteristics were relevant.

For the organisation, characteristics such as 'the accommodation was suitable for our needs' and 'the equipment worked well' are associated with an organisation that is providing a learning environment, which enables quality learning to take place.

Social (Eight Characteristics)

These were characteristics that were associated with the sociability of those involved in learning.

For the learner, it included the characteristics 'I found the group friendly' and 'I was treated with respect' – qualities of the learners which revealed their sense of sociability and positive attitude towards fostering fruitful relationships.

For the tutor, it included characteristics such as 'involving learners in learning' and 'asking for the opinions of learners' which generate a sociable approach to learning identified as being a component of quality learning sessions.

For the organisation, the characteristic that the 'group had a friendly feeling' was an expression of how the organisation enables a sociable environment to be created and maintained. It was important to the focus group participants.

Cognitive (Six Characteristics)

These were characteristics that were associated with the mental processes associated with learning in general and learning in quality informal later-life learning sessions in particular.

For the learner, it included characteristics such as 'I definitely learned new things' and 'I was challenged in my learning'. These were qualities of the learner that revealed their internal processes of learning and the 'changes' said to need to take place for learning to occur (Illeris, 2007; Findsen, 2014).

For the tutor, it included the characteristic associated with 'challenging [the learner] to learn new things' which alludes to the 'challenge' also associated with the learners themselves as identified by the participants in this research.

There were two characteristics that were associated with the tutor. One is specifically related to his or her 'being qualified as a teacher'. The other is whether they 'are experienced in what they are teaching' and relates to the ability and expertise of the tutor to provide the information and learning opportunities that can lead to a 'change' in the learners. The association of each of the three stakeholders and the 28 quality characteristics with each of the four dimensions is outlined in Table 7.1.

The Relative Importance of the Learning Dimensions

It can be seen from the responses of the focus groups in revealing the 28 characteristics of quality informal later-life learning that these cover four dimensions of learning. From the number of statements associated with each we can see that the 'attitude' of learner, tutor, and organisation to learning had more characteristics aligned with it (10) suggesting that this dimension is the most important ingredient to quality, informal later-life learning.

The dimension with the second most characteristics associated is 'social' indicating that the social dimension of learning is a clear importance to later-life learners in a quality-learning environment. The third most characteristic-rich dimension is the 'cognitive' demand and includes the expectations of the learners about the demands likely to be made on them from attending the session.

TABLE 7.1 Profile of the four dimensions of learning across the 28 characteristics of quality associated with the three stakeholders involved in quality later-life learning

	DIMENSIONS			
Stakeholders	Cognitive	Attitudinal	Social	Physical
		CHARACTERISTICS of QUALITY		
Tutor	They were qualified as a teacher	They made the learning interesting	They let me ask questions	
	They are experienced in what they are teaching	They motivated me to want to learn	They treated me with respect	
	They challenged me to learn new things	They made learning fun	They involved learners in their learning	
		They gave me confidence	They asked for my opinions	
		They encouraged me to keep on learning		
Learner	I definitely learned new things	I was, myself, motivated to learn	I was treated with respect	
	I was challenged in my learning	I took part in the learning activities	I found the group friendly	
	I had my individual learning needs me	I encouraged others to learn too		
Organisation		The organisation would listen to complaints	The atmosphere was safe and non-threatening	The accommodation was suitable for our needs
		The organisation selected the tutors with care	The group had a friendly feeling	The equipment worked well
				The group was not too large
				The room was organised for everyone to see & hear

The 'physical' environment dimension appears less important (four characteristics) suggesting 'quality' learning can, perhaps, take place if the other three dimensions are present even in a poorly supportive physical environment and especially if the social and attitudinal (emotional) climate is right for the learners.

Analysis of the findings from the focus groups identified the number of references associated with each characteristic. When these were associated with the four dimensions, a further, and slightly different, picture is revealed. The attitudinal features are still the most regularly mentioned as important in quality learning sessions with social features also highlighted strongly. However the cognitive demands through learning new things and involving challenge are as strongly represented by numbers of references as the social dimension. The cognitive dimension is now well above the physical environment dimension that it was close to through aligning the characteristics of quality alone. This illustrates that the cognitive demand in quality learning sessions is a well-supported dimension and includes characteristics referencing the academic ability and experience of the tutor.

Summary

In presenting the focus group findings in this chapter, comments made by the participants were categorised under the three stakeholders associated with quality learning; the learners, the tutor and the learning organisation. Further thematic qualitative analysis identified 28 themes, interpreted as characteristics of quality, and their relative numbers (eight characteristics associated with the learners, twelve with the tutor, and eight with the organisation) illustrated the relatively significant role of the tutor.

The focus groups also provided a great deal of detail about the importance of each characteristic making up quality learning. The ranking of the characteristics of quality, based on the number of comments linked with each, provided some indication of the relative perceived importance of a characteristic. As highlighted earlier, the support for the central role of the tutor was illustrated by the higher rankings compared to those for the learner characteristics, which in turn were higher in general than those for the organisation characteristics. However, even within the three stakeholders, further thematic analysis identified the influence of four 'dimensions' of later-life learning. These were to do with the attitudinal, cognitive, social, and physical dimensions of informal later-life learning and through the alignment of references, their relative importance began to emerge. In the next phase of research, (Phase 3), these perceptions of quality espoused by the focus groups were put before a wider group of fellow later-life learners, using a questionnaire, to identify to what extent they were supported.

Phase 3 – The Quality Learning Survey

Introduction

The third phase of fieldwork involved a survey, using a questionnaire, that involved a greater number of later-life learners within Golden Gates (202) and from across a wider range of types of learning. This fieldwork provided an opportunity to explore whether the characteristics of quality, which had arisen out of the focus groups, were supported by other learners. It also provided an opportunity to identify and gather any additional perceptions associated with quality learning by including a free response option within the questionnaire (Figure 7.2).

This chapter presents the findings and statistical analysis of the Quality Learning Questionnaire (QLQ). Where relevant, these findings are supported by comments from the participants collected either in the free response part of the questionnaire or directly from the participants during the process. A copy of the final questionnaire is presented in the appendices (Appendix C). As the changes to the pilot questionnaire were procedural, all responses to both the pilot questionnaire and the questionnaire proper were included in the final analysis.

Profile of the Groups Taking Part in the Survey

In total, 28 learning groups were involved in the survey and were drawn from a range of activities in order to ensure cohorts of learners taking part in particular types of learning were included. The groups concerned are outlined in Table 7.1. As with the nine focus groups, the learning groups taking part in the survey were drawn from a series of geographical locations as the learning hubs used (seven) represented the provision available to different learning communities within Golden Gates.

Within the level of anonymity agreed with the participants themselves, the management of Golden Gates and the Ethics Committee of the Institute of

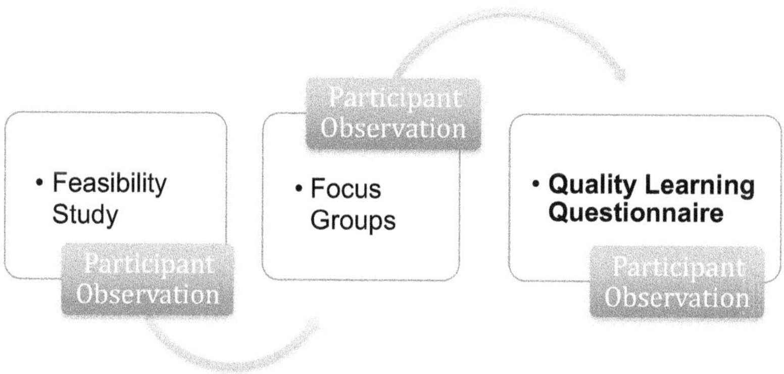

FIGURE 7.2 The survey within the mixed-method approach adopted.

Education, a specific set of demographic features was gathered from the participants. These data provided the opportunity to investigate whether each feature had an impact on the perceptions of the learners concerning what they considered quality informal later-life learning to be. These were:

- Sex.
- Age.
- Ethnicity.
- Level of educational qualifications.
- Number of classes attended each week.

Table 7.2 outlines the types of learning participant learners were involved in as well as the associated venues where they were held. In all, six types of learning

TABLE 7.2 Learning groups participating in the Quality Learning Questionnaire indicating types of learning and venues

Type of Learning	*Learning Group (Code)*	*Venue*
Physical Exercise	Steady and Stable (SS)	6
	Stretch and Tone (ST)	6
	Zumba (ZU)	5
Creative	Creative Threads (CT)	6
	Drama and Theatre (DT)	5
	Beginners Painting (BP)	6
	Drama (DR)	5
	Art Painting (AP)	6
	Sewing Class (SW)	7
Information Technology	Ipad for Beginners (IP)	6
	Digital Photography (DP)	6
	Beginners Internet (BI)	6
Humanities	Music Appreciation (MA)	4
	In the News (1) (NO)	5
	In the News (2) (NT)	5
	Philosophy (PH)	6
Languages	French (Advanced) (FA)	5
	English Conversation (EC)	5
	Russian (Advanced) (RA)	5
	Advanced French (AF)	6
	Spanish Conversation (SC)	5
Literature	Life Stories (LS)	5
Social Event	Westbourne Social (WS)	8
	Queen's Social (QS)	8
	Monthly Meeting (MM)	4
	Park Social (PS)	10
	Harrow Road Social (HS)	9
	Stroke Recovery (SR)	5

were covered, resonating with the profile of learning opportunities offered by Golden Gates' weekly programmes. The six types were:

(a) physical
(b) languages
(c) literature
(d) humanities
(e) creative
(f) information technology.

These categorical descriptions of types of learning were drawn from the titles described in the Golden Gates programmes and are also analogous to terms used by other later-life learning organisations. They were useful groupings of similar learning activities. In addition a number of 'social groups' of learners were included not aligned to a particular type of learning.

Questionnaire Groups – Sex and Age Profiles

The majority of learners participating in the questionnaire phase were women (Table 7.3), which was in line with the stated profile of later-life learners at Golden Gates although no exact overall figures for informal learning cohorts at the charity were available (Figure 7.3).

TABLE 7.3 Gender profile of participants involved in the Quality Learning Questionnaire

Questionnaire Participants	*Male*	*Female*
Totals (202)	27	175
Percentages of 202 Participants	13.4%	86.6%

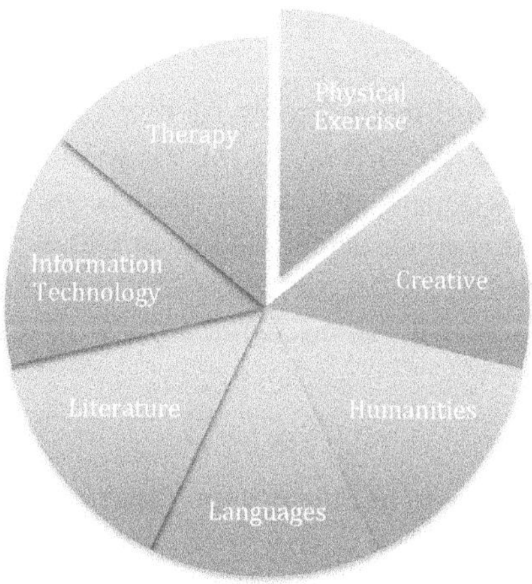

FIGURE 7.3 Profile of types of learning represented within the Quality Learning Questionnaire survey.

TABLE 7.4 Age profile of participants involved in the Quality Learning Questionnaire

Questionnaire Participants	*Aged 50–59*	*Aged 60–69*	*Aged 70–79*	*Aged 80+*
Totals (199)*	18	59	88	34
Percentages of 199 Participants	9.0%	29.6%	44.2%	17.1%

* Of the 202 participants, three did not respond to the request to provide their date of birth giving an overall response rate of 98.51%.

TABLE 7.5 Ethnicity profile of participants involved in the Quality Learning Questionnaire

Group	*White*	*Mixed*	*Asian*	*Black*	*Chinese*
Totals (from 192)	156	1	4	29	2
Percentages of 192 Participants*	81.3%	0.5%	2.1%	15.1%	1.0%

* Of the 202 participants, ten did not respond to the request to state their ethnicity giving an overall repose rate of 95%.

Table 7.4 indicates that the age group with the smallest number of questionnaire participants was 50–59 and that this was because the classes were scheduled to accommodate those who were post-work or other such full-time responsibilities. The majority of learners were in the 60–69 and 70–79 age ranges, corresponding to active retirees (the 3rd Age) while a smaller number were aged 80 years and older.

Questionnaire Groups – Ethnicity

Table 7.5. outlines the ethnicity profile of those involved in the questionnaire phase of fieldwork. According to the Head of Learning, the make up of the cohort of learners participating in the questionnaire was representative of the profile of later-life learners at Golden Gates. However, once again, the exact statistical patterns of those involved in informal learning were not available as such figures are not gathered locally, or used centrally, by the organisation.

Questionnaire Groups – Level of Educational Qualifications

As Table 7.6 indicates, a slight majority of learners participating in the questionnaire phase had a qualification of some kind. Over a quarter of learners had a degree or higher degree, which constituted over 50% of those with qualifications of some kind (Table 7.7).

TABLE 7.6 Qualification profile of participants involved in the Quality Learning Questionnaire

Group	*No Qualification*	*Qualification*
Totals (from 200)	91	109
Percentage from 200 Participants*	45.5%	54.5%

* Of the 202 participants, two did not respond to the request to state whether they had a qualification or not giving an overall response rate of 99.0%.

TABLE 7.7 Profile of participants involved in the Quality Learning Questionnaire by level of qualification

Group	*School Level*	*Diploma*	*Degree*	*Higher Degree*
Totals (from 106)	28	21	47	10
Percentage from 200 Participants*	14.0%	10.5%	23.5%	5.0%
Percentage from 106 Participants stating their qualifications**	26.4%	19.8%	44.3%	9.4%

* Of the 202 participants, two did not respond to the request to state whether they had a qualification or not giving an overall response rate of 99.0%.

** Of the 109 participants who stated that they had a qualification, three did not respond to the request to state the level of the qualification giving an overall response rate of 97.2%.

TABLE 7.8 Profile of participants involved in the Quality Learning Questionnaire by level of participation in learning

Group	*1 Class*	*2 Classes*	*3 Classes*	*4+ Classes*
Totals (192 responses)*	68	57	38	29
Percentages (%)	35.4%	29.7%	19.8%	15.1%

* Of the 202 participants, ten did not respond to the request to state the number of classes they attended per week giving an overall response rate of 95.0%.

Questionnaire Groups – Number of Classes Attended Per Week

Table 7.8 indicates that the majority of learners participating in the questionnaire, representing approximately two-thirds, attended more than one informal learning class per week.

The relationship between educational qualifications and the number of classes attended is illustrated in Table 7.9. A Chi-square test for independence indicated no significant association between the number of classes attended and the presence of educational qualifications (chi = 0.634).

Further analysis considered whether the level of qualification affected the level of participation (number of classes attended) and the profile is outlined in Table 7.10. It indicated that the greater the number of classes the fewer number of participants attended and that this held true for different levels of qualification. Of those learners with a higher degree, none of the participants

TABLE 7.9 Profile of participants involved in the Quality Learning Questionnaire by qualification and level of participation in learning

	1 Class	*2 Classes*	*3 Classes*	*4+ Classes*	*Total*
No Qualifications	29 38.2%	22 29.9%	13 17.1%	12 15.8%	76
Qualifications	37 35.3%	31 29.2%	25 23.7%	13 12.3%	106
Total (182 Responses)*	66	53	38	25	182

* Of 202 participants in the questionnaire, 182 provided a reponse to both the number of classes they attended and their qualification status giving a response rate of 90.0%.

TABLE 7.10 Profile of participants involved in the Quality Learning Questionnaire by level of participation in learning compared to level of qualification

	1 Class	*2 Classes*	*3 Classes*	*4 Classes*	*Total*
School level	11 39.3%	9 32.1%	7 25.0%	1 3.6%	28
Diploma level	2 9.6%	7 33.3%	7 33.3%	5 23.8%	21
Degree level	22 46.8%	7 14.9%	11 23.4%	7 14.9%	47
Higher Degree level	2 20.0%	8 80.0%	0	0	10
Total of responses*	37	31	25	13	106

* Of the 91 participants who said they had no qualifications, 76 responded to the number of classes attended too giving a response rate of 83.5%; Of the 109 participants who said they had qualifications, 106 also said the number of classes they attended too giving a response rate of 97.2%.

with this level of qualification attended more than two classes per week. The relationship between the level of educational qualifications and the number of classes attended was subjected to a Chi-square test for independence indicated no significant association between the number of classes attended and level of educational qualifications (phi = 0.271).

Venues

Two of the seven venues used for the questionnaire had previously been used for focus group meetings but two others had not and differed also from where the initial Feasibility Study was held. Altogether the responses to the overall research fieldwork were gathered from a total of ten different venues (Table 7.11).

TABLE 7.11 Profile of venues used throughout the mixed-method fieldwork

Research Phase	*Venues Used**
Phase 1. Feasibility study	1
Phase 2. Focus groups	2, 3, 4, 5
Phase 3. Quality Learning Questionnaire	4, 5, 6, 7, 8, 9, 10

* Once again, the names of the particular venues are not provided in order to preserve anonymity for the learning organisation concerned.

Analysis of Questionnaire Responses

In total, 205 participants were invited to participate from the 28 groups and 202 did so constituting a participation rate of **98.53%**. The participants

Physical Exercise (PHI)	*Creative (CRE)*
Steady and Stable	Art and Painting
Balance and Health	Drama and Theatre
Zumba	Creative Threads
Yoga	Mosaic and Pottery
Aerobics	Cooking and Sewing
Tai Chi	Beginners Painting
Stretch and Tone	Sewing
Keep Fit	Gardening
Line Dancing	
Ballroom Dancing	Humanities (HUM)
Dance (Latin)	Art History
Exercise	Current Affairs
Pilates	Philosophy
	Art Appreciation
Languages (LAN)	Music
English Language	Local History
Languages	Discussion Group
French	Social Learning
English Conversation	Singing
Russian Conversation	
Advanced Russian	Therapy (THE)
English Language	Physiotherapy
	Play Reading
Information Technology (ITC)	Lip Reading
Building Websites	Speech Therapy
Intermediate Computer	
IPad for Beginners	Literature (LIT)
Computers	Life Stories
Beginners Computer	Creative Writing
	English

were asked to consider a 'quality learning session' in which they had been involved and to indicate the presence of the quality characteristics and their relative value using a Likert Scale (1–5). They identified a wide range of classes (48) outlined below and a further type of learning, therapy, emerged.

Stakeholder Data Analysis

The responses to the indicator statements concerned with the characteristics of quality learning were subjected to quantitative analysis, firstly by entering the data into Excel spreadsheets and then using SPSS software as an analytical tool. Participants were asked to say, for each of the characteristics of a quality learning experience, if they: Strongly Agree (5), Agree (4), Neutral (3), Disagree (2), and Strongly Disagree (1). that each was a feature of 'quality' informal later-life learning they had experienced. Overall the survey results demonstrated that there was strong support for the characteristics of quality learning that had been identified in the focus groups. In other words, the perceptions of quality, expressed in the focus groups, were found to be shared more widely across Golden Gates. The mean response across all 28 characteristics of quality learning was **4.59**, which was between 4 (Agree) and 5 (Strongly Agree), the highest possible score.

Table 7.12 shows the results for the collated responses across the characteristics corresponding with the three stakeholders in informal later-life learning and illustrates that they were all positively supported. There were slightly more positive responses in relation to tutor characteristics (mean score – 4.67) being features of quality learning environments than those concerned with learner characteristics (mean score – 4.59). Both tutor and learner characteristics were more positively supported than organisation characteristics (mean score – 4.50). This was in line with the balance of comments arising out of the focus groups where more coded references were made about the tutors' characteristics contributing to quality learning than the learners and, in turn, than those of the organisation.

TABLE 7.12 Combined quality characteristic means aligned with the three stakeholders from the Quality Learning Questionnaire

Section	*Three Stakeholders in the Questionnaire*	*Focus*	*Combined Characteristic Means*
A	About You	Learner	4.59
B	About the Tutor	Tutor	4.67
C	About the Organisation	Organisation	4.50

Characteristics and Dimensions Data Analysis

As described previously, the identification of the four dimensions under which the quality characteristics are grouped, namely, cognitive (COG), attitudinal (ATT), social (SOC) and physical (PHY), arose from the categorical analysis association of the 28 characteristics of quality informal learning in later life arising from the focus group comments and subsequent coded references.

Tables 7.13–7.16 outline the findings from the statistical analysis of the data arising from the questionnaire concerned with the 28 characteristics of quality and the extent to which the participants supported each characteristic. Here, the outcomes of the analysis are discussed as characteristics both under the three stakeholders in later-life learning and the four dimensions of learning.

Cognitive Characteristics of Quality

The data and analysis associated with the cognitive characteristics of quality are set out in Table 7.13. As with the outcomes of the analysis of the focus groups, the tutor characteristics were more strongly supported (mean score 4.66) than those of the learners (mean score 4.60) although only slightly.

Of particular note is that the qualification and/or experience of the tutor, often not overtly strong through number of coded references associated with these quality characteristics in the focus groups, had shown itself to be important within the cognitive dimension when raised with a greater number of learners.

Indeed, the characteristic of the tutor being 'experienced in what they are teaching' was the most positively supported characteristic (mean score – 4.76) and more important than if the tutor was 'qualified as a teacher' (mean score – 4.65).

For the learners as a stakeholder, although there was less support for the characteristic of 'I had my individual learning needs met', it was still strongly supported with a mean score of 4.46. This finding reveals that a number of 'quality' learning sessions took place where this characteristic was perceived to be less of a feature than other characteristics.

There was strong support for 'definitely learned new things' being a characteristic of quality learning (mean score 4.74) while 'I was challenged in my learning', with a mean score of 4.42, was the lowest positively supported characteristic within the cognitive dimension. Although this was still seen as a positive characteristic, as a mean score of 4.42 is still very high, it was not perceived to be a feature of a number of quality learning sessions by the participant learners. As one member of the French (Advanced) group put it:

> *I like to be challenged when I learn but I don't think everyone does. It depends on your personality I think. [QFAG-2]*

TABLE 7.13 Questionnaire responses for the quality characteristics associated with the cognitive dimension and the three stakeholders

Dimension	*Characteristic*	*Strongly Agree*	*Agree*	*Neutral*	*Disagree*	*Strongly Disagree*	*Mean Score*	*Stand Dev.*
	Tutor							
	They were qualified as a teacher (14)	148	35	18	0	0		
		73.6%	17.4%	9.0%		4.65	0.641	
	They are experienced in what they are teaching (15)	158	41	2	0	1		
		78.2%	20.3%	1.0%		0.5%	4.76	0.514
	They challenged me to learn new things (17)	132	57	12	1	0		
		65.3%	28.2%	6.0%	0.5%		4.58	0.627
	Sub-Total for Cognitive Tutor Characteristics	438	133	32	1	1		
Cognitive		72.3%	22.0%	5.3%	0.2%	0.2%	4.66	
	Learner							
	I definitely learned new things(1)	154	43	5	0	0		
		76.2%	21.3%	2.5%			4.74	0.494
	I was challenged in my learning (3)	116	60	21	5	0		
		57.4%	29.7%	10.4%	2.5%		4.42	0.776
	I had my individual learning needs met (4)	116	64	21	1	0		
		57.4%	31.7%	10.4%	0.5%		4.46	0.698
	Sub-Total for Cognitive Learner Characteristics	386	167	47	6	0		
		63.7%	27.6%	7.7%	1.0%		4.54	
	Sub-Total for All Congnitive Characteristics						4.60	

Nevertheless, the contribution the tutor was perceived to have made to quality learning sessions was a very positive one. Whether a learner was 'challenged in my learning' or whether they 'had my individual learning needs met' are both subjective aspects of learning and depend upon how an individual learner responded to the same piece of learning before them. Hence both these characteristics had the largest standard deviation figures at 0.776 and 0.698 respectively indicating the greatest variability in responses.

Attitudinal Characteristics of Quality

As the data in Table 7.14 indicates, within the attitudinal dimension of quality, the characteristics associated with each of the three stakeholders were all positively supported. The mean scores being between 4.00 (Agree) and 5 (Strongly Agree) indicate that all three stakeholders were perceived to be contributors to quality learning.

As with the outcomes of the analysis of the focus groups' data, the tutor characteristics were more strongly supported (mean score – 4.68) than those of the other two stakeholders. However, within the attitudinal dimension, the characteristics of the organisation were more strongly supported (mean score – 4.55) than that of the learners (mean score– 4.52) albeit only slightly. Therefore, the approach of those organising and administering later-life learning sessions was found to be perceived as having contributed to the quality of learning taking place.

With a mean score of 4.77, the most positively supported attitudinal characteristic was that the tutor 'made learning interesting' while motivation was also seen to be important too. Both external motivation by the tutor through the 'they motivated me to want to learn' characteristic (mean score – 4.72) and internal motivation through the 'I was, myself, motivated to learn' characteristic (mean score – 4.72) were seen to be important and equally so. 'Encouraging others to learn too' although important, had a relatively low mean score (4.24) and was less of a strong feature of quality learning sessions.

The quality characteristic 'the organisation would listen to complaints', although positively supported as being a feature of quality learning, was less strongly supported than other attitudinal characteristics (mean score – 4.33). This could depend on whether a complainant had a positive response to their complaint or not and hence, perhaps, the greater standard deviation score for this characteristic (0.788). One learner in the Stroke Recovery class felt the members of staff of the organisation were not available to listen to their complaints, especially about holding their meetings in the noisy café, which she had raised previously as an issue. She suggested during the questionnaire fieldwork that:

> *Managers etc. should be in classes – participate – listen to us. [QSR-3]*

TABLE 7.14 Questionnaire responses for the quality characteristics associated with the attitudinal dimension and the three stakeholders

Dimension	*Characteristic*	*Strongly Agree*	*Agree*	*Neutral*	*Disagree*	*Strongly Disagree*	*Mean Score*	*Stand Dev.*
	Tutor							
	They made the learning interesting (9)	158	41	3	0	0		
		78.2%	20.3%	1.5%			4.77	0.457
	They motivated me to want to learn (11)	152	43	7	0	0		
		75.2%	21.3%	3.5%			4.72	0.524
	They made learning fun (12)	144	49	9	0	0		
		71.3%	24.2%	4.5%			4.67	0.560
	They gave me confidence (19)	139	49	14	0	0		
		68.8%	24.3%	6.9%			4.62	0.613
	They encouraged me to keep on learning (20)	136	54	12	0	0		
		67.3%	26.7%	6.0%			4.61	0.598
Attitudinal	Sub-Total for Attitudinal Tutor Characteristics	729	236	45	0	0		
		72.2%	23.4%	4.4%			4.68	
	Learner							
	I was, my self motivated to learn (6)	152	44	6	0	0		
		75.2%	21.8%	3.0%			4.72	0.510
	I took part in the learning activities (7)	134	55	12	1	0		
		66.3%	27.2%	6.0%	0.5%		4.59	0.617
	I encouraged others to learn too (8)	91	75	30	5	1		
		45.0%	37.1%	14.9%	2.5%	0.5%	4.24	0.830
	Sub-Total for Attitudinal Tutor Characteristics	377	174	48	6	1		
		62.2%	28.7%	7.9%	3.0%	0.1%	4.52	

Organisation							
The organisation would listen to complaints (26)	97	70	27	0	2		
	49.5%	35.7%	13.8%		1.0%	4.33	0.788
The organisation selected the tutors with care (27)	130	47	17	0	0		
	67.0%	24.2%	8.8%			4.58	0.648
Sub-Total for Attitudinal Organisation Charavteristics	227	117	44	0	2		
	58.2%	33.0%	11.3%		0.5%	4.45	
Sub-Total for All Attitudinal Characteristics						4.45	

Social Characteristics of Quality

The analysis of the questionnaire responses to the characteristics of quality associated with the social dimension is set out in Table 7.15. The questionnaire revealed that the social dimension of learning was perceived to have been of greater importance than any of the other three dimensions in quality informal later-life learning. The social dimension of informal later-life learning was the most strongly supported with a mean score of 4.72, indicating its importance to quality learning. It was more strongly supported than the next two strongly supported dimensions – the cognitive dimension (mean score – 4.60) and the attitudinal dimension (mean score – 4.55).

This strong support for the social dimension was apparent across all three stakeholders through their high mean scores – the tutor (4.67), the learners (4.77), and the organisation (4.72) – and highlighted that the learners and the organisation were perceived to have the greatest roles to play in ensuring their characteristics influenced sessions to make them ones of quality.

The most popular characteristics were associated with the notion of 'respect'. For the learners as stakeholders, 'I was treated with respect' by fellow learners (mean score – 4.80), and for the tutor as a stakeholder 'they treated me with respect' (mean score – 4.79) had the strongest support indicating their importance to quality learning. Also above the mean score for the social dimension characteristics (4.72) was that the learners 'found the group friendly' (mean score – 4.74) and that the organisation, as a stakeholder in quality informal later-life learning had ensured 'the group had a friendly feeling' (mean score – 4.73).

The standard deviation measures for the mean scores of all the social dimension quality characteristics were relatively low and all but one were below 0.575. For 'they asked for my opinion', however, the standard deviation score was higher (0.734) indicating that not all quality learning sessions provided opportunities for learners to express their own opinions.

Physical Characteristics of Quality

The analysis of the questionnaire responses to the characteristics of quality associated with the physical dimension is set out in Table 7.16. All four characteristics are associated with the organisation as a stakeholder in quality learning. With a mean score of 4.43, this dimension too was strongly supported by the participants in the questionnaire but was the least strongly supported of all four dimensions. This suggests that quality learning was considered to have taken place even where the physical environment did not encompass all the characteristics valued by the learners.

Table 7.17 indicates that for the different organisation characteristics of quality, the one receiving the lowest mean score (4.31) was 'the equipment worked well'. This contrasts with the overall findings and illustrates that the role of the equipment is significant to some participants perceiving it to be

TABLE 7.15 Questionnaire responses for the quality characteristics associated with the social dimension and the three stakeholders

Dimension	*Characteristic*	*Strongly Agree*	*Agree*	*Neutral*	*Disagree*	*Strongly Disagree*	*Mean Score*	*Stand Dev.*
	Tutor							
	They let me ask questions (10)	148	50	3	0	0		
		73.6%	24.9%	1.5%			4.72	0.483
	They treated me with respect (13)	159	43	0	0	0		
		78.7%	21.3%				4.79	0.410
	They involved (16) learners in learning	149	42	11	0	0		
		73.8%	20.8%	5.4%			4.68	0.571
	They asked for my opinions (18)	121	58	20	3			
		59.9%	28.7%	9.9%	1.5%		4.47	0.734
	Sub-Total for Social Tutor Characteristics	**577**	**193**	**34**	**3**			
		71.5%	**24.0%**	**4.2%**	**0.3%**		**4.67**	
	Learner							
Social	I found the group Friendly (2)	152	47	3	0	0		
		75.2%	23.3%	1.5%			4.74	0.473
	I was treated with respect (5)	164	36	2	0	0		
		81.2%	17.8%	1.0%			4.80	0.423
	Sub-Total for Social Learner Characteristics	316	83	5				
		78.2%	20.6%	1.2%			4.77	
	Organisation							
	The atmosphere was safe and non-threatening (22)	151	44	6	1	0		
		74.7%	21.8%	3.0%	0.5%		4.71	0.547
	They group had a friendly feeling (25)	152	45	5	0	0		
		75.2%	22.3%	2.5%			4.73	0.501
	Sub-Total for Social Organisation Characteristics	303	89	11	1	0		
		75.0%	22.0%	2.72%	0.3%		4.72	
	Sub-Total for All Social Characteristics						4.72	

TABLE 7.16 Questionnaire responses for the quality characteristics associated with the physical dimension and the three stakeholders

Dimension	*Characteristic*	*Strongly Agree*	*Agree*	*Neutral*	*Disagree*	*Strongly Disagree*	*Mean Score*	*Stand Dev.*
	Organisation							
	The accommodation was suitable for our needs (21)	117	59	19	7	0		
		57.9%	28.2%	9.4%	3.5%		4.42	0.788
	The equipment worked well (23)	101	55	25	6	2		
		53.4%	29.1%	13.2%	3.2%	1.1%	4.31	0.913
Physical	The group was not too large (24)	125	55	18	3	1		
		61.9%	27.2%	8.9%	1.5%	0.5%	4.49	0.761
	The room was organised for everyone to see and hear (28)	125	56	14	6	0		
		62.1%	27.9%	7.0%	3.0%		4.49	0.755
	Sub-Total for Physical Organisation Characteristics	468	225	76	22	3	4.43	
		59.0%	28.3%	9.6%	2.8%	0.3%		

a quality learning session or not. As one participant in the Creative Threads group said on handing in her questionnaire:

> *I came to the new class at the end of the 'season'. The sewing class had no sewing machine. I especially came for that class and I was disappointed.*

This characteristic, relating to equipment working well, had the largest standard deviation of all (0.913). Once again, the 'accommodation was suitable for our needs' (mean score – 4.42) was strongly supported but was highlighted as less of a feature of some quality learning sessions than other characteristics. The qualitative comments provided in response to the open question section of the questionnaire indicated that a number of learning sessions perceived as high quality had taken place in physical environments that were not optimal in terms of meeting the learning needs of the group or individuals. For example, even within one In the News class, which was very strongly supported by the participants, one learner wrote, in the open response section of the questionnaire, that they were in:

> *Need of a larger classroom, more space and a desk.*

Neutral or Disagreeing Responses to the Quality Characteristics

Although only a small number of learners provided responses to statements that were not positive (positive being scores of 4 or 5) it is valuable in looking at the pattern of neutral scores (score 3) or those Disagreeing or Strongly Disagreeing (scores 2 and 1 respectively).

For the different learner characteristics, the characteristic that received most responses that were not positive, (17.9%), was 'I encouraged others to learn too' (outlined in Table 7.15) with 36 of the 202 responses. Other learner characteristics not receiving scores of agreement were 'I was challenged in my learning' (12.9%) and 'I had my individual learning needs met' (10.9%). Once again the positive support for the tutor is highlighted by the fewer number of scores for the characteristics of quality that were not positive.

Some of the features already outlined could also be gleaned through reflection of the Neutral or Disagree/Strongly Disagree columns. For example, 12.9% of participants maintained that 'I was not challenged in my learning' while 17.5% of participants could not agree that in the quality learning session they were considering that 'the equipment worked well'.

Demographic Analysis

Having analysed the responses according to the dimensions of learning and categorising the characteristics by stakeholder, I went on to check for any differences in participant responses to the questionnaire that may have been attributable to demographic characteristics including sex, age and ethnicity. The findings are presented here.

Sex

From Table 7.17 it can be seen that the mean scores for men and for women, expressed through their responses across the Likert Scale, were not different. Through their mean scores for all the quality characteristics, both genders responded equally positively to the characteristics presented being features of quality learning.

Age

An analysis of variance (ANOVA) test was carried out, which compared the age groups with the mean scores for each indicator statement on the questionnaire. The analysis showed that for 24 of the 28 characteristics of learning there was no significant statistical difference in responses across the age groups to the presence of the particular characteristic within quality learning sessions. For four characteristics, 'I had my individual needs met', 'I was treated with respect', 'I was, myself, motivated to learn' (all Learner characteristics), and 'The organisation selected the tutors with care' (an Organisation characteristic) there were differences between the responses of different age groups.

Table 7.18 presents the F statistic and the p values for these four characteristics where the F ratio indicates where there is more variability between the groups than there is within the groups and the p value indicates where this variability can be found.

TABLE 7.17 Comparison of the sex of the participants responding to the questionnaire with mean scores and standard deviations

Sex	*Number Participating*	*Mean Scores*	*Standard Deviation*
Male	27	4.59	0.18
Female	175	4.60	0.16

TABLE 7.18 Comparison of the age groups of the participants responding to the questionnaire with mean scores where there is significant variability between groups

Statement	*Stakeholder*	*F Statistic*	*p value*
I had my individual needs met	Learner	4.402	0.002
I was treated with respect	Learner	3.645	0.007
I was, myself, motivated to learn	Learner	3.614	0.007
The organisation selected the tutors with care	Learner	3.149	0.016

TABLE 7.19 Comparison of White and Non-White participants and their mean scores and standard deviations

Ethnicity	*Number Participating*	*Mean Scores*	*Standard Deviation*
White	156	4.59	0.17
Non-White	46	4.63	0.13

In all four cases the older learners (age 80–89 or over 90 years old) were less positive than the younger later-life learners (50–59 or 60–69) that each of the four characteristics of quality featured in the quality learning sessions that they were considering when replying to the questionnaire.

Ethnicity

From Table 7.19 it can be seen that the mean scores for White and Non-White participants, expressed through their responses against the Likert scale, showed a slightly more positive response from the Non-White participants from two very positive sets of responses. Through their mean scores, both groups responded equally positively to the characteristics being features of quality learning.

An ANOVA test was once again carried out on the data collated, this time comparing the ethnic groups with regards to the mean scores for each indicator statement on the questionnaire. The analysis identified that there were no significant differences across the ethnic groups for any of the 28 characteristics of quality. Therefore all the characteristics were equally strongly supported across the profile of learners from different ethnic backgrounds.

Features of Quality Learning Sessions

Having analysed the responses to the questionnaire about quality learning it is now appropriate to look at the findings from the analysis of the types of learning sessions that participants reported as ones being the focus of their attention when considering the characteristics of quality. The questionnaire asked participants to identify four features of a learning experience, which they considered to have been of high quality. These were:

a Type of 'High Quality Learning Session or Activity'.
b The size of such a group.
c The time of day it took place.
d Whether the session was tutored or not.

Not all participants answered this part of the questionnaire, as not all the participants had necessarily directly experienced a learning session they considered to be of 'quality'. Overall 157 of the 202 participants responded and gave the details on their questionnaire. It is the analysis of those responses that is presented here.

Type of 'High Quality Learning Session or Activity'

In analysing the findings to this part of the questionnaire the learning sessions were grouped under the type of activity it belonged to. All seven types of learning (Table 7.20) were identified which were:

a Physical Exercise/Dancing (PHI).
b Creative (CRE).
c Information Technology/Computer (ITC).
d Humanities/Discussion Groups (HUM).
e Foreign Languages/English 2nd language) (LAN).
f Literature/Writing (LIT).
g Therapy (various) (THE).

Table 7.20 indicates that the humanities learning opportunities featured in almost a third of responses (30.0%) as displaying the characteristics of quality learning. Creative sessions (21.0%) and those involving physical exercise (18.4%) were also well supported. Table 7.20 outlines the profile of responses across the various learning activities. Although there was a strong correlation between the type of group participants were currently in and the type of group they identified as being one of quality (110 from 157 or 70.0% matched), this was, perhaps, likely to be the case in non-compulsory education where learners will be attending, in large numbers, classes they enjoy and not attending classes (and types of subject) they do not enjoy or have no interest in.

To this extent it was important that social groups were included in the spread of groups involved in the survey as they were not choosing the learning activity they were currently engaged in but reflecting on other quality learning experiences they were engaged in on other occasions or had been in the past (Table 7.21).

TABLE 7.20 Overall chosen quality learning session by learning type

Types of Learning	*PHI*	*CRE*	*ITC*	*HUM*	*LAN*	*LIT*	*THE*
Total Responses (N = 157)	29	33	16	47	21	7	4
Responses (%)	18.4%	21.0%	10.2%	30.0%	13.4%	4.5%	2.5%

TABLE 7.21 Chosen quality learning session responses by learning type

Group	*PHI*	*CRE*	*ITC*	*HUM*	*LAN*	*LIT*	*THE*
1. Steady and Stable	5	1					1
2. Drama and Theatre	2	4	1				
3. Creative Threads		6		1			
4. Beginners Painting*		3					
5. Music Appreciation*	1			3			
6. Westbourne Social*	3	1		1			
7. French (Advanced)*	1	1			7		
8. English Conversation*						2	
9. Stretch and Tone*	6				1	1	
10. Russian (Advanced)					3		
11. Zumba*	4						
12. Drama		5					
13. In the News (1)				14			
14. In the News (2)*		1		15	1		
15. iPad for Beginners*			4				
16. Art Painting*		6					
17. Philosophy*				6			
18. Advanced French*	1				3		
19. Queens Social*	1			2	1		
20. Life Stories*					1	3	
21. Stroke Recovery^							
22. Spanish Conversation	1				3		
23. Monthly Meeting*	2	2	3	2			2
24. Digital Photography*	1		3	1			
25. Park Social*				2	1		
26. Sewing Class		3				1	
27. Beginners Internet*			2				
28. Harrow Road Social*	1		3				1
Total Responses (N = 157)	**29**	**33**	**16**	**47**	**21**	7	**4**
Responses (%)	**18.4%**	**21.0%**	**10.2%**	**30.0%**	**13.4%**	**4.5%**	**2.4%**

* Not all participants responded to this question.
^ This question was not responded to by this particular group in the time available.

Analysis of Type of Quality Learning Session Data

Table 7.22 outlines the mean score for all the participants choosing each type of learning session, using the composite mean scores from across all 28 characteristics using the Likert scale. In total 157 of the 202 participants identified and named a specific type of learning.

TABLE 7.22 The number of respondents and composite mean scores for the 28 characteristics of quality

Type of Learning Session	*Number of Responses*	*Composite Mean Scores for perceptions of quality*
Physical	29	4.70
Creative	33	4.54
Technological	16	4.64
Humanities	47	4.63
Language	21	4.49
Literature	7	4.74
Therapy	4	4.65

All sessions were, overall, perceived as very positive (with mean composite scores of between 4 'Agree' and 5 'Strongly Agree') with regards the quality characteristics, with little difference between them. This outcome might be expected, as these 157 respondents had perceived that they had experienced actual quality learning environments while the other respondents had answered the question from a more theoretical standpoint.

Of the responses, the literature sessions had the highest composite mean score at 4.74 but this outcome was produced by only a small number of learners. Of those with a larger number of attendees, physical (exercise) classes such as Zumba, Tai Chi and dancing had the highest mean composite score at 4.70.

The Size of Group Associated with Perceptions of 'Quality Learning'

In analysing the findings relating to group size and its potential link with quality, reported class numbers were grouped together to get an idea across the range of classes rather than each class separately. As part of the questionnaire the participants were asked not only to think of a class they considered one of quality but also how many people were in that class as far as they could gauge or remember.

Therefore, the focus was not on the accuracy of the group numbers *per se* but an indication of where on the spectrum of sizes of learning classes the participants perceived quality learning sessions to be characterised (Table 7.23).

From the analysis of the findings associated with group size, (Table 7.23), the majority of respondents (over half) identified the classes in the 6–10 group range as being a feature of the quality learning session. At 54.1% this was much higher than any other grouping. It was significantly higher than the groups on either side. Only 5.1% chose classes within the smaller group and only 15% chose a class with more learners in the 11–15 range. This equates well with the characteristic of quality learning, which states that the group should be 'not too large', perhaps to enable individual learners to participate more (Figure 7.4).

TABLE 7.23 Profile of size of groups of class numbers across chosen quality learning sessions

Groups of Class Numbers	*1–5*	*6–10*	*11–15*	*15+*
Totals (N = 157)	8	85	25	39
Percentages (%)	5.1%	54.1%	15.9%	24.8%

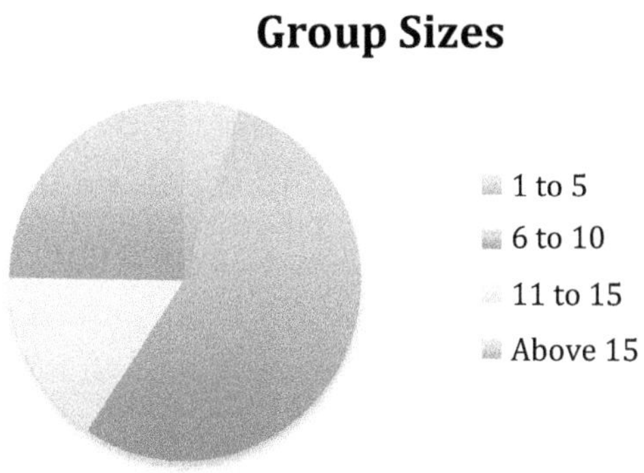

FIGURE 7.4 Chart highlighting the relative popularity of groups in class sizes across chosen quality learning sessions.

However, a significant number of learners (39 or 24.8%) chose sessions with over 15 learners suggesting that quality learning was not necessarily just number-dependent for many learners. This may be associated with many physical activity classes such as Steady and Stable and Tai Chi which proved popular or humanities classes such as In the News and Current Affairs, the former taking place in larger spaces and therefore holding larger numbers and the latter being talk-based and accepting larger numbers to promote fruitful discussion.

In fact, in some cases, such as dancing, larger numbers were needed to be maintained at a certain level to ensure there were enough partners to take part in certain dance routines. As one member of the Zumba class wrote on the questionnaire about her dancing class:

> *The class I do on a Monday needs to be bigger, especially for ballroom/Latin {American}.*

Table 7.24 outlines the profile of responses across the various individual groups. Although there is some association with the participants in a particular type of activity choosing that type of activity as one of the size they associated with quality, this is again more likely to be the case where learners attend classes they enjoy and, perhaps, would have stopped attending classes they did not enjoy or do not find had the characteristics of quality they seek. Once again, the inclusion of social groups proved to be valuable, as they learners were not necessarily choosing to focus a current learning activity.

TABLE 7.24 Profile of size of group across chosen quality learning sessions with respect to individual learning activities

Group/Numbers	*1–5*	*6–10*	*11–15*	*15+*
1. Steady and Stable		2	4	1
2. Drama and Theatre		7		
3. Creative Threads	1	5		1
4. Beginners Painting*		2	2	
5. Music Appreciation*		2	2	
6. Westbourne Social*			4	1
7. French (Advanced)*		8	1	
8. English Conversation*		1		
9. Stretch and Tone*		3	3	2
10. Russian (Advanced)	3			
11. Zumba*		1	3	
12. Drama		5		
13. In the News (1)				14
14. In the News (2)*	1			16
15. IPad for Beginners*		4		
16. Art Painting*		6		
17. Philosophy*		6		
18. Advanced French*		3	1	
19. Queens Social*		4		
20. Life Stories*	3	1		
21. Stroke Recovery^				
22. Spanish Conversation		4		
23. Monthly Meeting*		6	2	3
24. Digital Photography*		3	1	1
25. Park Social*		2	1	
26. Sewing Class*		4		
27. Beginners Internet*		2		
28. Harrow Road Social*		4	1	
Totals (from 157/157)	**8**	**85**	**25**	**39**
Percentages (%)	**5.1%**	**54.1%**	**15.9%**	**24.8%**

* Not all participants responded to this question.
^ This question was not responded to by this particular group in the time available.

The Time of Day Associated with Perceptions of 'Quality Learning'

In analysing the findings to this aspect of the questionnaire, start times were grouped together as either morning (AM) or afternoon (PM). Where the session straddled both sessions (recorded as am.pm or, say, 11.00 am to 1.00 pm by the respondents) the session was allocated to the morning, as that's when the learning began.

TABLE 7.25 Profile of start times of chosen quality learning sessions

Group Attendance	*Morning (am)*	*Afternoon (pm)*
Totals (from 157)	113	44
Percentages (%)	72.0%	28.0%

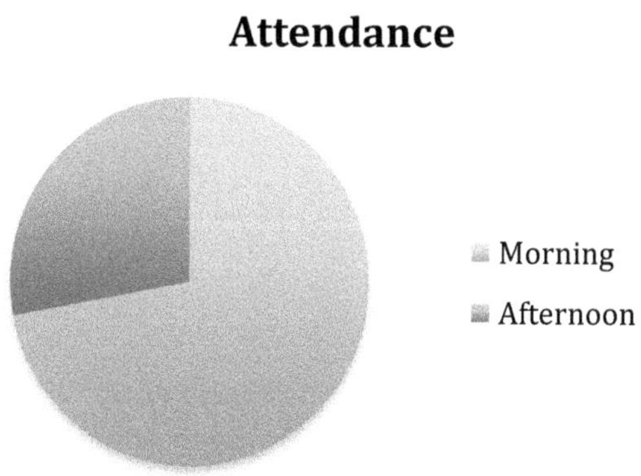

FIGURE 7.5 Chart highlighting relative popularity of start times across chosen quality learning sessions.

The groups taking part in the QLQ survey mirrored the range of classes provided by Golden Gates who operate learning sessions equally in the mornings and the afternoons. From the analysis of the findings associated with time of day (Table 7.25), the majority of respondents (almost three-quarters) identified the morning (am) sessions to be ones of quality compared to the afternoon (pm) sessions (Figure 7.5).

On the other hand, as one member of the Digital Photography class mentioned, the choice is a personal one, assuming there is a choice of both morning and afternoon sessions to attend:

Sleep for me is difficult, so courses starting later in the day suit me better

Tutor Presence Associated with Perceptions of 'Quality Learning'

In analysing the findings to this aspect of the questionnaire, it was simply a case of whether a tutor was present in the quality learning session the respondents had identified or not. From the results shown in Table 7.26, a tutor was present in almost all the sessions under consideration as ones of quality (97.4%).

This is in line with the greater number of characteristics associated with the tutor aspect of quality learning than the learners or organisation and the more positive response to the tutor characteristics throughout the survey. However,

TABLE 7.26 Profile of tutor presence within chosen quality learning sessions

Group	*Tutor Present*	*No Tutor Present*
Totals (from 155)	151	4
Percentages (%)	97.4%	2.6%

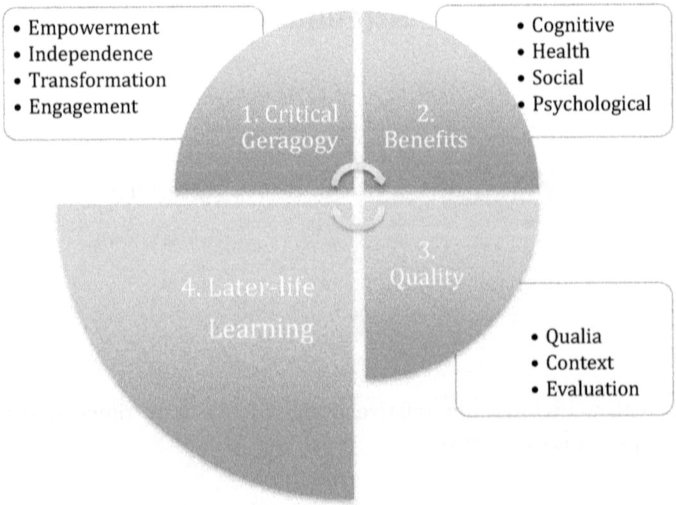

Facet 4 **Later-Life Learning**

- *Stakeholders* - identifying the importance of three contributors to quality informal later-life learning: the tutor, the learners and the organisation
- *Characteristics* - revealing the perceived characteristics of the quality learning environment associated with the three stakeholders
- *Dimensions* - understanding how the characteristics of quality learning coalesce within four overarching dimensions of quality later-life learning

FIGURE 7.6 The quality cirque for informal later-life learning (part 4).

it does also suggest it is possible to have a quality learning session with no 'tutor' present and that the learners, perhaps, take on many of the characteristics associated with the tutor.

The Quality Cirque (Part 4)

Figure 7.6 illustrates the fourth component part involved in the Quality Cirque arising from the analysis of data within the findings chapters (Chapters 6 and 7). Part 4 outlines what quality is for learning in informal later-life learning and suggests that understanding the relative roles of the three stakeholders, recognising, and adopting the characteristics of quality learning and giving attention to the four dimensions which allow the characteristics to flourish will maximise the benefits for the learners within a quality learning environment.

Summary

The analysis of the QLQ strongly supports each of the 28 characteristics of quality being present in sessions of informal later-life learning identified by participants as being ones of quality. The pattern of the tutor having the most impact on quality learning sessions followed by the learners themselves and the organisation as three stakeholders was maintained. For the four dimensions, the social dimension was highlighted as being the most important in quality learning and the physical dimension the least.

For the individual characteristics, the friendliness of the group (generated by the learners and the organisation) and the motivation to learn (generated by the learners and tutor) were of particular importance. In quality learning sessions, the learners learned new things but they were not necessarily challenged in doing so. Finally, the key role of the tutor was in making the learning interesting and being experienced in what they were teaching.

The absence of additional elements arising out of the questionnaire suggests the initial discussions were successful in teasing out and capturing the perceptions of the learners involved and that they spoke on behalf of their fellow learners. This profile was drawn from a larger number of participants who were involved in a greater number of types of learning and an even wider range of learning activities than members of the focus groups.

When identifying quality learning sessions, the greatest number of learners chose a 'humanities' session which strongly focused on characteristics such as 'asking the opinions of learners' and enabling the learners to 'take part in learning'. At the same time, they provided opportunities to 'keep up-to-date' which is something expressed as being valuable in the Feasibility Study discussions. At the same time, the strongest support for types of learning was in the 'physical' types of learning where, because of its very nature perhaps, 'individuals have their learning needs met' and were 'challenged in their learning'. They were also able to recognise where 'progress' had been made.

The presence of a tutor was also a key feature of quality learning sessions as would have been expected judging by the strong support for the tutor's role in quality learning both through the relative number of indicators identified and the larger quantity of comments associated with their role in such sessions. At the same time, and on the information provided, a greater number of such quality learning classes took place in the mornings rather than the afternoon. However, evidence of why this might be is limited.

Finally support for classes of a mid-range size 6–10 strengthens the quality characteristic of having classes that were 'not too large'. However, in some types of learning such as discussion groups or dancing, larger numbers of participants are required to aid participation and valued by the learners for this. As all these findings have been applied to informal later-life learning for the first time, it presents, perhaps, a unique evidence base on which to reflect.

8

WHAT DOES QUALITY LATER-LIFE LEARNING LOOK LIKE?

Introduction

When outlining the research Methodology used (Chapter 2), my role as a participant observer was both described and justified. Throughout the three phases of fieldwork, I made notes from any observations and used the framework of the 28 characteristics of quality to thematically analyse them. I then extracted relevant data to illustrate each characteristic in action and here the findings from my observations are presented under the four dimensions of informal later-life learning outlined earlier.

Each dimension section contains observations outlining where, when, and how the characteristics of quality were observed. At the same time I also identify where, in specific learning sessions, the features of quality that had been articulated by later-life learners were not observed. Where I have used quotes from the learners to illustrate or exemplify a point, these quotes were made either directly to me or within the group observed during the sessions when I was acting as a participant.

The questionnaire results indicated that the majority of participants (70%) identified an activity in the same domain or topic area they were currently participating in when asked to consider and identify a learning session that they perceived to be one of 'quality'. Therefore it seemed quite likely that the characteristics of quality they had experienced would be present in the learning sessions under observation.

DOI: 10.4324/9781003269892-8

The Cognitive Dimension

I Definitely Learned New Things

Whether a learner has actually learned new things is hard to determine objectively without an initial assessment and some measure of progress. Therefore, within the informal later-life learning context I was researching, I drew upon the subjective opinion of the learners. In learning sessions identified as ones of quality, the majority of learners identified learning new things as a characteristic of quality. Such progress was most readily articulated and demonstrated by learners during physical exercise activities and sessions such as English literature. In these classes, the learners, when presented with new moves to try or writing to tackle, were able to demonstratively achieve these by the end of the session.

The tasks outlined at the outset were often the same for all the class. They were rarely differentiated and so at that point did not take into account relative abilities or any individual's preferred way of learning. For example, in one Tai Chi class, the familiar exercises were well within the abilities of all the learners. Therefore the 'new things' that participants were learning were not often supported through the presentation and differentiation of tasks targeted to an individual's needs at the outset.

By contrast participants in many classes demonstrated that novel things were indeed learned or produced by outcome. Examples included the gaining of new skills in creative classes such as painting or the apparent gaining of new understanding in philosophy classes, which suggested that the teaching strategies employed by the tutors supported new learning.

> Learning new things by outcomes, through opportunities presented by the tutor, is what many learners said they wanted in quality informal later-life learning. One learner said of her practising artist tutors: *They [the tutors] are very skilled in their department and they are ever willing to share their knowledge. We are not too old to learn new tricks.*

I Was Challenged in My Learning

> During observations I found significant evidence of learners being challenged. For example, in humanities classes through targeted and probing questioning, in physical classes through individualised tasks taking into account learners' abilities and in information technology classes where the learners demonstrated new techniques they had been challenged to use. One learner in a literature class excitedly welcomed such 'challenge' when she said: *We're writing an anthology of our stories – I never thought I'd be part of [something like] that.*

In other classes, albeit a small number, there was a very similar routine each week and the tutor appeared disengaged with the participants. In one literature class, the tutor did not look at the performance of individuals at all and certainly not identify if they were being 'stretched' out of their 'comfort zones'. In one creative class, the learners complained that they had already done the task they had been asked to do on a previous occasion and by that same tutor.

> One learner stressed that challenge could only come about where the relative abilities of the learners were taken into account or they all suffered. She said: *Some classes need to be geared to beginners, intermediate and advanced. Mixing the classes slows others down.*

I Had My Individual Learning Needs Met

> Learning cohorts, as has been identified previously, are at their most diverse amongst those in later life. In most cases I observed such needs were catered for. In many physical exercise classes, for example, by enabling some participants to sit down in a chair for particular exercises while most stood. Such a sensitive approach was clearly valued by learners and one participant said that: *Before I came here I couldn't get out of the bath – I thought I was going to have to have a walk-in shower but now [bathing] is no problem. I love a bath.*

In non-physical classes, the learning needs of individual learners were not as well understood; such needs were not made overt or shared between learners and the tutor. For example, in a humanities session, the confident learners were very vocal and participated well throughout the session while others, more insular and needing encouragement, remained silent.

They Were Qualified as a Teacher

> This characteristic of quality learning was something that was not evident through participant observation. As discussed previously, the tutor being qualified, for some later-life learners, is a statement of their own worth as learners while other learners wanted to know that their tutor 'knew how to teach' and, for some, 'knew how to teach older learners'. Therefore this complex contribution to quality learning needs further research to identify how the 'qualification' aspect affects the practices seen in the classes. In one class the skills of a trained tutor were valued by one learner who remarked: *This is an exceptional class led by an exceptional man who engages us and encourages us all hugely. We exchange views on current affairs and he oversees our exchanges with great skill.*

They Are Experienced in What They Are Teaching

There were many good examples of where the current or previous experience of the tutor added value to the learning process. In such cases, the tutor was often of a similar age to the learners and had a background in the subject being studied. In one creative class, the tutor brought examples of students' work he was responsible for in another learning environment to show the learners examples of techniques being taught. In another humanities class, the tutor was able to make effective use of personal anecdotes to illustrate and enliven his input.

> Where the tutor appeared less experienced, they often avoided offering opportunities for the learners to interrupt or ask questions and therefore, perhaps, inadvertently challenge their knowledge or experience. For example, in one physical exercise session, the tutor went through the whole session without allowing feedback and in one literature class, the choice of what texts to study was reduced by the tutor to one book to discuss the nature of a protagonist, despite requests to use other books. In discussing another class she had attended recently, one learner differentiated her thoughts on the two classes, her current one being valued, by saying: *I am basing [my comments] on a specific lesson but I couldn't say the same about another language class I go to in which the tutor is inexperienced and often has material she hasn't prepared well.*

They Challenged Me to Learn New Things

In most classes there was evidence of the learners being challenged and if not in that particular session, the learners described how they had made progress, through challenge, throughout the course. In a foreign language class, new words introduced at the start were regularly attempted during the session and used correctly by the end.

> In a humanities class featuring discussions on 'current affairs', the learning was through the exchange of information and the challenge to previously held opinions and ideas. This was what the learners wanted as one learner said: *Our opinions or ideas are always varied and far-reaching - resulting in a stimulating and interesting session. The topics are always of immediate interest and all views are welcomed and discussed.*

However, in some creative and humanities classes, the work was too 'low level' and easily mastered by the learners. For example, in one sewing class, the learners used the machines available to complete a product using the skills they had rather than using new or better skills to address the task in hand. In one language class, the learners were all given the same task and worked through it for the duration of the session – some successfully while for others, the expectations were clearly too high and they floundered.

The Social Dimension

I Found the Group Friendly

Almost all the learning sessions observed were characterised by learner actions that put fellow learners at ease. Through the volume of smiles and warmth of expressions, the friendliness of the sessions shone through. This extract from my notes is provided by way of illustration.

> In an exercise class, some learners arrive early and put the mats and equipment out for all the learners knowing where each person will participate by name. They place a chair by one mat for a learner who requires it. A new member is introduced and warmly welcomed by all and learners volunteer to pair up with each other to help each exercise. They praise each other as they do so and laugh when things go array, as they often do. At the end they applaud each other and different learners stay behind to put away the equipment. Some learners leave together, chatting, having arrived alone.

Occasionally a group was less friendly. In one social session, for example, the chairs had been arranged so a latecomer had to sit on their own at the back unacknowledged by other learners (or the tutor) throughout the session.

I Was Treated with Respect

This indicator of quality is one that is 'in the eye of the beholder' and not always easy to observe directly. However, it was much in evidence in turn taking during discussions, the ready sharing of resources during painting classes and the making and fetching of refreshments for one another. There was very little sharp disagreement with just one example where one learner was perceived to have used up all of one colour of paint in a creative class. Overall, opinions were expressed freely without fear of adverse comment as this extract from my field-notes illustrates.

> In a humanities class, on the life and beliefs of Thomas Aquinas, the learners encourage each other to give opinions on their perceptions and feelings. These range from the political to the religious. When one learner contradicts the views of a fellow speaker, it is done respectfully and with the intention of adding something rather than disparaging what has been said before. The tutor did not have to intervene and each comment is as valued as another. At the break, individuals take the opportunity to talk freely with those they had 'challenged' during the exchange of views.

In one literature class, I mentioned to one learner that the features of their lives the group had been sharing to practise word-processing appeared to be quite personal. She had no problem with such sharing and said that for her: *Learning is not the only important thing – mutual respect amongst the group is also important.*

They Let Me Ask Questions

This characteristic of quality was a key feature of most learning sessions and was much appreciated by the learners. In social learning situations, for example, learners were encouraged to share what they had been doing and others were asked to join. There was regular dialogue between the learners and the tutors on most occasions whether to answer a question raised or to seek clarification of what was expected of them. Such dialogue did not just have to be about the learning. One learner said that she felt that: *We can ask questions whenever we want to – about anything.*

There were less opportunities to ask questions across some creative and humanities classes, where the tutor seemed intent in getting through the planned material more than focusing on learning. In one creative activity class, hands raised to signal the wish to ask a question led the tutor to respond that there was no time for questions as 'there is too much [work] to get through'.

They Treated Me with Respect

There were good examples of this quality characteristic observed such as in some humanities classes where praise for the contributions of the learners lent value to their experience or expertise. In some, large humanities (current affairs) discussion classes, the tutor openly valued the courage the learners showed in standing up and expressing themselves. In one creative class, the tutor positively accepted the lack of relative ability of some as one

> member of the class mentioned: *Although I was completely ignorant about the subject, the tutor never made me feel stupid when I asked basic questions. We were all treated with respect and made to feel worthwhile.*

However, this was not always the case although it was never expressed as overt disrespect. For example, in one creative class, learners were often told they could do better without any evidence to suggest they could. In one literature class, there was no recognition of what learners were clearly achieving in analysing a text.

They Involved Learners in Learning

In most cases the learners were fully involved in their learning. In humanities classes, this was often through question and answer sessions while in creative classes it was through active participation in group working. In a language class, participants had to carefully listen to the 'homework' of fellow learners and then assess it. Once again, an extract from my notes is provided by way of illustration.

> In a drama class, the tutor sets the scene and describes the background to the play they are to create and perform that afternoon. Each member of the group is given a role and is provided with a few characteristics of the person they are to play and encouraged to elaborate on them. In turn, pairs of leaders are asked to come up and act out a scene the tutor describes and make up the dialogue in character. After each vignette the 'actors' are applauded warmly by their fellow learners before having their contributions critiqued by their peers, prompted by the tutor, which helps them to prepare for their next scenes later in the afternoon.

In some classes, the format was said to be repetitive by the participants and where all learning was auditory, or physical, there was no opportunity to bring other ways of learning to the fore. For example, in physical exercise classes, the learners routinely followed the tutor, but if asked to do an exercise themselves, having been given its name, they were unable to do so.

They Asked for My Opinions

This characteristic of quality was readily evident in classes where discussion was a key feature of the learning. As one learner put it: *What I really like about current affairs is that we get to give our opinions – good or bad, it doesn't matter.*

This supports the quality characteristic of 'showing the learners respect' mentioned previously but it goes beyond that in capturing the experience and expertise of the learners. This involves the learners bringing new information to their learning, and that of others, either from their past work or life experiences. In one social setting, the speaker drew on the science background of one learner to help put the technical language and ideas into a more easily understood format. In a humanities session, the tutor allowed a learner to explain the doubts that had arisen in his mind about issues from his working practices to stimulate discussions. As learning can be enhanced by such experiential learning, (Wolfe, 2006), this was an important feature.

The Atmosphere Was Safe and Non-Threatening

Golden Gates is a well-organised and well-staffed learning organisation and there is a clear focus on ensuring the learners are entering well-supervised and comfortable learning environments. The classes are held during the day and finish early when it is likely to be daylight outside. They are offered in well-populated areas and in as many venues as possible to reduce the need to travel. A series of managers oversee the welfare of the learners in certain venues irrespective of the courses on offer. As well as course satisfaction surveys concerned with the organisation or learning sessions, each manager in a particular geographical area offers a programme of social sessions where personal as well as learning issues can be raised and addressed. No negative comments were made about this issue to me during my observation fieldwork.

> One learner offered the reminder that it is not straightforward being a later-life learner and that the provision needs to ensure there are no additional barriers to get in the way of them attending. She said: *Learning is important. If you don't keep on learning you'll just waste away and die. I know it's an effort to get there sometimes but it's always worth it.*

The Group Had a Friendly Feeling

It was noticeable that new members were warmly welcomed to individual sessions and that the tutors often used the first names of the learners. At the start of learning sessions, some tutors also enquired about learners who were not present. However, not all learning environments (for example a canteen) or social areas (such as a shared rest-home lounge) lent themselves to the promotion of positive interaction during or between learning sessions.

Indeed, the good management of the Golden Gates as an organisation, and the learning environments they oversaw, were conducive to creating a friendly feeling to both the learning sessions and the social areas around them. This extract from my notes is provided to illustrate that point.

> In the bright and welcoming reception area, details of the classes for the day and courses for the term are displayed. Artwork by learners provided a temporary exhibit and shelves of books entreat learners to borrow them freely. One member of staff helps a nervous, potential new learner to complete a brief application form with reassuring tones. She also welcomes attending learners warmly by their first names and with clear knowledge of the classes they were attending. A second member of the office staff is on the phone with a learner who had not attended a class, asking if they were 'all right' as some members of the class had asked after her. She said she would let her fellow learners know about her situation. The atmosphere appears friendly, encouraging, purposeful, and engaging.

The Attitudinal Dimension

I Was, Myself, Motivated to Learn

There were many good examples of motivation amongst learners. In a painting class a number of learners arrived early to work on their paintings well before the tutor arrived. In two language classes, the 'homework' set had been completed by all the learners while in a humanities session, the learners were eager to voice their anticipation of what was coming up in the class. The learners often suggested that when others had left the classes (dropped-out) it was those who were 'motivated' who still attended regularly. For one learner, learning itself can provide motivation. In his opinion: *Once you are out of proper school it is harder to get motivated and the classes totally help with that.*

I Took Part in the Learning Activities

Once again this was a feature of the majority of classes I observed. In creative classes, everyone 'had a go' at the task set and physical exercise classes always saw full participation, albeit at a variety of levels. In humanities classes, where opinions were asked for, more responses were often forthcoming than could be handled by the tutor. In information technology classes, learners worked together to present contributions from every learner.

There were a few examples of learners not participating, mainly in humanities sessions when the much larger groups of learners appeared to provide a barrier to those less confident from speaking out. In some social groups, however, the constant talk from the tutor to a room of static, passive listeners provided no opportunity to actively participate.

I Encouraged Others to Learn too

> This was an important feature of some classes but one that was not observed in all sessions or indeed regularly. Such opportunities to encourage others to learn depended upon the approach the tutor took in planning the learning session. In some creative lessons, learners moved freely around the tables (painting) or machines (sewing or information technology) where learners were working and praised the efforts or the craftsmanship of their peers. In some physical exercise classes, there were very good examples of pairs of learners encouraging each other to 'do better'. In a language class, a learner expressed her pleasure by saying: *This is really friendly group – we really help each other.*

However, in many classes, there was less interaction than might have been, as the focus was on what the tutor was doing or saying rather than any planned pair or group work. Therefore, opportunities for greater levels of social learning, in my view, were lost.

They Made the Learning Interesting

Overall the tutors were very good at making learning interesting. They used a wide variety of activities in physical exercise classes, employed humour and anecdotes in humanities classes, or introduced well-thought-out conversation exercises in language classes. Some tutors employed games such as listening to musical compositions and suggesting composers or looking at a variety of paintings and identifying the artists through their various styles.

> Where the sessions followed a too familiar pattern, such as routine physical exercise classes or where the teaching approach ignored the learners' previous knowledge, the learners appeared less interested and engaged. For example, one tutor ignored the stated previous reading experience of learners when tackling a book chapter – although new to some, it was overly familiar to others whose interest waned. The learners always had views on what they valued; one learner let me know his thoughts about how a drama class he had attended could have been more engaging. He said: *I think if we had [had] some videos about plays, which took place and made comments about the characters and the role of each actor, [it] would have made the course more interesting.*

They Motivated Me to Want to Learn

Most tutors were adept at motivating learners in their sessions and some were good at motivating learners to learn *per se* whether in their own subject area or not. In one instance, the tutor did this by identifying good progress and suggesting that the learner should explore taking further opportunities to learn new facts or skills such as in literature classes.

In one creative class, the tutor stopped the whole class to display and explain the good work one learner had produced, which was very motivating to the others. This extract from my notes is provided for further illustration.

> Just before one class, involving music appreciation, the learners sit fidgeting in anticipation of the arrival of the tutor and the start of the session. One learner has just arrived back in the country that morning from a holiday abroad but has come straight to the session so as not to miss it. The learners talk about what they hope to hear that afternoon, how they had listened to the recommended music from their last session and how they had got better at recognising the characteristics of different composers. The tutor arrives, excitement rises and the learners struggle to take turns to let him know about the new music they had been involved with since the last session and how good it had made them feel.

> One learner turned to me and said: *This is marvellous. I've learned so much from [the tutor] and I [now] listen to a great range of music.*

By way of contrast, in one physical exercise class, the tutor remained quite separate from the learners throughout. Although she directed the learners, she did not focus on their actions and, therefore, their learning. In such cases, the motivation was down to the learners alone.

They Made Learning Fun

> Almost all classes I participated in were fun to attend – the learners and tutors were positive from the outset. They looked to see how their relative inputs could contribute to a light-hearted atmosphere in which the learning was to take place. This was true in humanities, creative and physical exercise classes in particular with one learner saying that: *[The tutor] is marvellous – a good tutor. He makes the class in fact. It's a joy to come and meet up with him and the rest of the group.*

In a small number of classes, such as some creative and information technology classes, the learning was functional rather than 'fun'. In such sessions, the learning took place amongst a group of largely disconnected individuals who did not interact to any great extent.

They Gave Me Confidence

There were many instances where the tutors gave confidence to the learners about the work they were learning and their ability to cope with its demand. This was certainly true in some physical exercise, humanities, and language classes where learners felt more able to tackle tasks unaided and extend themselves, whether by tackling a new exercise movement, speaking a new foreign word or considering a new way of looking at the world.

> Sometimes that confidence was more personal than 'educational' in nature as one learner explained when speaking about her humanities class: *We're used to giving our opinions here. I wouldn't have stood up [and spoken] at one time.*
>
> For another learner, however, that was the purpose of her attending. She said: *My aim in joining the drama class was to increase my self-confidence. This has been achieved and the classes are always fun.*

They Encouraged Me to Keep on Learning

This characteristic of quality informal later-life learning manifested itself in two ways – the first was an encouragement to learn outside the learning session and the second was to carry on learning once a course had finished. The former was sometimes structured, such as in the use of between-session homework exercises and sometimes unstructured such as encouraging participants to carry out daily physical exercises prior to the next session. In humanities, it simply involved thinking about an issue before the next session, as this would be the starting point for the discussions. In all cases the opportunity to carry on learning outside the session appeared to be readily accepted.

In some cases, there was no such encouragement or direction to extend the learning opportunities that had begun to take place at the day's session. In one literature class, the learners asked, to no avail, for a task to be set for them for the following week while in an information technology class, two learners arranged to get together themselves to use the computer room, when it was free, to move their projects forward.

> Encouragement to keep on learning *per se* came from two tutors who asked their learners what courses they were going to sign up for the following term when their own courses had come to an end. They had high expectations of the learners and were positive about the suggested new courses they raised. This gave life to the observation of one learner about the nature of Golden Gates describing it as providing: … *a culture of encouragement as opposed to cynicism; an opportunity to contribute, myself. An opportunity to apply what I learn outside the class.*

The Organisation Would Listen to Complaints

This was a further characteristic of quality informal later-life learning that was not directly observable but information was gleaned from learners during the participant observation fieldwork. The Satisfaction Surveys, used by Golden Gates at the end of courses, or annually across the organisation, were welcomed and most learners felt they provided the opportunity to raise issues and 'complain' if necessary. The members of staff were also universally approachable and helpful they said. Examples were given where complaints about accommodation or tutors had led to change and improvement.

> However, the complaints of the language classes concerning noisy or open environments had gone unheeded and there was no evidence of the café staff ameliorating the noisy situation by changing practices. One learner said: *Wonderful class but it's hard to hear in the café, you know.*

The Organisation Selected the Tutors with Care

There was no direct or observable evidence in the learning sessions but the tutors were all employed through the Head of Learning and had to demonstrate their expertise and experience in the area they were teaching. This did not demand a formal teaching qualification although all such tutors had to successfully go through the safeguarding hurdle overseen by the Disclosure and Barring (DAB) service.

However, the organisation did not operate a monitoring and evaluation scheme and so was reliant on learners to identify if the academic abilities, personal qualities and teaching approaches of the tutor met their needs. Golden Gates also had no policy on teaching and learning either, which can be one way of outlining the expectations of a learning organisation with respect to operation and approach in the 'classroom'.

The Physical Dimension

The Accommodation Was Suitable for Our Needs

In many cases the organisation provided accommodation that was applicable to the needs of the group and the nature of the activity being undertaken. For example one physical exercise class now used a large, warm church hall and a creative class used a large bright room with tables able to accommodate the learners' paintings. In another example, the information technology classes were held in clean and well-equipped computer rooms.

> Occasionally, rooms were allocated to courses early and proved too small for the numbers of learners eventually attending. One literature class was

open to other learners to use while the class was going on and caused disruption. Therefore, it very much depended on specific classes in the accommodation available and even one physical exercise class venue was thought not to be large enough to enable effective learning. As one leaner said, tactfully: *The room used for [this] exercise class is not really as big as it might be.*

The Equipment Worked Well

In most cases the equipment used to support learning worked well and this was for two reasons. Firstly, individual tutors were often responsible for the equipment and had checked it beforehand. Secondly, the equipment had been tailored to make it appropriate. For example, language classes were discussion and paper-based not using, say, interactive whiteboards or international Skype sessions as they might be in schools or universities. Where the organisation was able to have new and up-to-date equipment, such as a set of iPads for information technology classes, the learners fully appreciated the value they provided. As one learner said: *I never thought I'd be able to do this in a million years, but the photos we've taken are amazing.*

On just two occasions, one humanities session and one literature session, the equipment or materials did not work and on both occasions the tutor was not able to adequately deal with the issue to ensure the learning was as effective as it might have been. The lack of readily available alternative rooms or technical support, as would be available in more formal education environments, appeared to restrict the range of learning being undertaken.

In some classes, it was the use of the equipment available rather than the equipment itself that, I felt, restricted the level of learning taking place. In one physical education class, the sound box was placed at the front of the class and was very loud there but was much less audible at the back of the room. In a humanities class, the tutor's handwriting on the flip chart was illegible.

The Group Was Not too Large

Once again the groups were mostly of an appropriate size for the learning being undertaken and the accommodation and equipment available to them. In two physical exercise classes, the numbers reduced the space available to exercise fully while in two humanities classes, the numbers were so large that many learners found it hard to contribute as fully as they wanted to. One learner said that this issue was being attended to when he said: *There are too many for the space – it's under review.*

In one language class, relatively high learner numbers restricted the amount of conversation any one learner could be involved in the target language while in an English literature class the numbers were so large that learners expressed that they did not all get a chance to contribute to meaningful discussions during the sessions. One learner suggested that, for her: *Language classes should be limited to 6.*

The Room Was Organised to Enable Everyone to See and Hear

In the vast majority of cases the accommodation was managed to enable all the learners could see and hear with the learners themselves often taking charge of this aspect prior to the session starting. Learners with disabilities moved themselves to be closer to where the tutor was guiding the learning. Fellow learners often knew who needed additional support and aided them.

However, the participants in such physical exercise classes were usually organised in rows facing the tutor who was demonstrating the 'moves' to be made as the session progressed. As the floor was flat, those in the back rows struggled to see the tutor and the moves being made by their feet.

Nevertheless, overall the accommodation was appropriate for the type of learning taking place. This extract from my notes is provided by way of illustration.

> At the request of the learners, a physical exercise class has been moved from a small and windowless room within the Golden Gates building to a church hall not too far away. Here, there is ample room for the learners to change from their outdoor clothes to their kit while their possessions remain in sight. There is also sufficient room now for the learners to 'spread out' and to carry out space-consuming exercises with freedom and confidence. The tutor is able to use the helpful small platform at the front to demonstrate the moves to be followed in clear sight of the learners and it gives her an opportunity to see, talk to and assess the progress of those at the back of the group. After the session, the learners change and move to a separate, comfortable seating area in the same hall and socialise as volunteers from the church bring them refreshments.

Capturing the Voice of the Learners

One of the features that came to the fore during my participation in the classes was the gratitude of the older learners for having a spotlight shone on them as an important part of society. One learner said; *And can I say how grateful we are to you for doing this on behalf of older people.*

The opportunity to take part in the research, and the value it gave to them, was also recognised and expressed by one learner said: *It is so important the group feels involved [in the research]. It helps us to know we are important too.*

> Learners who valued such an opportunity also encouraged fellow learners, who were less inclined to participate, to do so. One woman saying to her scrabble partner: *I 'lent my voice' earlier this week. Would you have a go?*

These comments resonate with the critical educational gerontology (CEG) framework where the 'education' in which these later-life learners were participating provided an opportunity to feel important, to take a part in society and not to be 'left behind'. It also provides an opportunity for them to feel empowered by giving their own opinions and in that way adding value to themselves and, as they see it, to society as a whole.

Reflection as a Participant Observer

Throughout my time as a participant observer the characteristics perceived by the learners to be attributed to quality informal learning, as outlined earlier, were readily observed. Their presence positively affected the learners from, for example, the learners being motivated by the tutor to learners encouraging each other causing levels of participation to rise as a result. Where learning or participation was not taking place, it could readily and directly be related to the lack of quality characteristics. For example, the lack of challenge in the material being explored or the lack of opportunities for participation provided by the tutor resulted in the learning being of less interest to the participants.

Indeed, the key role of the tutor, identified through the focus groups and supported through the questionnaire research, was very evident with their individual experience, expertise, and approach significantly determining the quality of learning taking place in the sessions. The idiosyncratic nature of teaching and learning at Golden Gates led to a great variability in the number of quality characteristics being present in any one learning session. Where the tutor used a restricted range of teaching strategies or ones less appropriate for the needs of the older learners, such as using exclusively oral explanations with no written material to refer to, learning was clearly restricted.

By contrast where teaching and learning techniques had been amended to take account of the needs of the participants other than by outcome (such as the finished paintings or their level of exercise abilities) learning was more clearly evident. For example, where tasks had been set between sessions to enable older learners to remain 'hooked on' what they had learned previously and prepare for the next session, the learners were able to articulate and demonstrate that they had made progress in their learning and were more motivated at the start of the following session.

The organisation provided warm and comfortable learning environments and even where accommodation was not totally appropriate, it was possible to learn. However there was less focus by the organisation on 'learning' *per se*. For example, there was little display of work to demonstrate good practice or promote learning and the library contained no books on learning or its benefits either in general or in old age in particular.

This focus on provision rather than the quality of teaching and learning was evident by a lack of presence or involvement by the managers or Head of Learning in learning sessions. There was no formal monitoring of the teaching and learning occurring and therefore the organisation garnered no direct evidence, which could be used for evaluation purposes.

Summary

The information gained from being a participant observer in a wide range of informal later-life learning environments enabled me to observe almost all the characteristics of quality identified by the learners through the focus groups and supported so strongly through the questionnaire. Those characteristics not featured, such as those involving the qualifications of the tutors, the care in their selection or the willingness of the organisation to listen to complaints, were not directly observable. Therefore my observations identified that all the observable characteristics of quality informal later-life learning perceived and valued by the learners were evident in their own learning. The characteristics were, therefore, a set of practical features of teaching and learning that help to improve the quality of learning not just suggestions of aspirations that could not be realised in reality.

I do not know if any one session revealed all the observable characteristics of quality but certainly most, however, were present on most occasions and it was their absence that was noticeable. Such absences sometimes highlighted the inconsistency across informal later-life learning sessions and gave life to the assertion that was raised at the start, in the Feasibility Study, of 'some sessions being better than others'.

9

ADOPTING OUTCOMES TO IMPROVE THE QUALITY OF LATER-LIFE LEARNING

Introduction

In Chapters 6 and 7, I outlined the findings from my fieldwork and the subsequent analyses of data. In the Feasibility Study, semi-formal discussions clarified my research focus and revealed the participants' perceptions of three stakeholders influencing quality in learning in later life; the learners, the tutor, and the organisation. Subsequently through qualitative analysis of the comments made from the main study focus groups, 28 characteristics of learning were identified as contributing to 'quality' learning in informal later-life learning sessions.

The outcomes of the Quality Learning Questionnaire revealed the high levels of agreement with the newly emerged characteristics of quality from across a wider section of those participating in informal learning at Golden Gates. Further thematic analysis identified that the characteristics represented four dimensions of learning – cognitive, attitudinal, physical, and social. The comments of the participants across all aspects of the fieldwork provided a context, and support, for each finding and provided insightful commentary in answer to my research question and sub-questions:

What are older learners' perceptions of quality, in informal later-life learning?

a What are the learners' perceptions of the environmental factors that underpin quality, learning experiences?
b How does informal learning reflect the principles of quality as defined by the participants themselves?

DOI: 10.4324/9781003269892-9

In addressing the first sub-question, I interrogated the reported experiences and perceptions of informal learning, amongst a representative sample within a case study organisation. The evidence presented from my involvement as a participant observer, and comments made by group participants during those sessions, also helped to address the second sub-question concerned with how such informal learning embodies the newly unearthed perceptions of quality.

In this chapter, I discuss these findings in relation to the literature concerned with informal learning amongst older people, as well as relevant literature concerned with more formal adult education, and reflect on how my findings may be framed by what has been discussed and documented by those working in this field. Where the evidence produced differs from views previously expressed including where my findings offer a contribution to knowledge in the field of later-life learning, it will be revealed. Throughout this chapter I use the 28 characteristics of quality (italicised) as a framework for discussing the stakeholders, characteristics, dimensions, and both contextual and demographic features associated with quality informal later-life learning.

The Quality Cirque

Figure 9.1 presents all four parts of the Quality Cirque previously outlined in the thesis (see Chapters 2, 3, 4, and 8). As such, the figure represents an 'unpacking' of the constituents contributing to the overarching concept of quality

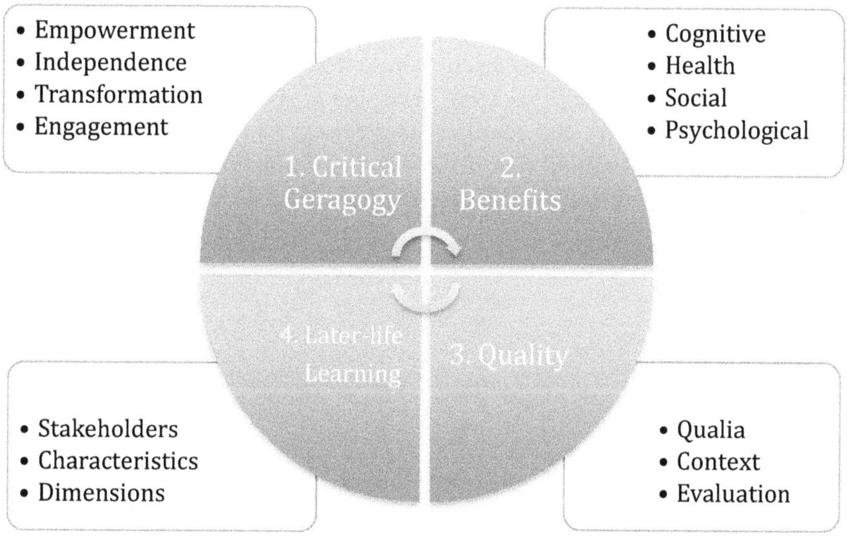

FIGURE 9.1 The quality cirque for informal later-life learning (parts 1, 2, 3, and 4).

in informal later-life learning. Framing informal later-life learning with a critical geragogical approach provides the opportunity for nurturing the potential benefits that later-life learning can bring, which would then be enhanced by a supportive context delivered through a quality informal later-life learning environment.

Key Findings

Stakeholders in Quality Informal Later-life Learning

The first finding came from the Feasibility Study with the emphasis on the central importance of interpersonal dynamics in general and the interaction between the learners in particular, contributing to learning sessions they valued. In addition, the participants highlighted the importance of the actions of the tutor and the value of his or her aptitudes and approaches; the role of learners themselves and what they contributed to the learning process and the influence of the environment or organisational arrangements in affecting the 'quality' of learning both positively and negatively.

Therefore, one key finding is that responsibility for quality was shared amongst a number of stakeholders in learning (Figure 9.2). This finding, that learners perceived themselves to be an equal partner in quality later-life learning, resonates with the theory of critical geragogy (Battersby, 1987; Formosa, 2002) which focuses on the empowerment of individual later-life learners and their engagement both in the practice of learning and in society in general. It also lends support to earlier research where these three stakeholders of quality informal later-life learning have been represented within expressed theories of older adults learning (Bandura, 1986; Merriam et al., 2007).

For Bandura (1976), the cognitive component of learning was only part of the picture. He proposed that behaviour was a function of the person with the environment and went on to describe his model of learning as a triangle

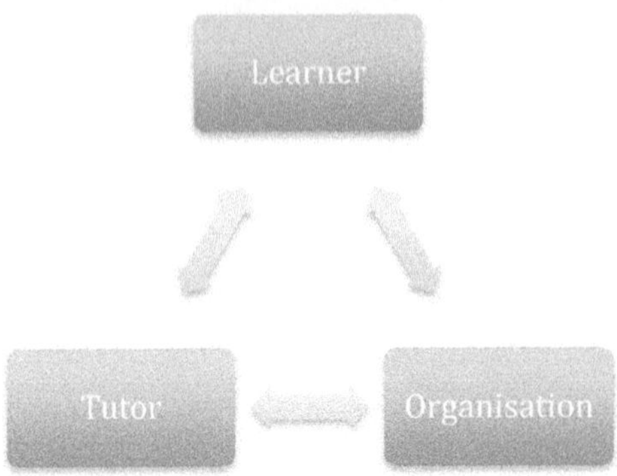

FIGURE 9.2 The three stakeholders of quality informal later-life learning.

in which the learning, the person and the environment are interactive and reciprocal (Bandura, 1986). Merriam et al. (2007) further reinforced the importance of the three stakeholders in later-life learning by offering a framework for adult learning that distinguishes it from child learning according to the characteristics of the learner, the process, and the context provided by the organisation. The importance of the learners playing an active role in quality learning is supported by theorists such as Hergenhahn and Olson (2005) who similarly argued that observation and imitation of behaviour were not enough for learning to occur.

The evidence that emerged from the survey strengthened the finding that the responsibility for quality was shared amongst three stakeholders in learning. The data confirmed the perceptions of the focus groups by strongly supporting all the characteristics associated with quality learning under the three stakeholder categories (Table 8.11). Merriam and Bierema (2014) later went on to expand their framework, which highlights the roles of tutor, learner, and organisation as partners in learning, to move from a generic process of learning to specifically include the role of the educator (tutor). They concluded that the work of helping adults learn begins with the mindset of the educator:

> Effective learning for adults is cognizant of the intersecting roles the educator, learner, process and context play in the design and facilitation of learning. The design and facilitation of learning is the bridge between theory and practice in adult education.
>
> *(p. 253)*

The Tutor

This key role of the tutor was supported in my own research findings where the participants in the focus groups identified a larger number of characteristics of quality associated with the tutor as a stakeholder (12 characteristics) in comparison with the role of the learners (8 characteristics) and the organisation (8 characteristics). Support for the importance of the tutor in fostering quality in informal later-life learning came about by the emergence of specific characteristics such as the tutor *lets me ask questions.* In quality learning experiences, the learners felt free to ask questions, which can help to secure their engagement in learning (Wlodkowski, 2008) and foster the notion of respect (Creech et al., 2014b). The question asked by the learners may be to further their understanding of something new or it may be a question borne out of an individual's experience, which requires airing and sharing. Wlodkowski (2008) supported such a notion by saying: 'By making the learners' goals, interests and cultural perspectives the context of challenging and engaging learning experiences, instructors can secure their continuous participation' (p. 109).

He goes on to recommend addressing this condition throughout the lesson with strategies specifically including questions and answers.

Quality learning was perceived to take place when the tutor is *experienced in what they are teaching*. This is not necessarily something that is made overt to the learners and it is more likely they could be discerned from the sessions through the use of personal examples or where the tutors were able to answer questions based on their experience.

In addition, in later-life contexts such as the u3a, there is fluidity in the roles in the learning sessions, and learners take on the role of teachers at times, leading to a context where 'peer teaching' may often be found. Peer teaching, or peer interaction, offers a powerful vehicle for learning (Wood, 2010) and is supported by a number of commentators (Brady et al., 2003; Choi, 2009; Erickson, 2009). Indeed Simson et al. (2001) reported surveys indicating clearly that the peer teaching experience is an overwhelmingly positive one, with peer teachers noting many rewards such as personal satisfaction and intellectual stimulation. However, in this study, 97.4% of the learning sessions perceived by the learners as ones of quality had a tutor present and that tutor being both 'experienced' and 'qualified' were characteristics of quality identified by the learners too. The benefits accrued to the peer tutor in such sessions may not translate to benefitting the learners if quality learning is to take place. For example, they may not be 'challenged' or 'motivated' by such fellow learners acting as tutors.

However, that is not to say such characteristics could not be provided by a 'peer' and therefore does not negate peer teaching as a way of providing the experiences valued by learners in quality informal later-life learning. It may certainly be possible within organisations offering informal later-life learning, such as u3a, that those who act as tutors are eminently qualified and experienced while in any group of learners there will be valuable life experiences, and often expertise, that can be drawn upon.

In this case study, because of the structure where tutors are employed by the organisation, the value of peers as tutors may well have gone unrecognised. In peer learning in general, the practices are often introduced in an ad hoc way, without consideration of their implications (Boud, 1988). Boud goes on to say that it is not a substitute for teaching and activities designed and conducted by 'staff' members', but an important addition to the repertoire of teaching and learning activities that can enhance the quality of education.

Motivation to learn can often come in the form of engagement between learning sessions. According to Rogers and Horrocks (2010) adult learning should be seen as an on-going process and the tutor should ensure that continued learning occurs outside of the 'group meetings'. There were good examples of the learners engaging in such reinforcement in language classes where they relished opportunities to do 'homework' to keep learning fresh.

These practices reinforced the learners' perceptions that, in quality informal later-life learning, ***the tutors encouraged me to keep on learning*** too.

The Learners

The learners also wanted to be ***treated with respect*** by their peers (as well as by their tutors) with a need to feel comfortable in the learning environment and, partly, that comes from the shared respect of fellow learners, which reduces stress (Wlodkowski, 2008). That can be through physical manifestations such as the openness of the learning environment or equal availability of the resources. It can also be through the way participants are spoken to, or engaged with, and respect for them as people through recognition of the experience and expertise they embody. For MacKeracher (2004), such respect comes from being treated as an equal. She says:

> When interaction in learning is effective, participation is based on equality, co-operation, collaboration and shared power and control. Both facilitator and learner must understand that such characteristics are not based on some altruistic process in which one 'gives' control and power to the other.
> *(p. 196)*

Feedback on individual progress was informally given. The employment of 'assessment' or 'tests' was a concern for many learners from the Feasibility Study onwards as it harked back to unhappy school days and therefore whether feedback was sought or accepted was the choice of individual learners. However, in order to be able to see their own progress, learners must receive frequent information about changes in their knowledge, skills or behaviour relative to what they anticipated or desired. However, learners can also judge their own progress through self-evaluation strategies, in music for example (Creech et al., 2014a). Therefore, the information about progress can come from a multitude of sources, including learners' own self-evaluation, cues in the environment and informal feedback as well as formal assessments.

For Wlodkowski and Ginsberg (1995), such feedback can only be provided following activities where the learner is permitted to test out new behaviour (knowledge, understanding, skills). For example, they say that if the point comes early in the session, then the good feelings from success will motivate the remainder of that session. If feedback is delayed, especially from one session to the next, the learner may have trouble connecting it to the behaviour that was tested out previously and consequently the impact and reinforcement from feedback loses its value. Opportunities for self-evaluation too, must be provided so that learners may exercise their own judgement and take control of their own learning, which can lead to more powerful engagement in learning activities (Spigner and Anderson, 1999).

The Organisation

Finally the organisation was also identified as a stakeholder in quality informal later-life learning. For example, the learners saw the organisation as being responsible for creating a *safe and non-threatening atmosphere.* Maslow (1970) suggested that people could not move towards positive goals such as 'growth' until adverse conditions such as 'survival and security of themselves or their families' have been reduced and, for Strange and Banning (2001), the feeling of safety and inclusion is a 'basic requirement' before learning can occur. For many, if they could not attend later-life learning classes in safe and accessible environments, then they would not attend at all (Withnall, 2010).

Hebb (1972) pointed out that although adults and children both experience emotions, stress and anxiety arousal processes, the level, strength, and duration of the reaction increases with intellectual capacity and age. Therefore adults need a supportive, encouraging and non-threatening learning environment (Kidd, 1973; Rogers and Roethlisberger, 1991). As stakeholders, the learners wanted to be *challenged in their learning* which often involves looking at what one already knows or believes and 'challenging' it with new information or new ways of looking at things (Bialystok et al., 2012). This is one way of building up cognitive reserve (Zull, 2006) to strengthen and enhance the mind. Once again it is for the learner to describe what is a challenge. In the case of Golden Gates this was especially true as the organisation had no mechanism for formally charting the knowledge, understanding or skills of individual learners at the start of sessions and could not, therefore, engage in *planned* challenge for individuals with any certainty.

Concurrently, the learners expected the organisation to *select the tutors with care* in order to ensure they embodied the qualities and practices the learners valued. Where possible, the organisation did engage tutors with experience and, on many occasions, with qualifications. However, as with many charitable organisations, such tutors were not always available.

The performance of a tutor involved in formal learning is usually monitored internally on a regular basis by senior staff and, periodically, in England, by external inspection teams. However, with informal learning, as at Golden Gates, internal evaluation is unlikely to happen and external evaluation not at all. Organisations do, however, act where a complaint has been received about a tutor. However, direct performance 'in the classroom', and what tutors do before to prepare for or follow up learning afterwards, is rarely monitored or evaluated.

According to Caine and Caine (1991), adult learners expect the choice of tutors to be to a certain standard and, that such tutors would understand that whatever is learned, is embedded in the context in which it is learned. They go on to say that the 'context' consists of many components, including social interactions, physical environment, personal comfort, the language being used, and the information being learned. As the brain processes all these contexts, not just the information to be learned, learning experiences can be enhanced when the facilitator takes this embedded quality into account (Caine and Caine, 1991).

To summarise, the first finding from the fieldwork was the identification of three stakeholders in quality informal later-life contributing to learning sessions they valued. The participants highlighted the importance of the actions of the tutors and the value of their aptitudes and approaches; the role of learners themselves and what they contributed to the learning process and the influence of the environment or organisational arrangements in affecting the 'quality' of learning. The following section highlights and discusses the characteristics of the learners, the tutor, and the organisation underpinning the positive involvement of each of the three stakeholders.

Characteristics of Quality Informal Later-Life Learning

A second key finding was the 28 characteristics of quality, which were identified by the learners in the focus groups as being features of quality informal later-life learning. There was very positive support for the quality characteristics by the questionnaire participants who were largely either in agreement or strong agreement with the characteristics presented. From the balance of comments arising out of the focus groups, the older learners perceived the tutors' contributions to quality learning to be more substantial than the learners' and, in turn, than the organisation's.

For example, the learners perceived that in quality learning the tutor *made the learning fun*, which resonates with the views of other commentators (Rogers, 2001; Brophy, 2008). Rogers (2001) singled out fun as a key ingredient of successful learning and advised those coming new to tutoring with adults that:

> While it is important for [the tutor] to know what the motivation is, of the learners, remember that initial motivation is just the pleasure of learning ... In a successful group it grows and develops. In an unsuccessful group it shrivels and dies.
>
> *(p. 20)*

This focus on 'learning for pleasure' contrasts with the structured curriculum and assessments associated with formal adult learning in schools or universities. Jarvis (1987) postulated that learning is more than just a psychological process, taking place in an individual's head, but a social phenomenon. The learners, he contested, were seeking first enjoyment, pleasure, and enrichment in a social atmosphere as knowledge itself could be accumulated from a range of other sources. Tutors can use the power of emotions to affect learning and retention positively. By intensifying the learners' emotional state, they may enhance both meaning and memory (Wolfe, 2006).

In addition, the learners expected the tutor to be *qualified as a teacher*. As previously mentioned, there were not as many coded references about this in comparison with other characteristics. However, opinions on this issue were expressed strongly and attracted a great deal of non-verbal support from other learners, such as nodding, demonstrating wider agreement. Within a critical geragogy framework, education is seen as a way of empowering older people and ensuring they have a 'worth' recognised by both themselves and by others. Therefore, not only is it important that their learning is a quality experience in itself, so the participants may receive the maximum benefits from it, it should be to the same standard for this section of the society as any other. If not, what does this say about life-long learning, its part within the life course of older adults and the value placed on citizens in later life? The importance of qualifications has also been discussed and highlighted by Findsen and Formosa (2011) who, when referring to 4th Age learning among older people, argued that in the future, to ascertain what qualifies as good practice in 4th Age learning: '… requires an examination of the range of available qualifications for those who provide learning activities for frail elders, to ensure that educators are not left out in the development of a curriculum …' (p. 115).

The idea of peer learning and teaching, such as in the u3a model, chimes well with the framework of critical geragogy with its emphasis on engagement and empowerment by putting the learning and the teaching in the hands of the learners themselves. On the other hand, could this just be a way of using the critical geragogy argument as a justification for practices that enable other would-be providers, such as local or national governments, to save money by not providing informal learning opportunities and, in doing so, expressing the extent to which society really values later-life learning?

As Formosa (2002) points out, the u3a organisation attracts largely well-educated individuals, those who Sargant (2000) termed the 'learning-rich'. Comfortable with acting as both teachers and learners, they may well constitute a different clientele to those who in later life participate in the Golden Gates provision with its tutor-led learning sessions. Therefore, it might be that there needs to be different types of models of informal later-life learning to reach different types of people or could organisations such as Golden Gates adopt a more peer-focused u3a type model for some of its provision in order to more readily embrace all the characteristics of quality identified by the learners themselves?

The learners also wanted to be *involved in their learning*. Adults learn best when they are involved in developing learning objectives for themselves congruent with their current self-concept and ideal self (hooks, 2010). Many adult learners are quite willing to accept some pre-established learning goals but it helps if the facilitator offers opportunities to set some goals for themselves (Tough, 1979). Good facilitation should be understood as a process of orchestrating the learners' experiences through providing a variety of activities and resources (Caine and Caine, 1991).

Tutors who were involved in active participatory learning were also valued for their ability to *give confidence* to the learners (Thibodeau, 1979). It was clear from the Feasibility Study that many older learners, returning to learning, brought negative experiences of schooling with them. Just as Withnall (2010) discussed, memories of secondary school, for many later-life learners, had been coloured by poor or bored teachers who were felt to have lacked interest in helping children to learn. In this way, prior experiences had discouraged interest in learning for many people as they became older. Individuals may be very self-directed in learning activities related to their own work but very dependent in learning activities related to knowledge and expertise lying outside their experience (Candy, 1991). Therefore, learners need help in achieving and, in doing so, building their confidence through direct encouragement and support.

Certain other characteristics of quality learning were also the responsibility of the learners themselves. In their perceptions of quality learning environments the learners *found the group friendly* and the need for them, as learners, to feel part of a friendly and supportive group helped them to take part in 'social learning' and get the most from learning alongside and through others (Cozolino and Sprokay, 2006). This supports research indicating that a friendly atmosphere reduces the levels of stress in the learners and that this lack of stress makes for more effective learning too (Thistle, 1968). In this way the learners feel connected in a way that Wlodkowski (2008) identified as 'promoting learning'. This fostering and manifestation of helpful relationships arising from social learning is lost where it takes place in isolation. As such 'independent learning alone' has expanded greatly in recent years as provision by the public sector has shrunk (McNair, 2012) it is timely to research any benefits such learning may bring.

At times of quality learning, identified by the learners, the learners also *motivated themselves to learn* and this was evident in both their decision to participate in learning and their continuing attendance. In informal learning, learners choose what they wish to learn (usually from a menu of courses) and so they are involved in learning that they have chosen for themselves. Motivation in learning is often described as being either a drive to 'reduce uncertainty' and meet unmet needs or a drive towards 'positive growth' through exploring the unknown. Kidd (1973) suggests that adults who attend learning experiences on the basis of personal growth tend to be relaxed, do not require much structure or direction from facilitators and are able to negotiate and plan their own structure, directions, feedback and reinforcement with minimal assistance. The learners recognised that, unlike statutory schooling, they did not have to attend and that the choice to do so was already a contribution to learning and an expression of their motivation to learn. This resonates with the theory of critical geragogy where the later-life learners exert their independence in deciding to engage in learning, where and when to learn and what to learn.

In quality learning the learners also perceived that they *took part in the learning activities*, which, according to Rogers (1983), requires internal motivation. Rogers went on to say that the learning that follows active participation is 'significant'; it has a quality of personal involvement where the whole person, in both feeling and cognitive aspects, is involved in the learning event. However, external factors to ensure active participation in learning are important too: firstly providing the opportunity to get involved and secondly to motivate involvement from outside. Wlodkowski (2008), in answering the question of what tutors need to do to gain learners' attention, addresses both factors. For the latter he espouses that though adults may feel included, and have a positive attitude, their involvement will diminish if they cannot find learning meaningful; while for the former, he suggested engaging activities such as role-play and shared problem solving. The benefits of taking part in learning with others or 'social learning' are quite different from simply being in a social group (Hallam et al., 2011).

In quality learning, identified by participants in my study, characteristics of quality were perceived to be the responsibility of the learning organisation too. For example, the physical or technical equipment used to support and enhance the learning experience *worked well.* In other words, the equipment needs to work as expected and in 'quality' learning sessions it did. As later-life learning takes place in a variety of settings, often in multi-purpose rooms not created for learning, the equipment is often portable and more likely to suffer problems from constant moving. The tutors are often without technical support in such environments.

Tutors also need to understand the drawbacks of using technology too as the benefits of using equipment *per se* do not necessarily lead to quality learning. Burge (2000) stressed that 'any technology that appeals to only one learning style, will be used by only half the learners'. For example, the use of power point presentations is now a common visual aid used by tutors to improve the quality of presentations but Mayer (2002) found that recounting even interesting stories while using an otherwise straightforward multimedia presentation (a common occurrence) was actually distracting to learners.

The 'equipment' does not need to be sophisticated but if it is lacking in any way, it can negatively affect the learning experience. In one case, the handouts to support a literature class were not in the right order and were incomplete causing confusion to such an extent they were unusable. Notwithstanding these issues around resources, it must be emphasised that the findings reported here suggest that this area was not as important as the interpersonal issues, in terms of contributing to quality later-life learning. Quality learning, the perceptions of learners suggested, can take place despite ill-functioning equipment.

A further characteristic of quality learning associated with the organisation was that in such classes the *room was organised to enable everyone to see and hear* as, with increasing age, the acuity of the sensory receptors for vision and hearing decline, albeit very slowly. Some individuals remain unaware of such changes while, for others, these declines can be corrected. However, such declines affect learning by reducing the quantity and quality of the information input to the learning process. Adults experiencing such declines, typically, develop coping behaviours to compensate and even use information from past experiences to replace unseen or unheard material (Hiemstra and Sisco, 1990; Novak, 1993).

Hearing loss, in particular, can have a profound effect in group settings and communicating with other people, who are finding hearing hard, can tax the ability of those who hear normally too. Holding language classes in a noisy canteen, for example, encounters the negative effect of background noise, which is more acute in foreign language learning where the accuracy of that hearing is a key feature of successful learning.

The Dimensions of Quality Informal Later-Life Learning

A further key finding was that the characteristics of quality learning affiliated into four dimensions of learning – attitudinal, physical, social, and cognitive. These dimensions also reflect the critical geragogy framework (Formosa, 2002) where the cognitive dimension of learning can lead to the transformation underpinned by the theory, the social dimension aligns with the engagement within the theory and the attitudinal dimension parallels the decision-making role of learners within later-life learning that leads to continued, or further, empowerment of individuals.

The attitudinal dimension was associated with ten characteristics of quality that were concerned with the attitude of those involved in learning. The physical dimension was associated with only four characteristics of quality that were concerned with the physical environment associated with quality learning sessions. The social dimension was associated with eight characteristics of quality that were concerned with the sociability of those involved in learning while the cognitive dimension was associated with six characteristics of quality concerned with the mental processes associated with such learning.

The Attitudinal Dimension

In comparative terms, the 'attitude' of the learners, tutors, and the organisation during quality informal later-life learning and the 'social' dimension of learning have the most quality characteristics associated with them. Both are embedded in the development of positive relationships – a positive attitude by the learners and a positive response from fellow learners, the tutor, and the organisation through its staff. For example, the positive attitude of the tutor in *making learning interesting* was seen as being important. To be interesting, learning is often new and challenging not boring and repetitive (Bjorklund, 2011) and even a lecture can be enjoyable if the lecturer is prepared to deviate from the ground rules (McIntyre, 2003). Again knowing the background of the individual learners and their specific learning needs would increase the chances of the learning opportunities being individually relevant.

One way to make learning interesting is to present information or tasks according to a particular learner's preferred way of learning (Messick, 1976) or using individualised teaching strategies (Adey et al., 1999) and includes cognitive as well as affective, social, and physiological ways of responding to learning tasks. The connection between the tutor and learner is then forged. This happens in learning sessions, perceived as ones of quality by later-life learners, by being the second most strongly supported tutor characteristic but not, perhaps, in other situations when, due to a lack of interest, learning of 'quality' is less likely to happen.

A positive attitude was also evident through the learners perceiving that, in quality learning, the tutor *motivated them to want to learn*. Earlier comments on motivation in quality learning experiences, focused on the internal motivation of the learners themselves but the external motivation from the tutor was also highlighted as a characteristic of quality (Wlodkowski, 2008). Such external motivation is seen to establish inclusion amongst adult learners, develop positive attitudes towards learning, enhance the meaning of learning, engender competence, and deal with ethical considerations – all important parts of a tutor's role in motivating learners (Brophy, 2004).

The attitudinal dimension was not just the responsibility of the tutor as the learners identified that in quality learning they *encouraged others to learn too*.

Such informal learning groups, especially where they have been in place for some time, are often seen as good examples of learning communities or communities of practice (Wenger, 1998; Wenger and Snyder, 2000). According to Wenger (1998), a community of practice becomes a learning community when learning is not only a matter of course in the history of its practices but is at the very core of its enterprise. He views communities of practice as being made up of learners who have different levels of knowledge, behaviours, attitudes, and norms of the group. It is the sharing of this expertise, which makes for this quality experience.

The organisation can also display characteristics of quality associated with a positive attitude. For example, where the *organisation would listen to complaints*. As a participant observer, I received feedback from learners about situations where complaints had been listened to and where they had not. However, listening to complaints and the setting up of an appropriate dialogue does not necessarily have to involve change and some requests by learners were simply not possible to address as the learners understood.

The Social Dimension

The social dimension was supported by characteristics of quality such as where the teacher *treats the learners with respect.* Adults who value their own experience as a rich resource for further learning, or whose experience is valued by other people too, are better learners (Combs, 1974; Thibodeau, 1979). A positive rapport between teacher and learner provides a feeling of social inclusion that generates much motivation and enthusiasm and, consequently, a sense of community. In such situations, where learning experiences are embedded in respectful relationships, older adults thrive (Wlodkowski, 1999).

The social dimension was also supported where the tutor *asked for the opinions* from the learners. Hiemstra and Sisco (1990) point out that instructors can unknowingly create a surplus 'load' for learners by assuming a traditional authoritarian stance and not respecting learners' opinions or experiences. Following good adult education practice, that honours and respects the learner, is important for giving learners more power to engage in informal later-life learning. According to the learners, quality learning depends on the learners being asked for, and giving, an opinion and letting the tutor know what they, as individuals or as a group, already know. That opinion is not just to engage the learners in the learning or even to demonstrate the value that the tutor is giving to their expertise and life experience.

The social dimension of quality learning was also supported when the learning group was perceived to *have a friendly feeling.* For adults to become fully engaged in learning, they must be aroused, feel relatively safe and be willing and able to channel their motives into positive change processes. For these reasons, adults need a supportive and encouraging learning environment that does not threaten them (Kidd, 1973; Rogers and Roethlisberger, 1991). At the same time, involving learners in the session in this way enables the tutor to provide an environment in which learners can find their voice in a supportive and safe atmosphere (Tisdell, 2000). The approach of the organisation to factors, such as how learners can be helped to pay for courses, can generate a 'friendly feeling' to classes.

The Physical Dimension

The physical dimension of quality learning was supported when the *accommodation was suitable to the needs* of the learners. This characteristic of quality refers to the physical environment and those things affecting the comfort and wellbeing of the learners and the tutor. In quality learning sessions, it was perceived, the learning environment contributed positively. The parameters such as size of the room, adequate lighting, and the lack of distracting background noise all helped to support learning. The nature of the hall or room was specific to the subject under study and the size or abilities of the group concerned.

For example, Art for All students required accommodation with good, natural light while the Steady and Stable group required an accessible venue. Other features, such as cleanliness, are important and even the finer points such as room temperature can have an effect on learning (Dunn and Dunn, 1978). Indeed, manipulating the physical shape of the group, and where individual participants sit, can have an enormous influence on how they behave (Rogers, 2003). Armstrong (2012) suggested that, for older people, fair and equitable access to valued space was related to 'spatial justice' and aids both learning and participation.

The physical dimension was enhanced when the *learning group is not too large* which incorporates two important features. The first is that the group is not too large for the physical environment and secondly that the members of the group are not too numerous so that taking part in the activities of the sessions, such as by answering questions, is not restricted as reported by Gifford (1997) in relation to schools. For some learners, it may simply be intimidating to have such large numbers which, being stressful, gets in the way of quality learning. This characteristic resonates with others such as learning sessions being enhanced by having a *friendly feeling* or where the learners *feel safe*. In classes of an appropriate size, learners can receive more individual attention and, perhaps, develop those positive relationships that appear to matter so much to learners if quality learning is to take place.

The Cognitive Dimension

The cognitive dimension was evident through characteristics such as where the tutor *challenges them to learn new things*. Brown et al. (1989) first articulated the steps involved in learning where the tutor first demonstrates what they are doing and thinking and helps the learner to develop a conceptual model of the process involved. The learner then attempts to imitate these new skills or behaviours with on-going support. This is often known as scaffolding and is an attempt to get the learner to a level just beyond what they could accomplish by themselves. Vygotsky (1978) referred to this as the 'zone of proximal development' and, referring to children, believed that fostering development within this zone enables learning so that 'what the child is able to do in collaboration today he will be able to do independently tomorrow' (Vygotsky, 1978, p. 211).

Challenge to rise to new 'zones' can also come in the form of physical activity, which, when used alternatively with mental activity, enhances learning by providing the brain with 'time out' to process ideas and experiences (MacKeracher, 2004). Learners who take part in just one type of activity whether creative, cognitive, or physical for example, may, therefore, benefit from the enhanced learning that new challenges, ideas, and experiences bring. Race (2010) recommends that teachers should structure lessons so that students are engaging higher order learning processes such as practising, applying, comparing and contrasting. In this way a greater amount of brain networks are used in constructing an individual's own understanding.

Having high expectations of learners also introduces the element of risk in learning (Lightfoot, 1997) – the risk that, as a learner, you may not be successful in achieving what you set out to achieve. However, the positive identification of this characteristic of quality learning resonates with the work of Asen (2004) and Biesta (2007) who see it as a 'vital part of learning'.

Within the cognitive dimension of informal quality learning, the learners themselves need to ensure they *definitely learned new things*. This characteristic is a feature of individual learners as only they can say or show with any certainty through self-evaluation, in the absence of formal or informal assessment practices, whether they have learned anything new. The provision of opportunities for such forms of evaluation can depend upon the skill of the tutor (Wlodkowski and Ginsberg, 1995). For some learners they know that they have learned something new because of the changes in their knowledge, understanding or skills and can gain the cognitive benefits arising from doing so (Zull, 2006). This is in line with learning as 'change' previously outlined (Illeris, 2007) where the learner is more capable afterwards than before within the subject being studied.

This characteristic, concerning learning new things, was strongly supported from analysis of responses to the questionnaire and this important part of the learning process resonates with recent research into neuroscience where 'cognitive dissonance' arising from new memories being formed is a way of strengthening the brain's capacity (Zull, 2006). There is also an element of empowerment that comes from learning something new and the satisfaction it can provide. By learning new things, and therefore updating oneself, later-life learners are able to continue to take an active part in the world and not be 'left behind' as new technology, for example, becomes embedded in society and moves from being desirable to essential.

The cognitive dimension is further evident where learners *have their individual learning needs met*. Critical Educational Gerontology (CEG) theory reminds us that those in later life do not compose a homogeneous group and their learning needs, as with other needs in their lives, are both varied and unique to each individual (Glendenning and Battersby, 1990). Therefore any actions to meet learning needs must be, by definition, differentiated to take account of this variety. Involving adults in clarifying their own ambiguous needs, and in defining clear learning objectives, is acknowledged as an important aspect of adult learning (Knowles, 1990).

Most adults, however, have little experience of orally articulating their own needs and may need considerable assistance in clarifying and specifying them (MacKeracher, 2004). If this does not happen, then both sensory overstimulation (information overload) and under-stimulation (boredom) can produce physical stress responses that interfere with learning as outlined previously. Hart (1975) asserted that adults who are getting too much or too little information, as when their current learning task is not meeting their learning needs, may, in fact, not be learning at all.

Unfortunately there is little clarification of learning objectives in informal later-life learning classes in the same way there are in formal classes leading to assessment and/or qualifications. It became clear to me, as a participant observer, that the physical exercise classes were ones where the needs of individuals were more consistently identified at the outset and therefore progress could be identified during the course by both the tutor and the learners themselves. Partly this was because there is a need to test the physical health and abilities of participants before starting such classes. It is also partly that the improvements that come about by participation in this type of learning are physically evident and do not require a test or intrusive questioning to reveal them. Where learning needs are understood by both learners and the tutor, and are met through appropriate learning experiences, then the learners will develop (Tough, 1979; Knowles, 1990) but progress should not be forced or demanded.

Relative Strengths of the Dimensions of Learning

Altogether, four dimensions were identified: attitudinal, physical, social, and cognitive through the association of similar characteristics of quality identified by the later-life learners. Fewer characteristics were coded as being associated with the 'physical' environment than the other three dimensions, which suggests 'quality' learning is perceived by learners to be able to occur even in poorly supportive physical environments if the characteristics of quality associated with the other dimensions are present.

Through the analysis of references associated with the underpinning characteristics of each dimension a further, and slightly different, pattern emerged. The attitudinal dimension (171 references) was still the most regularly mentioned as important in quality learning sessions while the social dimension was also strongly supported (136 references). However the cognitive dimension (141 references) was as strongly represented as the social dimension highlighting that through the perceptions and conceptualisations of quality, the participants placed as much emphasis on the cognitive as the social dimension. This importance of challenge was highlighted by Creech et al. (2014a) in their research into the benefits of music in the 3rd Age where 'being successful in meeting the challenges posed led to a great sense of achievement that in itself was enjoyable, stimulating and rewarding' (p. 47).

Finally, analysis of findings from the Quality Learning Questionnaire revealed the strength of the relative support for the specific characteristics (which underpinned the four dimensions of learning) being contributors to quality. Participants were able to say not only whether they agreed with the characteristics of quality learning perceived by members of the focus groups, but how strongly they agreed when they identified 'what makes a "quality learning experience" in later life' using the Likert grading scale. Such findings arose from the summation of the scores for the various characteristics, as previously outlined, under each dimension and calculating the mean scores. Once again, the social dimension of quality informal later-life learning (mean score – 4.72) received the greatest strength of support from the questionnaire responses just above the cognitive dimension (mean score – 4.60) and attitudinal dimension (mean score – 4.55) with the physical dimension supported too (mean score – 4.43) but less strongly.

Parameters – Contextual and Demographic Variables

Altogether, seven types of learning were identified from the provision at Golden Gates namely physical, creative, information technology, humanities, languages, literature, and therapy. Examining the types of activity chosen as ones of quality experienced by the learners, the humanities learning opportunities featured in almost a third of responses (30%) as displaying the characteristics of quality learning, which was then followed by creative sessions (21%) and those involving physical exercise (18.4%). However, there was a strong correlation with the participants in a particular type of activity choosing that type of activity as one of quality. Therefore, this finding was influenced by the number of participants responding from different classes of different sizes.

When groups involved in different types of learning were compared, all types of learning identified the tutor as the most important stakeholder in the learning process and in some cases significantly (physical, literature, and social sessions). However, for humanities and for creative sessions, often involving discussions or joint activities, the learners were almost as important. Although the organisation was the third most important stakeholder in informal quality later-life learning across all types of learning, for humanities and literature classes, it was significantly more important than for the other groupings.

It was clear from the findings that the group size of 6–10 participants was greatly favoured – a size that was not too small or too large. The participants also identified the morning as the time when they experienced quality learning rather than the afternoon. Finally, as previously mentioned, the later-life learners participating in the questionnaire also strongly identified the presence of a tutor as an important factor in almost all the learning sessions they perceived to be ones of quality. These factors all contribute to learning contexts that Manheimer (2009) termed 'senior friendly spaces'.

Analysis of the questionnaire data comparing the mean responses of men and women highlighted that their support for the characteristics of quality was equally strong (4.59 and 4.60 respectively) although it is acknowledged that the groups were not of equal size (27 and 175 respectively). Although the comparison of mean scores highlighted that White participants showed a slightly more positive response than Non-White participants from two very positive sets of responses, further analysis of the qualitative data across all ethnic groups did not reveal any significant differences in the strength of support. Once again, the groups of participants from the various ethnic groupings were not of an equal size.

Further analysis showed that for 24 of the 28 characteristics of learning there was no difference in responses across the age groups to the presence of the particular characteristic within quality learning sessions. For four quality characteristics, the responses from the older later-life learners (age 80–89 or over 90 years old) were less positive than those of the younger later-life learners (50–59 or 60–69). Three of these four characteristics were concerned with the learners, and the presence of positive relationships amongst them in particular, which appeared to be a more important feature for older learners.

Empowering the Voice of the Learners

These new findings from research into the quality of informal later-life learning are in accordance with the principles of critical geragogy, challenging the idea of later life as a time of 'deficit', promoting engagement and enabling reflection by older learners about what they themselves value (Formosa, 2002). The findings also have 'ecological validity' through being gleaned directly from the learners themselves (Campbell and Stanley, 1963) and, according to Messiou (2014), engaging with such students' voices can in itself be considered a manifestation of being inclusive. Participants in learning in later life have something important to say and as Boulton-Lee and Tam (2012) observed:

> There is very little research that describes what older people themselves say they want and need to learn … there is no doubt we need more data from older people themselves about what their attitudes to learning and why, how and what they want to learn.
>
> *(p. 3)*

Listening to the voice of learners is, therefore, a valuable way of gaining insight into their ideas, beliefs, and ways of thinking (Withnall, 2010). The relationship of the learner to the tutor and to the learning organisation was identified as being applicable to later-life learners as it had been identified in formal adult settings previously (Boshier, 2006).

Finally, the evidence to support the presence of each of the characteristics of quality in practice across a range of learning activities through participant observation demonstrated that the characteristics are not a set of theoretical ambitions for informal learning but manageable possibilities. Such findings validated the voice of the learners and added strength to their perceptions.

A First focus on Quality

Despite the rise in the elderly population and the increasing numbers of older people engaging in informal later-life learning, there has been no prior research into the quality of provision and especially from the point of view of the learners themselves. However, if such participants are going to maximise the chances of reaping the benefits from learning in the 3rd Age (Hultsch et al., 1993; Rowe and Khan, 1999; Schuller et al., 2004), it needs to take place within learning environments, which enable this to happen.

In defining quality as 'meeting the customers' needs' a further important element in the research was clarified and a shared understanding was gained. When discussed with the learners, a variety of more colloquial expressions, such as 'did you get out of it what you wanted or were expecting?' were used. The identification of the learners, tutor, and organisation as all having an effect on the quality of learning drew in a wide range of influences on quality but, in this research, quality was always perceived from the learners' (customer's) position not that of the teacher (the tutor) or the provider (the organisation).

The characteristics of quality also described a very wide learning context in line with the 3P model (Biggs, 2003) outlined earlier (Chapter 4). Some characteristics were 'presage' features (before the learning sessions) with 'selection of the tutors with care' or 'the accommodation was suitable to our needs' being appropriate examples. Most were 'process' features (during the learning sessions) such as 'letting me ask questions', 'being treated with respect', and 'the equipment worked well' being suitable examples. Fewer were of the 'product' type (after the learning sessions) as in the 3P model itself. An example would be 'they [the organisation] listened to complaints' but this also strengthens the notion that products such as skill development or qualifications were valued features of quality informal later-life learning.

Summary

Through the exploration of the beliefs and experiences of quality learning amongst older people in informal learning contexts, I have been able to identify the learners' perceptions of the environmental factors that underpin quality learning experiences. The comments of the participants in the Feasibility Study identified the tutor, the organisation and the learners themselves to be three key stakeholders in quality informal later-life learning. This position was reinforced during the focus groups leading to the identification of 28 indicators of quality. These were strongly supported by a larger number of participants in informal learning through the questionnaire and identified in practice through participant observation.

In this chapter, each of the characteristics has been shown to be valuable in quality later-life learning and supported as such through the work of other writers on education. They were also evident across a range of types of learning and aligned themselves to four dimensions of learning – cognitive, social, physical, and attitudinal – with the social and attitudinal dimensions consistently valued and the physical environment being less important.

The positive identification of each of these characteristics in learning sessions, through participant observation, enabled me to experience how the characteristics of quality learning, as identified by the informal later-life learners, were articulated in practice. It was identifiable that informal learning can, and does, reflect the principles of quality as defined by the participants themselves. In the final chapter, the importance of this study, while also acknowledging its limitations, is stressed together with recommendations for both future research in this area and how the findings from this study could aid the quality of everyday practice in informal later-life learning.

10

CONCLUDING REMARKS

Introduction

This chapter briefly reflects on the context of the study and the questions that underpinned the research. It references the empirical evidence outlined in the findings chapters and the ideas and assertions made in the previous discussion chapter. Its main focus, however, is on drawing conclusions from this research and, within the inevitable limitations of this study, making both recommendations for the current policies and practices of informal later-life learning and alluding to areas for possible future activity and research.

Withnall (2010) asserts the position that the connections between research, practice, and policy in later-life learning do not appear to be well made and that comparatively little is known about the experiences of education and of learning of later-life learners over the course of their lives. In addressing this gap, the outcomes of this research bridged research and practice through the direct involvement of the learners from the outset, by narrowing down the research parameters, through the Feasibility Study, on an aspect that was valuable to the older learners and privileging their perspectives as later-life learners. The addressing of my research question and sub-questions recognised that this research was new and, although based on a case study of one later-life informal learning provider, could, potentially, be of value to other later-life learners, to those involved in leading learning, and to other organisations providing informal learning experiences for older learners.

This study took place against a background of demographic change indicating that average lifespans are increasing (Harper, 2006), as are numbers participating in informal later-life learning (McNair, 2012). It explored later-life learners' perceptions of what makes a quality informal learning experience while

DOI: 10.4324/9781003269892-10

identifying the benefits that have been shown to be accrued from such learning (Schuller and Field, 1998; Withnall, 2010). Given the costs to society, economically and socially, of addressing the physical and psychological changes associated with ageing (Stuart-Hamilton, 2000) it is advantageous to identify the features of learning experiences that older learners identified as having most value for them. This research revealed the nature of quality learning, which has the potential to maximise the benefits outlined and, altogether, seven key findings have emerged. Each is identified here with comment and conclusions drawn from the findings (Chapters 6–8) and the discussions arising from them (Chapter 9).

Key Findings

1 The participants identified and reinforced support for the idea that there are three key stakeholders in informal later-life learning that together produce quality experiences: the tutor, the organisation, and the learners themselves.

The three stakeholders were congruent with academic literature, as they have been identified previously as influences on teaching and learning situations (Illeris, 2007). However, these aspects have rarely been applied to informal learning and especially in later life. The tutor in particular was identified as the most supported positive influence on quality learning being in a position to create valuable and valued 'emotionally healthy learning environments' (Johnson, 2006) when 'optimum learning' can take place.

2 Twenty-eight characteristics associated with quality learning experiences were identified. The study also revealed the extent to which the later-life learners valued some characteristics more than others.

The characteristics of quality in informal later-life learning emerged from the focus groups and were supported through the quality learning questionnaire. The mean scores from the use of the Likert scale identified the relative strength of support for each characteristic. The lack of additional characteristics being put forward by the participants during the questionnaire suggests, perhaps, that, within this case study, a full range of characteristics have been identified.

Now that later-life learners have identified the characteristics that are associated with quality learning, the issue that this understanding raises concerns the extent, in informal later-life learning, that participants encounter the full range of characteristics. Over one third of the participants in the questionnaire took part in just one class and therefore, by definition, one type of learning. Indeed, even where learners took more than one class, the learning experiences could, perhaps, have been of a similar types such as Tai Chi and Stretch and Tone, both physical exercises, or French and Spanish sessions, both being language classes.

3 The characteristics of quality could be interpreted as being clustered around four learning dimensions, attitudinal, social, cognitive, and physical underpinning a quality learning environment.

The four dimensions of learning, identified by learners as being important in quality informal later-life learning through the analysis of the characteristics, also resonate with the four groups of benefits of learning identified through research; cognitive, health, social, and psychological. The cognitive characteristics may lead to the gaining of cognitive benefits, the attitudinal to psychological benefits, and the social benefits from the social characteristics.

One relevant question in relation to 'quality' is how, perhaps, could any course of informal learning sessions be structured so that it is as holistic as possible in demonstrating the incorporation of the dimensions of quality. For example, does a sewing course have to be sedentary? A really innovative approach for older people might be that any one course of learning could be much more 'cross curricular' or, more accurately, inter-dimensional in nature, incorporating some gentle exercise, some cognitive challenge, some social learning and some creative activity.

4 The research identified to what extent these generally well-supported 28 characteristics of quality later-life learning experiences were associated with different features of learning, such as types of learning, and identified ways in which the characteristics were articulated in practice.

The profile of the learners involved in this research was representative of the organisation involved and has smaller number of those groups under-represented in later-life learning as a whole such as men, ethnic minorities and the less well-educated (Sargant, 2000). Men, for example, are not involved in learning to the same extent as women despite being given the same opportunities to do so. The relatively small number of learners in the 50 to 60 year old age group illustrates that opportunities for informal learning are not taken up as younger later-life learners and could work against the participation of members of this section of the population later in life.

Nationally, those from the ethnic minorities are also under-represented, as are those from poorer backgrounds, and this pattern is mirrored by the groups of participants within Golden Gates. Finally, the profile of learners participating in this research shows them, as in the national picture, to be educated (Formosa, 2002). As prior education has been shown to support cognitive reserve, it is those without an education who are more likely to be in greater need of later-life learning and benefit most from offsetting dementia (Rowe and Kahn, 1999).

Nevertheless the characteristics of quality informal later-life learning were all shown to be supported, to various extents, across the age-rages of the participants, the sex of the learners, their ethnic origin, and their level of education. They were also supported across different types of learning too.

5 This research shows that later-life learners had strong views related to quality in their informal learning,

Through this research the authentic voice of a sample of the later-life learners was heard and the depth of perceptions about what quality learning looks like for them was revealing. Critical geragogy had been established as an underlying theoretical base for my research as it is a framework which champions the independence of older people, their empowerment to make decisions about their own lives and their continued participation in, and influence on, society. My research underpins this framework and the value of participation of those in later life. Cusack (2000) suggests that the actual purpose of learning opportunities for older people should be 'empowerment', which means reframing the established notions of 'power over' to 'power to' and 'power with' approaches. This research highlights that older adults are able to have a greater role in setting the local community learning agenda and shaping the policies and the programmes that affect them.

6 For the first time an understanding of 'quality' in informal later-life learning, grounded in the perceptions of older learners, has been proposed.

Whether as an 'absolute' term or a 'relative' term, the drive to ensure the provision of 'high quality' learning for later-life learners is a movement towards providing what the learners value and, in doing so, meeting their needs. This research, in identifying what the characteristics of quality are, has established a benchmark, which can be discussed and addressed by those learning, leading or providing informal later-life learning.

Quality learning would, potentially, be better able to provide the new information or develop the new skills that the learners require to improve their abilities and their wellbeing or use to secure future employment or educational opportunities. Continued participation, in society and life in general, is supported through the social settings such informal learning provides. The acquisition of contemporaneous knowledge and the development of skills, such as computer literacy involving the use of social media, lead to greater and more meaningful engagement with society.

7 The outcomes of this research raised the possibility of using this 'framework of quality' as guidance for the three stakeholders in informal later-life learning to increase the chances of the benefits available through later-life learning to be gained.

Opportunities for learning informally in later life may need to be provided cost-free, locally and for everyone if learning is to fully embrace the notions of independence and empowerment. Not only that, it may be cost-effective to support later-life learning through investment in facilities and providers through direct financial support rather than meet the social care or health demands on society from older people who are isolated, not well educated nor engaged in learning.

Leaving later-life learning largely up to charities or other voluntary organisations in the UK has enabled the current pattern of provision to be created where much good work in providing 'learning' occurs. However, it does not always provide learning now understood to cause the specific 'change' needed to accrue benefits (Illeris, 2007; Findsen, 2014) or necessarily embrace the characteristics of 'quality' learning that learners themselves have perceived. Therefore, this research raises the question that if engaging in such a range of learning types is beneficial to activate a greater number of regions of the brain, or to increase the oxygen flow to improve brain functioning, how can such learners be encouraged to take part in such a range of opportunities to accrue and maximise the benefits now recognised?

Finally, how can older people make such decisions to advantage themselves in this way when a growing number of learners state that they learn in isolation at home or do not participate in learning at all (McNair, 2012)? The element of compulsion in school education has long been established, accepted and, in many ways, jealously guarded. There is no such element of compulsion for employers to provide learning for adult employees and certainly not for those in later life who are post-work or post-responsibilities such as family or caring commitments.

My contribution to practice is:

- The generation of a format for capturing the perceptions of later-life learners to enable them to make a direct contribution to the development and enhancement of learning.
- The development of a framework, which can be used to gather information about the quality of teaching and learning in informal later-life sessions and provide a 'reflective tool' that could be used by all stakeholders.
- The creation of the Quality Cirque for informal later-life learning provides a framework for the way in which the rationale for learning in later life and the benefits arising from it can be garnered through an understanding and appreciation of the value of quality and the way it can flourish in supporting learning environments.

My contribution to research is ...

- providing new insights into the quality of learning within informal later-life learning that could lead to improvements for current learners,
- providing a 'reflective tool' that could enhance evaluation, practices by those providing or managing learning or developing policy to make improvements,
- providing evidence of how the benefits of later-life learning could, and should, be used to attract new learners through the provision and management of quality learning environments.

Potential for Further Research

The relative scarcity of studies into informal learning in later life leaves quite a fertile field for further research.

Enhancement of My Research

Carrying out this gathering of information could be extended to listening to the voice of the *tutors* involved in later-life learning. In this way support for the perceptions of learners could be gauged, any additional characteristics captured and any congruencies in the findings of the two groups addressed.

Some work could involve an application of my research into other types and areas of learning and other learning organisations. There is also the possibility of looking in more depth at the perceptions of participants arising from this research and looking deeper into aspects such as motivation and learning needs. There is also the possibility of involving a wider sample of learners.

The creation of instruments to identify and record the learning needs of later-life learners, so that progress in learning can be evaluated and fed back, will best be done with the learners themselves, as they can be wary of tests and assessments as judgements of them as learners can be considered to be personal judgements of them as people.

Further work on the types of learning and how the characteristics of quality are more aligned with some forms of learning than with others would have the advantage of ensuring the quality of provision meets the needs of particular learners across the range of types of learning they are personally involved in.

Finally, more in-depth studies on learner profiles including their sex, ethnicity, and education levels could be used to address the needs and expectations of those particular groups. In doing so, there is an opportunity to use such findings to consider how these under-represented groups within the later-life community could be better attracted to, and served by, learning.

Extension of My Research

The benefits of learning, which embody the characteristics of quality, could be identified through longitudinal studies to see if changes in delivery cause improvements in the lives of those involved. Such studies could look at specific individuals over longer periods of time rather than a greater number of older learners at particular times in their lives.

There is the possibility of considering to what extent the lack of quality provision, as revealed through the characteristics of quality, has been a barrier to learning for some older people. This could then be used to see if changes to practices can encourage greater numbers to participate, to be retained following participation and particularly participation from the groups within the UK population as a whole who are currently under-represented.

Further National and International Research

The providers of informal later-life learning opportunities, from local councils and charities to a national network of adult education colleges and the government itself through funding regimes, have an opportunity to listen to, and reflect on, the perceptions of older people about what, for them, constitutes quality provision.

As previously set out, there is recognition at all levels from charities such as The Alzheimer's Society to the government through the Foresight Mental Capital and Wellbeing Project (GOScience, 2008) that there are considerable social benefits from later-life learning. There is also possible improved value for money in preventing the need to access medical or social support in later life. This would lead to society as a whole, and governments in particular, considering new paradigms of learning throughout the life course and the extent to which it is supported and incentivised. An article in the Times Educational Supplement (Nash, 2015) highlighted the case of doctors in London prescribing courses of learning for elderly patients instead of prescribing drugs and other medicines. This is especially relevant to the less well-educated who require greater amounts of financial, medical and social support as they get older. Quality learning could help to bridge what Sargant (2000) called 'the large gulf between the learning-rich and the learning-poor'.

At the same time, as a researcher spending time within the wide range of courses offered by Golden Gates, which supports educational gerontology, I found no courses on gerontological education (Jarvis, 1990). This is where people, whether already in later life or other stages in life, are made aware of the process of ageing and gain an understanding of how they could and, perhaps, should age well. Research has identified how dementia can be offset by 'keeping the mind active' (Kemperman, 2006) and also by maintaining a healthy weight, eating a healthy diet, and taking exercise. Without an understanding of the range of factors involved, how they affect people as they age and how they can positively address them within their individual situations, the benefits of learning are diluted.

One way in which organisations or the government could get involved would be through pre-retirement training where preparation for an active later life could be fashioned at the start of later life so that the benefits of learning can be gleaned over as many years as possible.

Finally, sharing research into quality later-life teaching and learning practices across countries would lead to a more focused international view of quality learning. In this way, future pronouncements from bodies such as the United Nations, ostensibly talking about quality learning in later life, do not simply focus on the measurement of numbers 'attending' learning or numbers of 'classes offered' in different countries. Instead they could and, I assert, should focus on the provision of 'good practice' in those classes and the extent to which the characteristics of quality informal learning in later life, now identified, are being made manifest.

The Limitations of This Study

One limitation to this study is, firstly, that it is a case study within only one specific organisation and, secondly, the study comprises views from only a relatively small sample of learners within this case study organisation despite the sample being a representative one. Equally, not all types of learning represented within the organisation were encompassed through the research fieldwork. While outcomes cannot be generalised, the point of an instrumental case study, as outlined in the Methodology (Chapter 5), is that the findings can be transferred to other contexts. It is representative of that one organisation even though clearly not balanced regarding aspects such as gender or ethnicity.

This study also focused on those attending classes and there may be characteristics of quality later-life learning that non-attendees might suggest that were not perceived by those attending. As Lee (2003) noted: '... the adults from whom [Knowles] drew andragogical assumptions ... were over-represented by privileged individuals, who were primarily White, male, educated, and from middle-class backgrounds - a population that was not unlike himself' (p. 15).

This research did not seek to access those not attending learning who may have a different perspective on what constitutes quality later-life learning. Chen et al. (2008) stress that there is a great deal of work to be done in gaining the views of those adults currently not involved in formal education or, indeed, any form of organised learning and also those groups currently under-represented. If only 20% of adults in later life take part in any activities they describe as learning (McNair, 2012) then the vast majority do not. The research approach also did not engage later-life learners who are in the 4th Age either. Such older adults, in need of care and, usually, unable to attend external provision, may also have a different but valuable perspective on quality informal later-life learning.

Limitations were recognised at each phase of the fieldwork sessions. Firstly, the Feasibility Study consisted of just one meeting when a series of meetings involving a wider number of older people may have identified other aspects they valued in the learning. Initially, I hoped to establish a 'steering group' available to use as a sounding board throughout the study but, due to logistical difficulties, that did not happen. Therefore the input of the learners on the wider aspects of later-life learning they valued were captured on one occasion only and those assertions were not subject to amendment or 'fine-tuning' as the research continued.

During the focus group sessions, the way 'quality' was presented to the participants may have skewed their responses by hinting at what responses I, as the researcher, was looking for. Establishing a comfortable atmosphere and good relationships with the learners may have led to more subjective responses to my questions than otherwise might have been the case. Nevertheless, this aspect of focus groups is difficult to negate and the prior use of the Feasibility Study and familiar language of later-life learners themselves were ways adopted to address this aspect.

The administration of the survey and the way 'quality' was presented to the participants through the questionnaire may also have influenced the responses of the participants. However, structure and presentation are always limitations on the use of any questionnaire (Robson, 2011); the participants may respond according to what they think the researcher wants their responses to be, they may express views on concepts that they are, in fact, unfamiliar with and the researcher does not have any control over how the participants interpret the degrees of the Likert scale (one person's interpretation of 'very important' can be very different from another's). It must be acknowledged, therefore, that if the statements concerning quality were presented in a different form they may have achieved different results. Nevertheless, in using a checklist produced by de Vaus (2001), I was able to avoid the most obvious problems with question wording.

Finally, as a participant observer, I made contemporaneous notes on each occasion but I did not record actual practices by, for example, video-recording activity within the learning environment. This limited the amount of information I was able to consider, following the classes, as I was unable to look back and analyse what actually happened in the sessions I attended from a more objective perspective

Implications for Practice – Recommendations

The research findings described in the previous chapters have implications for a range of personnel involved with informal later-life learning from policy makers and providers, at both local and national levels, to practitioners and to learners themselves as outlined in the Introduction (Chapter 1). In summary:

For policy makers, the outcomes could help to guide social policy so that the agreed benefits of learning in later-life become a significant part of more older people's lives. In general terms, the characteristics could form part of any training leading to 'improving the quality of work', one of the recommendations in the report following the inquiry into the future for life long learning (Schuller and Watson, 2009) where it proposes the wider use of 'license to practice' requirements 'to promote the raising of the level and use of skills' (p. 3).

For providers the responses of the later-life learners can be used to inform and improve the learning 'environment' in which learning can take place and suggest ways in which the needs of those learning can be best met to maximise the benefits from learning in later life. It can also be used to look at ways in which policy can be devised, and practice influenced, to ensure consistency of practice and promote opportunities to embrace feedback from later-life learners over and above 'satisfaction surveys'.

For practitioners, those given the privilege of teaching older learners, from qualified facilitators to peer tutors, it is possible that the characteristics of quality provide a 'checklist' which can be used as a reflective tool to ensure the perceptions of learners on what they value, and especially the needs of individual learners, are taken into account both in planning and in delivery.

For learners, in general, the outcomes can be considered a set of guidelines on the learning provision learners, like them, say are valuable and likely to benefit them in later life. Therefore they have a set of expectations they can share with their providers including facilitators and organisations.

Such sharing of the characteristics of quality could reveal how learners themselves could contribute to the provision of quality in later-life learning, say, in the following four ways:

Teaching and Learning Policy

The creation of teaching and learning policies for organisations offering or supporting informal later-life learning will ensure what happens in sessions is informed by the perceptions of what learners themselves perceive to be quality learning experiences. It will also offer consistency of expectations across sessions and ensure all learners can benefit irrespective of whether the tutor is a peer or not and irrespective of the type of learning involved.

Informal learning sessions that involve later-life learners are usually led by tutors demonstrating a wide range of expertise and experience from those who are experienced and/or trained as teachers or lecturers to volunteers. Although the latter are willing and, although often experienced in the subject they are focused on, they can be new to leading learning. Later-life learning organisations, such as u3a, do not seek to impose a creed to direct or standardise teaching and learning and neither are organisations such as Golden Gates able to arrange meetings of staff to raise such matters, as this would entail paying the tutors from the limited funding available to them. Therefore, in such a climate, the benefits that could be gained from sharing and disseminating good practice amongst learners, tutors, and provider organisations could be lost.

During this study, it was clear from discussions that there was a general lack of awareness by both providers and participants about current research findings into later-life learning and an absence of opportunities for discussing them within the learning organisation. This applies to specific neuroscientific research but also to notions of the practice of geragogy and methods of identifying or measuring quality in both teaching and learning. Although some caution needs to be expressed about how such findings could, and should, influence practice, the Royal Society working group on Neuroscience and Lifelong Learning (2011) has an aim of disseminating such knowledge to enrich teachers' own experiences of how adults learn in later life.

Quality Assurance

Strategies to monitor and evaluate the presence and value of characteristics of quality in informal later-life learning offer an opportunity to assess if agreed teaching and learning policies are actually manifested in practice and to what extent they are having the desired beneficial effects on individual learners.

Through the use of the checklist of quality characteristics and the use of associated strategies such as focus groups and participant observation, later-life learners can be continually involved in improving the quality of learning.

The focus on extracting individual perceptions of quality in informal later-life learning was important in enabling individuals to be empowered and in control of the expression of their own opinions underpinning the critical geragogical framework. However, that did not preclude aggregating the individual expressions of characteristics of quality, which featured elements such as 'emotion', and 'feelings' (qualia) as well as more objective descriptions into a composite framework of what quality learning might look like. This framework is of value to each of the three stakeholders in later-life learning and can act as a template against which to reflect their practices and their own responsibility for, and participation in, them. In this way 'appropriate judgements' about the quality of provision can be made (Sallis, 2002).

This research also reveals the ability of the learners to 'evaluate' their learning internally and that they are in the ideal place to do so (McKen in Lomax, 1996). Such learning can therefore be monitored through self-evaluation using a framework and feedback from any 'assessment' could, and should, lead to improved learning (Cross and Steadman, 1996).

The variations in session delivery, and the differences in the expectations of tutors, can have benefits both as motivational tools and ways to meet the various needs of individuals or groups. However, where it happens in an uninformed way (about what works and about the characteristics of quality the learners require) it is less advantageous. This is exacerbated where there is a lack of policy for teaching and learning or the lack of a framework by which progress in different learning contexts and sessions could be evaluated.

Training and Professional Development

The implications for training and professional development about quality in informal later-life learning are three fold.

The first involves training for those already trained in teaching but for school children (pedagogy) or adults (andragogy). Here is an opportunity to focus on the characteristics of quality, the practices of teaching and learning and how to best meet the individual learning needs of those in later life (geragogy).

The second involves training for those not having undergone formal teacher training. Charitable organisations such as U3A value the notion of the learner also being the teacher but do not provide guidance on effective geragogical practice either to support tutors or later-life learners in their learning. Such provision is focused on the enjoyment of learning, which is valuable. However, many of the characteristics of quality learning may not be regular features of such sessions, and perhaps this is hardly surprising given the autonomy of each U3A area and the lack of training in geragogy. By adopting an evaluative framework, drawn from the perceptions of later-life learners directly involved, informal later-life learners could maximise the benefits such learning brings.

Finally, there is a need to link new and developing understandings about the benefits of later-life learning to geragogical practices. The developments in neuroscience, for example, have shone a light on the capacity of those in later life to continue learning throughout their life course and in doing so highlighted strategies by which their capacity can be maintained or strengthened. This information could and should be part of such guidance for all those supporting people in later life, including family members and assigned carers, and should be continually updated as new research findings are revealed.

National or International Policy Making

The information uncovered by this research could also be used to support the work of the UK and other governments looking to fund initiatives to improve the lives and wellbeing of those in later life. At the moment, in the UK, the relative profile of funding for adult (over 18) education is in terms of pence for each individual involved in later-life learning compared to pounds for those in higher education (Chapter 2). The government also has a role in funding ongoing research including the dissemination of good practices demonstrating the value placed on the thoughts and the voice of those in later life.

At the same time, there remains the question concerning how the knowledge of these benefits to be gleaned from learning in later life could, or should be, made available within a growing, and increasingly needy society. Gerontological education (learning about ageing and ageing successfully) does not feature as a distinct element either in general learning environments involving older adults or within the formal education provision at schools and colleges. In particular, how can older people choose such paths to follow when this is not even a feature of their centres of learning?

Reflection

Retirement from working in the field of education enabled me to study full-time and give my research the time and attention it required and deserved. There was, I believe, a value in being part of the age group that I was studying. It enabled me to converse more readily with the participants, to be able to empathise with their views on learning and later life and also to appreciate the nuances of what was said and done during the fieldwork that other, younger researchers, might not have picked up on or appreciated as being of significance.

At the same time, having been heavily involved in educating children and students, it is quite dispiriting to see the gains being made so quickly and fruitfully in early life not being built on in later life. After all, learning new information and skills to keep up-to-date with changes in daily activities and on the job is a necessary challenge throughout life (Stern and Spokus, 2019). Much of the good work in the early years is undone where learning is not applied throughout the life course and many people do not go on to use the abilities they have developed to improve the quality of their lives as they age. As Frith (2011) found, there is: '... an inverse relationship between educational attainment and risk of dementia, which means that keeping the mind active slows cognitive decline and improves cognitive abilities in older learners' (p. 4).

We all age and, if fortunate, grow old. We all continually learn too whether formally, informally or simply incidentally and gain various levels of benefit from doing so. This is valuable not just for individuals but a society as increasing levels of education may be the best long-term public health strategy for achieving national health goals (Mirowsky and Ross, 2015). If that learning can be organised and provided to be of the quality that would enable older learners to glean the most benefits from doing so, both individuals, and society as a whole, would be better for it. Our schools are charged with ensuring that 'no child is left behind'; using the outcomes of this research we have the opportunity to ensure throughout the life course that 'no one' is left behind either.

REFERENCES

Adey, P., Fairbrother, R. and William, D. (1999). *Learning styles and strategies – A review of research*. London: Kings College.

Ahl, H. (2006). 'Motivation in adult education: A problem solver or a euphemism for direction and control?'. *International Journal of Lifelong Education*, 25, 385–405.

Aldridge, F. and Lavender, P. (2000). *The impact of learning on health*. Leicester: NIACE.

Aldridge, F. and Tuckett, A. (2010). *A change for the better: The NIACE survey on adult participation in learning 2010*. Leicester: NIACE.

Armstrong, F. (2012). 'Landscapes, spatial justice and learning communities'. *International Journal of Inclusive Education*, 16 (5/6), 609–626.

Asen, R. (2004). 'A discourse theory of citizenship'. *Quarterly Journal of Speech*, 90, 189–211.

Bak, T. H., Nissan, J. J., Allerhand, M. M. and Deary, A. J. (2014). 'Does bilingualism influence cognitive aging?' *Annals of Neurology*, 75 (6), 959–963.

Baltes, P. B. (1997). 'On the incomplete architecture of human ontogeny: Selection, optimization, and compensation as the foundation of developmental theory'. *American Psychologist*, 52, 366–380.

Baltes, P. B., Reese, H. W. and Lipsitt, L. P. (1980). 'Life-span developmental psychology'. *Annual Review of Psychology*, 31, 65–110.

Bandura, A. (1976). 'Modelling theory'. In W. S. Sahakian (Ed.), *Learning: Systems, models and theories*. Skokie, IL: Rand McNally.

Bandura, A. (1986). *Social foundations of thought and action: A social cognitive theory*. Englewood Cliffs, NJ: Prentice Hall.

Banks, I. (2006). *Brain manual*. Sparkford: Haynes Publishing.

Baringer, D. K. et al. (2004). 'Instructural communication and older adults'. In J. F. Nussbaum and J. Coupland (Eds.), *Handbook of communication and aging research*. Mahwah, NJ: Erlbaum.

Battersby, D. (1987). 'From andragogy to geragogy'. *Journal of Educational Gerontology*, 1 (2), 4–10.

Battersby, D. (1993). 'Developing an epistemology of professional practice within educational gerontology'. *Journal of Educational Gerontology*, 8 (1), 17–25.

Battersby, D. and Glendenning, F. (1992). 'Reconstructing education for older adults: An elaboration of first principles'. *Australian Journal of Adult and Community Education*, 32 (2), 115–121.

Baumgartner, L. M. (2012). 'Mezirow's theory of transformative learning from 1975 to the present'. In E. W. Taylor and P. Cranston (Eds.), *The handbook of transformative learning*. San Francisco, CA: Jossey Bass.

BeLL Project (2014). 'About the project' [online]. Available at: http://www.bell-project.eu/cms/ (accessed 10 November 2016).

Berkman, L. F. (2000). 'Which influence cognitive functions: Living alone or being alone?'. *Lancet*, 355, 1291–1292.

Betts Adams, K., Leibbrandt, S. and Moon, H. (2011). 'A critical review of the literature on social and leisure activity and wellbeing in later life'. *Ageing and Society*, 31 (4), 683–712.

Bialystok, E. et al. (2012). 'Bilingualism: Consequences for mind and brain'. *Trends in Cognitive Sciences*, 16 (4), 240–250.

Biesta, G. (2007). 'The problem of "learning"'. *Adults Learning*, 18 (8), 8–11.

Biggs, J. B. (1989). 'Approaches to the enhancement of tertiary teaching'. *Higher Education Research and Development*, 8, 7–25.

Biggs, J. B. (1993). 'From theory to practice: A cognitive systems approach'. *Higher Education Research and Development*, 12 (1), 73–85.

Biggs, J. B. (2003). *Teaching for quality learning at university: What the student does* (2nd edition). Ballmoor: Open University Press.

Bissland, V. (2013). 'Older adults' voices: An exploration of preferred learning and communication styles and their fit with emerging insights from neuroscience'. *International Journal of Education and Ageing*, 3 (1), 43–62.

Bjorklund, B. R. (2011). *The journey of adulthood* (7th edition). Boston, MA: Prentice Hall.

Blakemore, S.-J. and Frith, U. (2005). *The learning brain: Lessons for education*. Oxford: Blackwell Publishing.

Blaikie, A. (1999). *Ageing and popular culture*. Cambridge: Cambridge University Press.

Blakie, N. (2007). *Approaches to social enquiry*. Cambridge: Polity Press.

Blunden, J. F., Buscha, P. and Urwin, P. (2010). *Measuring the returns to lifelong learning*. CEE Discussion Paper 110. London: Centre for Economics of Education.

Bonsang, E., Adam, S. and Perelman, S. (2010). 'Does retirement affect cognitive functioning?'. [Online]. *Netspar discussion papers*. Available at: http://arno.uvt.nl/show.cgi?fid=113197.

Boshier, R. (1991). 'Psychometric properties of the alternative form of the education participation scale'. *Adult Education Quarterly*, 41 (3), 113–130.

Boshier, P. (2006). *Perceptions of quality in adult learning*. New York: Continuum International Publishing Group.

Botwinick, J. (1984). *Aging and behaviour* (3rd edition). New York: Springer Publishing Company.

Boud, D. (1988). 'Moving towards autonomy'. In D. Boud (Ed.), *Developing student autonomy in learning*. London: Kogan Page.

Boud, D., Cohen, R. and Walker, D. (1993). 'Introduction: Understanding learning from experience'. In D. Boud, R. Cohen and D. Walker (Eds.), *Using experience for learning*. Milton Keynes: Open University Press.

Boulton-Lewis, G. (2012). 'Issues in learning and education for the ageing'. In G. Boulton-Lewis and M. Tam (Eds.), *Active ageing, active learning: Issues and challenges*. New York: Springer.

Boulton-Lee, G. and Tam, M. (Eds.) (2012). *Active ageing, active learning: Issues and challenges*. New York: Springer.

Brady, E. M., Holt, S. and Welt, B. (2003). 'Peer teaching in lifelong learning institutes'. *Educational Gerontology*, 29 (10), 851–868.

Braun, V. and Clarke, V. (2006). 'Using thematic analysis in psychology'. *Qualitative Research in Psychology*, 3, 77–101.

Brayne, C., Ince, P. G., Keage, H. A. D., McKeith, I. G., Matthews, F. E., Polvikoski, T. and Sulkava, R. (2010). 'Education, the brain and dementia: Neuroprotection or compensation?' *EClipSE Collaborative. Aug*; 133 (Pt8): 2210–2216.

Brine, J. (2006). 'Lifelong learning and the knowledge economy: Those that know and those who do not – the discourse of the European Union'. *British Educational Research Journal*, 32, 649–665.

Brookfield, S. D. (1986). *Understanding and facilitating adult learning*. San Francisco, CA: Jossey-Bass.

Brophy, J. (2004). *Motivating students to learn* (2nd edition). Mahwah, NJ: Erlbaum.

Brophy, J. (2008). 'Developing students appreciation for what is taught in schools'. *Educational Psychologist*, 43 (3), 132–141.

Brown, A. and Dowling, P. (1998). *Doing research*. Abingdon: Routledge.

Brown, J. S., Collins, A. and Duguid, P. (1989). 'Situated cognition and the culture of learning'. *Educational Researcher*, 18 (1), 32–42.

Burbules, N. and Burk, R. (1999). 'Critical thinking and critical pedagogy: Relations, differences and limits'. In T. Popkewitz and L. Fendler (Eds.), *Critical theories in education: Changing terrains of knowledge and politics*. New York: Routledge.

Burge, E. J. (2002). 'Synthesis: learners and learning are the issues'. In E. J. Burge (Ed.), *The strategic use of learning technologies, new directions for adult and continuing education*. San Francisco, CA: Jossey-Bass.

Burns, R. (2000). *Introduction to research methods* (4th edition). London: Sage.

Caine, R. N. and Caine, G. (1991). *Making connections: Teaching and the human brain*. Alexandria, VA: Association for Supervision and Curriculum Development.

Campbell, D. T. and Stanley, J. C. (1963). 'Experimental and quasi-experimental designs for research on teaching'. In N. L. Gage (Ed.), *Handbook of research on teaching*. Chicago, IL: Rand McNally.

Candy, P. C. (1991). *Self-direction for lifelong learning*. San Francisco, CA: Jossey-Bass.

Carstensen, L. L., Hansen, K. A. and Freund, A. M. (1995). 'Selection and compensation in adulthood'. In R. Dixon and L. Backman (Eds.), *Compensating for psychology deficits and declines*. Mahwah, NJ: Erlbaum.

Chen, L., Kim, Y., Moon, P. and Merriam, S. B. (2008). 'A review and critique of the portrayal of older adult learners in adult education journals, 1980-2006'. *Adult Education Quarterly*, 59 (1), 3–21.

Chène, A. (1994). 'Community-based older learners: Being with others'. *Educational Gerontology*, 20 (8), 65–78.

Cheng, M. (2011). 'The perceived impact of quality audit on the work of academics'. *Higher Education Research and Development*, 30 (2), 179–191.
Choi, I. (2009). 'The meaning of older adults' peer teaching: A phenomenological study'. *Educational Gerontology*, 35 (9), 831–852.
Chumley, L. H. (2013). 'Evaluation regimes and the qualia of quality'. *Anthropological Theory*, 13 (1/2), 69–183.
Chumley, L. H. and Harkness, H. (2013). 'Introduction: QUALIA'. *Anthropological Theory*, 13 (1/2), 3–11.
Clark, M. C. (1993). 'Transformational learning'. In S. B. Merriam (Ed.), *An update on adult learning theory. New Directions for Adult and Continuing Education, No. 57.* San Francisco, CA: Jossey-Bass.
Cohen, G. D. (2000). *The creative age: Awakening human potential in the second half of life.* New York: Avon Books.
Coleman, J. S. (1988). 'Social capital in the creation of human capital'. *American Journal of Sociology, Supplement: Organizations and Institutions: Sociological and Economic Approaches to the Analysis of Social Structure*, 94, 95–120.
Combs, A. W. (1974). 'Humanistic approaches to learning in adults'. In R. W. Bortner (Ed.), *Adults as learners.* University Park, PA: Pennsylvania State University.
Coombs, P. H. (1985). *The world crisis in education: A view from the eighties.* New York: Oxford University Press.
Coombs, P. H., Prosser, R. C. and Ahmed, M. (1973). *New paths to learning for children and youth.* New York: International Council for Educational Development.
Cooper, C. L., Field, J., Goswami, U., Jenkins, R. and Sahakian, B. (2010). *Mental capital and wellbeing.* Oxford and Ames, IO: Wiley-Blackwell.
Cozolino, L. and Sprokay, S. (2006). 'Neuroscience and adult learning'. In S. Johnson and K. Taylor (Eds.), *The neuroscience of adult learning: New directions for adult and continuing learning.* San Francisco, CA: Jossey-Bass.
Cranston, P. and Taylor, E. W. (2012). 'Transformative learning theory: Seeking a more unified theory'. In E. W. Taylor and P. Cranston (Eds.), *The handbook of transformative learning.* San Francisco, CA: Jossey-Bass.
Creech, A., Hallam, S., Varvarigou, M. and McQueen, H. (2014a). *Active ageing with music: Supporting wellbeing in the Third and Fourth Ages.* London: Institute of Education Press.
Creech, A., Varvarigou, M., Hallam, S., McQueen, H. and Gaunt, H. (2014b). 'Scaffolding, organisational structure and interpersonal interaction in musical activities with older people'. *Psychology of Music*, 42 (3), 430–447.
Creech, A. and Hallam, S. (2015). 'Critical pedagogy: A framework for facilitating older learners in community music'. *London Review of Education*, 13 (1), 43–57.
Creswell, J. W. (2003). *Research design: Qualitative, quantitative and mixed methods approaches* (2nd edition). Thousand Oaks, CA: Sage.
Cross, K. P. and Steadman, M. H. (1996). *Classroom research: Implementing the scholarship of teaching.* San Francisco, CA: Jossey-Bass.
Crowley, C. and Lodge, H. S. (2007). *Younger next year: Turn back your biological clock.* New York: Workman Publishing Company.
Cumin, E. and Henry, W. E. (1961). *Growing old: The process of disengagement.* New York: Basic Books.
Csikszentmihályi, M. (1990). *Flow: The psychology of optimal experience.* New York: Harper Row.

Cusack, S. A. (2000). 'Critical educational gerontology and the imperative to empower'. In F. Glendenning (Ed.), *Teaching and learning in later life: Theoretical implications.* Aldershot: Ashgate Publishers.
Daines, J., Daines, C. and Graham, B. (1993). *Adult learning, adult teaching* (3rd edition). Nottingham: University of Nottingham.
Daloz, L. A. (1999). *Mentor: Guiding the journey of adult learners.* San Francisco, CA: Jossey-Bass.
Damant, J., Knapp, M., Freddolino, P. and Lombard, D. (2017). 'Effects of digital engagement on the quality of life of older people'. *Health and Social Care in the Community*, 25 (6), 1679–1703.
Darkenwald, G. G. and Merriam, S. B. (1982). *Adult education: Foundations of practice.* New York: Harper Row.
Dawson, A. and Baller, W. (1972). 'Relationships between creative activity and the health of elderly persons'. *Journal of Psychology*, 82, 49–58.
de Vaus, D. (2001). *Surveys in social research* (5th edition). London: Routledge.
Dench, S. and Regan, J. (2000). *Learning in later life: Motivation and impact.* Nottingham: Department for Education and Employment.
Dennet, D. (1988). 'Quining Qualia'. In A. Marcel and E. Bisiach (Eds.), *Consciousness in Contemporary Science.* New York: Oxford University Press.
Department for Innovation, Universities and Skills (2008a). *Informal adult learning - Shaping the way ahead.* London: DIUS.
Department for Innovation, Universities and Skills (2008). *The learning revolution.* London: DIUS.
Dewey, J. (2010). 'The Democratic role of higher education in England'. In J. Sloam and M. Bacon (Eds.), *Journal of Political Science Education*, 6 (4), 336–352.
Dirkx, J. M. (2001). 'The power of feelings: Emotion, imagination and the construction of meaning in adult learning'. In S. B. Merriam (Ed.), *The new update on adult learning theory, New Directions for Adult and Continuing Education, No. 89.* San Francisco, CA: Jossey-Bass.
Duay, D. L. and Bryan, V. C. (2008). 'Learning in later life: What seniors want in a learning experience'. *Educational Gerontology*, 34 (12), 1070–1086.
Duncan, S. (2014). *Reading for pleasure and reading circles for adult emerging readers.* Leicester: NIACE.
Duncan, S. (2015). 'Biographical learning and non-formal education: Questing, threads and choosing how to be older'. *Studies in the Education of Adults*, 47 (1), 35–48.
Dunn, R. and Dunn, K. (1978). *Teaching students through their individual learning styles.* Reston, VA: Reston Publishing.
Elias, P. K., Elias, M. F., Robbins, M. A. and Gage, P. (1987). 'Acquisition of word-processing skills by younger, middle-age and older adults'. *Psychology and Aging*, 2 (4), 340–348.
Elmore, R. (1999). 'Education for older people: The moral dimension'. *Education and Ageing*, 14, 9–20.
Elton, L. (1992). 'University teaching: A professional model for quality and excellence', paper presented at the Quality by Degrees Conference at Aston University, 8th June 1992.
Erickson, D. (2009). 'Learning in retirement peer instructors: In over their heads or swimming comfortably'. *Educational Gerontology*, 35 (5), 393–408.

Evans, K. (1991). *Education for young adults: International perspectives.* London: Routledge.
Feinstein, L., Hammond, C., Woods, L., Preston, J. and Bynner, J. (2003). *The contribution of adult learning to health and social capital,* DCSF Research Report. London: Department for Children, Schools and Families.
Feinstein, L. and Symons, J. (1999). 'Attainment in secondary schools'. *Oxford Economic Papers,* 51, 300–321.
Field, J. (2009). *Well-being and happiness,* IFLL Thematic Paper 4. Leicester: NIACE.
Field, J. (2011). 'Researching the benefits of learning: The persuasive power of longitudinal studies'. *London Review of Education,* 9 (3), 283–292.
Field, J. (2012). 'Lifelong learning, welfare and mental well-being into older age: Trends and policies in Europe'. In G. Boulton-Lee and M. Tam, (Eds.), *Active ageing, active learning: Issues and challenges.* New York: Springer.
Findsen, B. (2014). *Making a difference: Learning in later life.* Hamilton: Wilf Malcolm Institute of Educational Research Faculty of Education, The University of Waikato.
Findsen, B. and Formosa, M. (2011). *Lifelong learning in later life.* Rotterdam: Sense Publishers.
Findsen, B. and Formosa, M. (2016). 'Concluding remarks'. In B. Findsen and M. Formosa (Eds.), *International perspectives on older adult education.* New York: Springer Cham Heidelberg.
Findsen, B. and McCullough, S. (2007). *Your money or your life? How policy and practices affect older FE and HE learners' participation.* Paper presented at the Proceedings of the 37th Annual SCUTREA conference, The Queen's University of Belfast, Northern Ireland, 3–5 July 2007.
Formosa, M. (2002). 'Critical pedagogy: Developing practical possibilities for critical educational gerontology'. *Education and Ageing,* 17 (1), 73–85.
Formosa, M. (2005). 'Feminism and critical educational gerontology: An agenda for good practice'. *Ageing International,* 30 (4), 396–411.
Formosa, M. (2007). 'A Bourdieusian interpretation of the University of the Third Age in Malta'. *Journal of Maltese Education Research,* 4, 1–16.
Formosa, M. (2011). 'Critical educational gerontology: A third statement of first principles'. *International Journal of Education and Ageing,* 2 (1), 323–338.
Formosa, M. (2012). 'European Union policy on older adult learning: A critical commentary'. *Journal of Aging and Social Policy,* 24 (94), 384–399.
Freire, P. (1970). *Pedagogy of the oppressed.* New York: Seabury Press.
Freire, P. (1973). *Education for critical consciousness.* New York: Seabury Press.
Freund, A. M. and Baltes, P. B. (1998). 'Selection, optimization, and compensation as strategies of life management: Correlations with subjective indicators of successful aging'. *Psychology and Aging,* 13, 531–543.
Frith, H. and Gleeson, K. (2004). 'Clothing and embodiment: Men managing body image and appearance'. *Psychology of Men and Masculinity,* 5, 40–48.
Frith, U. (2011). *Brain Waves Module 2: Neuroscience: Implications for education and lifelong learning.* RS Policy document 02/11. London: The Royal Society.
Gembris, H. (2008). 'Musical activities in the Third Age: An empirical study with amateur musicians'. In A. Daubney, E. Longhi, A. Lamont and D. J. Hargreaves (Eds.), *Musical development and learning.* Proceedings of the Second European Conference on Developmental Psychology of Music, Roehampton University, England, 10–12 September. Hull: G. K. Publishing.

Gerring, J. (2006). *Case study research: Principles and practice*. Cambridge: Cambridge University Press.

Gibb, B. J. (2012). *The rough guide to the brain* (2nd edition). London: Rough Guides Ltd.

Gibbs, G. (2010). *Dimensions of quality*. York: The Higher Education Academy.

Gifford, R. (1997). *Environmental psychology: Principles and practice* (2nd edition). Boston, MA: Allyn & Bacon.

Gilleard, C. and Higgs, P. (2000). *Cultures of ageing: Self, citizen and the body*. Upper Saddle River, NJ: Prentice Hall.

Gilleard, C. and Higgs, P. (2002). *The third age: Class, cohort and Community*. Cambridge: Polity.

Gillhooly, M. L. et al. (2007). 'Real world problem solving and quality of life in older people'. *British Journal of Health Psychology*, 12 (4), 587–600.

Giroux, H. A. (1994). 'Toward a pedagogy of critical thinking'. In K. S. Walters (Ed.), *Re-thinking reason: New perspectives in critical thinking*. Albany: SUNY Press.

Giroux, H. A. (2010a). 'Lessons from Paulo Freire'. *Chronicle of Higher Education*, 57 (9), 1–8.

Giroux, H. A. (2010b). 'Rethinking education as the practice of freedom: Paulo Freire and the promise of critical pedagogy'. *Policy Futures in Education*, 8 (6), 715–721.

Glendenning, F. and Battersby, D. (1990). 'Why we need educational gerontology and education for older adults: A statement of first principles'. In F. Glendenning and K. Percy (Eds.), *Ageing, education and society, readings in educational gerontology*. Association for Educational Gerontology: The University of Keele.

GOScience (2008). *Foresight mental capital and wellbeing project*. London: The Government Office for Science.

Graham, N. and Warner, J. (2009). *Alzheimer's disease & other dementias*. Poole: Family Doctor Publications.

Green, D. (1994). 'What is quality in higher education? Concepts, policy and practice'. In D. Green (Ed.), *What is quality in higher education*. Buckingham: Open University Press.

Greene, J. C. and Caracelli, V. J. (1997). 'Defining and describing the paradigm issue in mixed-method evaluation'. In J. C. Greene and V. J. Caracelli (Eds.), *Advances in mixed-method evaluation: The challenges and benefits of integrating diverse paradigms, New Directions for Evaluation*, 74. San Francisco, CA: Jossey-Bass.

Guillemard, A.-M. (2000). *Aging and the welfare-state crisis*. Newark: University of Delaware Press.

Hafford-Letchfield, T. (2009). 'The age of opportunity? Revisiting assumptions about the life-ling learning opportunities of older people using social care services'. *British Journal of Social Work*, 40 (2), 496–512.

Hallam, S. et al. (2011). *Music for life project: Promoting social engagement and well-being through community supported participation in musical activities: Final report*. London: IOE and Guildhall School of Music and Drama.

Hammersley, M. (1992). *What's wrong with ethnography?* London: Routledge.

Hanson, A. (1996). 'The search for separate theories of adult learning: Does anyone really need andragogy?' In R. Edwards, A. Hanson and P. Raggatt (Eds.), *Boundaries of adult learning. Adult learners, education and training vol. 1*. London: Routledge.

Harper, S. (2006). 'Mature societies: Planning for our future selves'. *Daedalus*, 135 (1), 20–31. Available at: http://www.mitpressjournals.org/doi/abs/10.1162/001152606775321040

Hart, L. A. (1975). *How the brain works: A new understanding of human learning, emotion and thinking*. New York: Basic Books.
Havinghurst, R. J. (1953). *Education and development.* New York: David McKay Company.
Hebb, D. O. (1972). *Textbook of psychology* (3rd edition). Toronto: W. B. Saunders.
Hergenhahn, B. R. and Olson, M. H. (2005). *An introduction to theories of learning* (7th edition). Englewood Cliffs, NJ: Prentice Hall.
Heron, J. (1999). *The complete facilitator's handbook.* London: Kogan Page.
Hesse-Biber, S. N. (2010). *Mixed method research: Merging theory with practice.* New York: The Guilford Press.
Hickson, J. and Housley, W. (1997). 'Creativity in later life'. *Educational Gerontology*, 23 (6), 539–547.
Hiemstra, R. (1991) 'Aspects of effective learning environments'. *New Directions for Adult and Continuing Education*, 1991 (50), 5–12.
Hiemstra, R. and Sisco, B. (1990). *Individualizing instruction.* San Francisco, CA: Jossey-Bass.
hooks, b. (2010). *Teaching critical thinking: Practical wisdom.* New York: Routledge.
Houle, C. O. (1961). *The inquiring mind: A study of the adult who continues to learn.* Madison: University of Wisconsin Press.
Hultsch, D. F., Hammer, M. and Small, B. J. (1993). 'Age differences in cognitive performance in later life: relationships to self-reported health and activity life style'. *Journal of Gerontology*, 48 (1), 1–11.
Illeris, K. (2004). *Adult education and adult learning*. Malabar, FL: Kreiger.
Illeris, K. (2007). *How we learn: Learning and non-learning in school and beyond.* London/New York: Routledge.
Illeris, K. (2009). 'A comprehensive understanding of learning'. In K. Illeris (Ed.), *Contemporary theories of learning: Learning theorists … in their own words.* New York: Routledge.
Immordino-Yang, M. H. and Damasino, A. (2007). 'We feel, therefore we learn: The relevance of affective and social neuroscience to education'. *Mind, Brain and Education*, 1 (1), 3–10. In V. Bissland (2013). 'Older adults' voices: An exploration of preferred learning and communication styles and their fit with emerging insights from neuroscience'. *International Journal of Education and Ageing*, 3 (1), 43–62.
Jacobi, M. and Stokols, D. (1983). 'The role of tradition in group-environment relations'. In N. R. Feimer and E. S. Geller (Eds.), *Environmental psychology: Directions and perspectives.* New York: Praeger Press.
Jamieson, A. (2007). 'Higher education study in later life: What is the point?' *Ageing and Society*, 27 (3), 363–384.
Jarvis, P. (1985). *Sociological perspectives on lifelong education and lifelong learning.* Athens: University of Georgia.
Jarvis, P. (1987). *Adult learning in the social context.* Beckenham: Croom Helm.
Jarvis, P. (1990). 'Trends in education and gegrontology'. *Educational Gerontology*, 16 (4), 401–409.
Jarvis, P. (1995). *Adult and continuing education: Theory and practice.* London: Routledge.
Jarvis, P. (2001). *Learning in later life: An introduction for educators and carers.* London: Kogan Page Limited.
Jenkins, A. (2011). 'Participation in learning and wellbeing amongst older adults'. *International Journal of Lifelong Education*, 30 (3), 403–420.

Jenkins, A. and Mustafa, T. (2012). *Learning and wellbeing trajectories among older adults in England.* (BIS Research Paper Number 92). Institute of Education, University of London: Department of Business, Innovation and Skills.

Jenkins, A. and Mustafa, T. (2013). 'Wellbeing and learning in later life'. *International Journal of Education and Ageing*, 3, (1), 9–24.

John, M. T. (1983). *Teaching and loving the elderly.* Springfield, IL: Charles C. Thomas.

John, M. T. (1988). *Geragogy: A theory for teaching the elderly.* Binghampton, NY: The Haworth Press.

Johnson, S. (2006). 'The neuroscience of the mentor-learner relationship'. *New Directions in Adult and Continuing Education*, 110, 63–69.

Jones, B. D. and Bayen, U. J. (1998). 'Teaching older adults to use computers: Recommendations based on cognitive aging research'. *Educational Gerontology*, 24, 675–689.

Kandel, E. R. (2006). *In search of memory: The emergence of a new science of mind.* New York: Norton.

Karnieli-Miller, O., Strier, R. and Pessach, L. (2008). 'Power relations in qualitative research'. *Qualitative Health Research*, 19 (2), 279–289.

Kempermann, G. (2006). 'Adult neurogenesis'. In P. B. Baltes, P. A. Reuter-Lorenz and F. Rösler (Eds.), *Lifespan development and the brain: The perspective of biocultural co-constructivism.* Cambridge: Cambridge University Press.

Kidd, J. R. (1973). *How adults learn.* New York: Association Press.

Kincheloe, J. and Steinburg, S. (1997). *Changing multiculturism.* Bristol, PA: Open University Press.

King, P., Kitchener, K. S. and Knowles, M. (1984). *Applying modern principles of adult learning.* San Francisco, CA: Jossey-Bass.

Kitzinger, J. (1995). 'Qualitative research: Introducing focus groups'. *British Medical Journal*, 311, 299–302.

Knowles, M. S. (1970). *The modern practice of adult education: Andragogy versus pedagogy.* New York: Associated Press.

Knowles, M. S. (1984). *Androgeny in action.* San Francisco, CA: Jossey-Bass.

Knowles, M. S. (1990). *The adult learner: A neglected species.* Houston, TX: Gulf Publishing.

Kolb, D. A. (1984). *Experiential learning: Experience as the source of learning and development.* Englewood Cliffs, NJ: Prentice Hall.

Kolland, F. (2013). 'The benefits of learning in later life: An editorial essay'. *International Journal of Education and Ageing*, 3 (2), 115–126.

Lamb, R. and Brady, E. M. (2005). 'Participation in lifelong learning institutes: What turns members on?' *Educational Gerontology*, 31, 207–224.

Laslett, P. (1989). *A fresh map of Life: The emergence of the Third Age.* London: Weidenfield and Nicholson.

Lawrence, P. R. and Nohria, N. (2001). *Drive: How human nature shapes our choices.* San Francisco, CA: Jossey Bass.

Lawrence, R. L. (2012). 'Intuitive knowing and embodied consciousness'. *New Directions for Adult and Continuing Education*, 134, 5–13.

Lebel, J. (1978). 'Beyond andragogy to geragogy'. *Lifelong Learning: The Adult Years*, 1 (9), 16–18.

Lee, M. (2003). 'Andragogy and foreign-born learners'. In L. M. Baumgartner, M. Lee, S. Birden and D. Flowers (Eds.), *Adult learning theory: A primer.* Columbus, OH: Center on Education and Training for Employment.

Lightfoot, C. (1997). *The culture of adolescent risk-taking*. New York: Guilford Press.
Lincoln, Y. S. and Guba, E. G. (1985). *Naturalistic enquiry*. Newbury Park, CA: Sage.
Lloyd, R. (1992). 'Foreword'. In D. Roberts and T. Higgins (Eds.), *Higher education: The student experience*. The findings of a research programme into student decision-making and consumer satisfaction. Leeds: Heist Roper.
Lomax, P. (1996). *Quality management in education: Sustaining the vision through action research*. London: Routledge.
MacKeracher, D. (2004). *Making sense of adult learning*. Toronto: University of Toronto Press.
Maginess, T. (2017). *Enhancing the wellbeing and wisdom of older learners*. New York: Routledge.
Mangrum, F. and Mangrum, C. (1995). 'An ethnomethodological study of concerted and biographical work performed by elderly persons during game playing'. *Educational Gerontology*, 21 (3), 231–246.
Manheimer, R. J. (2009). 'Creating meaningful senior-friendly spaces'. *Generations*, 33 (2), 60–65.
Marchese, T. (1991). 'Assessment's next five years'. *AIR Newsletter, Special Supplement*. Washington, DC: Fall-Winter.
Mark, R. (2004). 'The quality debate in lifelong learning: What are we measuring and for whom'. Retrieved from the web equipe.up.pt/RESOURCES/Articles/Article April 2016.
Marmot, M. (2004). 'Status syndrome'. *Significance*, 1 (4), 150–154.
Marsick, V. J. and Watkins, K. E. (2001). 'Informal and incidental learning'. *New Directions for Adult and Continuing Education, No. 89*. San Francisco, CA: Jossey-Bass.
Mårtensson, J., Eriksson, J., Bodammer, N. C., Lindgren, M., Johansson, M., Nyberg, L. and Lövdén, M. (2012). 'Growth of language-related brain areas after foreign language learning'. *NeuroImage*, 63 (1), 240.
Maslow, A. H. (1954). *Motivation and personality*. New York: Harper and Row.
Maslow, A. H. (1970). *Motivation and personality* (2nd edition). New York: HarperCollins.
Maxwell, J. A. (2005). *Qualitative research design: An interactive approach* (2nd edition). Thousand Oaks, CA: Sage.
Mayer, R. E. (2002). 'Cognitive theory and the design of multi-media instruction: An example of the two-way street between cognition and instruction'. In D. F. Halpern and M. D. Hakel (Eds.), *Applying the science of learning to university teaching and beyond. New Directions for Teaching and Learning*. San Francisco, CA: Jossey-Bass.
McCaffrey, J. R., Lockwood, D. F., Koretz, D. M. and Hamilton, L. S. (2003). *Evaluating value added models for teacher accountability*. Santa Monica, CA: RAND Corporation.
McCall, G. J. (1984). 'Systematic field observation'. *Annual Review of Sociology*, 10, 263–282.
McGivney, V. (1999). *Informal learning in the community: A trigger for change and development*. Leicester: NAICE.
McIntyre, D. (2003). 'Using foregrounding theory as a teaching methodology in a stylistics course'. *Pedagogy of Style and Stylistics*, 37 (1), 1–13.
McLeod, J. (2001). *Qualitative research in counselling and psychotherapy*. Thousand Oaks, CA: Sage.
McNair, S. (2012). *Older people's learning in 2012 – A survey*. Leicester: NIACE.

Merriam, S. B. (2001). 'Something old, something new: Adult learning theory for the twenty-first century'. *New Directions for Adult and Continuing Education*, 89, 93–96.

Merriam, S. B. and Bierema, L. L. (2014). *Adults learning*. San Francisco, CA: Jossey-Bass.

Merriam, S. B., Cafferella, R. S. and Baumgartner, L. M. (2007). *Learning in adulthood* (3rd edition). San Francisco, CA: Jossey-Bass.

Messick, S. (1976). 'Personality consistencies in cognition and creativity'. In S. Messick (Ed.), *Individuality in learning: Implications of cognitive styles and creativity for human development*. San Francisco, CA: Jossey-Bass.

Messiou, K. (2014). *Responding to diversity by engaging with students' voices: A strategy for teacher development*. Southampton: University of Southampton.

Mezirow, J. and Associates (1990). *Critical reflection in adulthood*. San Francisco, CA: Jossey-Bass.

Mezirow, J. and Associates (2000). *Learning as transformation*. San Francisco, CA: Jossey-Bass.

Midwinter, E. (2003). *500 beacons: The U3A story*. London: Third Age Press.

Mirowsky, J. and Ross, C. E. (2015). 'Education, health, and the default American lifestyle'. *Journal of Health and Social Behaviour*, (1), 297–306.

Morgan, L. and Kundel, S. (2001). *Aging: The social context* (2nd edition). Thousand Oakes, CA: Pine Forge Press.

Nash, I. (2015). 'What the GP ordered: A course of education'. *Times Education Supplement*, 5164, 44.

NDA (2013) *New Dynamics of Ageing Programme*. Online. www.newdynamics.group.shef.ac.uk/ (accessed 21 September 2016).

Newman, M. (2012). 'Calling transformative learning into question: Some mutinous thoughts'. *Adult Education Quarterly*, 62 (1), 36–55.

Newman, S., Ward, C., Smith, T., Wilson, J. and McCrea, J. (1997). *Intergenerational programmes: Past, present and future*. Washington DC: Taylor & Francis.

Noice, T. Noice, H. and Kramer, A. F. (2013). 'Participatory arts for older adults: A review of benefits and challenges'. *The Gerontologist* [Online] December 11, 2013. doi:10.1093/geront/gnt138

Novak, M. (1993). *Aging and society: A Canadian perspective*. Scarborough, ON: Nelson.

Ozuah, P. O. (2005). 'First, there was pedagogy and then came andragogy'. *Einstein Journal of Biology and Medicine*, 21, 83–87.

Padgett, D. K. (1998). *Qualitative methods in social work research: Challenges and rewards*. Thousand Oaks, CA: Sage.

Patton, M. Q. (1982). *Practical evaluation*. Newbury Park, CA: Sage.

Patton, M. Q. (1990). *Qualitative evaluation and research methods* (2nd edition). Thousand Oaks, CA: Sage.

Patton, M. Q. (2002). *Qualitative research and evaluation methods* (3rd edition). London: Sage.

Peeters, G., Kenny, R. A. and Lawlor, B. (2020). 'Late life education and cognitive function in older adults'. *International Journal of Geriatric Psychiatry*, 35 (6), 633–639.

Percy, K. (1990). 'The future of educational gerontology: A second statement of first principles'. In F. Glendenning and K. Percy (Eds.), *Ageing, education and society:*

Readings in educational gerontology. Keele: The Association for Educational Gerontology, University of Keele.

Perry, B. D. (2006). 'Applying principles of neurodevelopment to clinical work with maltreated and traumatized Children: The neurosequential model of therapeutics'. In N. Boyd Webb (Ed.), *Working with traumatized youth in child welfare*. New York: Guilford Press.

Peters, T. and Waterman, R. H. (1982). *In search of excellence*. London: Harper & Row.

Peterson, D. A. (1976). 'Educational gerontology: The state of the art'. *Educational Gerontology*, 1 (1), 61–73.

Peterson, D. A. (1983). *Facilitating education for older learners*. San Francisco, CA: Jossey-Bass.

Pfeffer, N. and Coote, A. (1991). *Is quality good for you?* Social Policy Paper No. 5. London: Institute of Public Policy Research.

Phillipson, C. (1983). 'Education and the older learner. Current developments and initiatives'. In S. Johnson and C. Phillipson (Eds.), *Older learners: The challenge to adult education*. London: Bedford Square Press.

Phillipson, C. (1993). 'The sociology of retirement'. In J. Bond, P. Coleman and S. Peace (Eds.), *Ageing in society* (2nd edition). London: Sage.

Phillipson, C., Ogg, J. and Universities UK Staff (2010). *Active ageing and universities: Engaging older learners*. Research report, Universities UK.

Platt, J. (1992). 'Cases of case ... of cases'. In C. C. Ragin and H. S. Becker (Eds.), *What is a case? Exploring the foundations of social inquiry*. Cambridge: Cambridge University Press.

van Praag, H., Kempermann, G. and Gage, F. H. (1999). 'Running increases cell proliferation and neurogenesis in the adult mouse dentate gyrus'. *Nature Neuroscience*, 2 (3), 266–270.

Prosser, M. and Trigwell, K. (1999). *Understanding learning and teaching. The experience in higher education*. Buckingham: Open University Press.

Race, P. (2010). *Making learning happen* (2nd edition). London: Sage.

Ramsden, P. (1992). *Learning to teach in higher education*. London: Routledge.

Reder, S. (2009). 'Scaling up and moving in: Connecting social practices views to policies and programs in adult education'. *Literacy and Numeracy Studies*, 16.2/17.1 (1), 35–50.

Reio, T. G. (2007). 'Exploring the links between adult education and human resource development: learning, risk taking, and democratic discourse'. *New Horizons in Adult Education and Human Resource Development*, 21 (1/2), 5–12.

Roberts, D. and Higgins, T. (1992). *Higher education: The student experience*. The findings of a research programme into student decision-making and consumer satisfaction. Leeds: Heist Roper.

Robotham, D., Morgan, K. and James, K. (2011). *Learning for life: Adult learning, mental health and wellbeing*. London: Mental Health Foundation.

Robson, C. (2011). *Real world research* (3rd edition). Chichester: John Wiley and Sons Ltd.

Rogers, A. and Horrocks, N. (2010). *Teaching adults* (4th edition). Maidenhead: Open University Press.

Rogers, C. (1969). *Freedom to learn: A view of what education might become*. Columbus, OH: Charles Merill.

Rogers, C. (1983). *Freedom to learn for the 80s*. Columbus, OH: Charles E. Merrill.

Rogers, C. R. and Roethlisberger, F. J. (1991). 'Barriers and gateways to communication'. *Harvard Business Review*, November–December, 105–111.

Rogers, J. (2001). *Adults learning* (4th edition). Buckingham: Open University Press.

Rogers, J. (2003). *Adults learning* (5th edition). Buckingham: Open University Press.

Ross, C. (2006). 'Brain self-repair in psychotherapy: Implications for education'. In S. Johnson and K. Taylor (Eds.), *The neuroscience of adult learning: New directions for adult and continuing* learning, *No. 110*. San Francisco, CA: Jossey-Bass.

Rowe, J. W. and Kahn, R. L. (1999). *Successful aging*. New York: Pantheon Books.

Sallis, E. (2002). *Total quality management in education* (3rd edition). London: Kogan Page Ltd.

Sallis, E. and Hingley, P. (1991). *College quality assurance systems*. Bristol, The Staff College, Mendip Papers, 20.

Sargant, N. (2000). *The learning divide revisited*. Leicester: NIACE.

Sauter, J., Widmer, E., Ihle, A. and Kliegel, M. (2019). 'The association of leisure activities in middle adulthood with cognitive performance in old age: Social capital mediates cognitive reserve effects'. *Psychology & Neuroscience*, 12 (2), 236–246.

Scarlett, C. and Winner, A. (1995). 'Quality issues in informal women's education in the voluntary sector'. *Adults Learning*, 7 (3), 53–76.

Schuller, T., Baron, S. and Field, J. (2000). 'Social capital: A review and critique'. In S. Baron, J. Field and T. Schuller (Eds.), *Social capital: Critical perspectives*. Oxford: Oxford University Press.

Schuller, T. and Field, J. (1998). 'Social capital and the learning society'. *International Journal of Lifelong Education*, 17 (4), 226–235.

Schuller, T., Preston, J., Hammond, C., Brassett-Grundy, A. and Bynner, J. (2004). *The benefits of learning: The impacts of formal and informal education on social capital, health and family life*. London: Routledge.

Schuller, T. and Watson, D. (2009). *Learning through life: Inquiry into the future of lifelong learning*. Leicester: NIACE.

Schwandt, T. (2000). 'How do we think about evaluation?' In Lifelong Learning and Experience Vol. 2. *Papers and Perspectives of the 1st international Summer School of the Graduate School in Lifelong learning*, Ed. K. Weber, Roskilde University and the Danish Research Academy, No. 109/99. Adult Education Research Group, Copenhagen: Roskilde University Press.

Schwandt, T. (2007). *Dictionary of qualitative enquiry* (3rd edition). Thousand Oaks, CA: Sage.

Simson, S., Thompson, E. and Wilson, L. (2001). 'Who is teaching lifelong learners? A study of peer educators in Institutes for Learning in Retirement'. *Gerontology & Geriatrics Education*, 22 (10), 31–43.

Simone, P. M. and Hass, A. L. (2013). 'Frailty, leisure activity and functional status in older adults: Relationship with subjective well being'. *Clinical Gerontologist*, 36 (4), 275–293.

Spigner-Littles, D. and Anderson, C. E. (1999). 'Constructivism: A paradigm for older learners'. *Educational Gerontology*, 25 (3), 203–209.

Stake, R. E. (1995). *The art of case study research*. Thousand Oakes, CA: Sage.

Stake, R. E. (2005). 'Qualitative case studies'. In N. K. Denzin and Y. S. Lincoln (Eds.), *Handbook of qualitative research*. Thousand Oaks, CA: Sage.

Stenhouse, L. (1975). *An introduction to curriculum research and development*. London: Heinemann.

Stenhouse, L. (1978). 'Case study and case records: Towards a contemporary history of education'. *British Educational Research Journal*, 4 (2), 21–39.

Stenhouse, L. (1982). 'The conduct, analysis and reporting of case study in educational research and evaluation'. In R. McCormick (Ed.), *Calling education to account*. London: Heinemann.

Stern, H. L. and Spokus, D. M. (2019). 'Training the older workers: Pathways and pitfalls'. In S. J. Czaja, J. Sharit and J. James (Eds.), *Current and emerging trends in aging and work*. New York: Springer.

Strange, C. C. and Banning, J. H. (2001) *Educating by design*. San Francisco, CA: Jossey-Bass.

Strauch, B. (2010). *The secret life of the grown-up brain*. London: Penguin.

Stuart-Hamilton, I. (2000), *The psychology of ageing* (3rd edition). London and Philadelphia: Jessica Kingsley.

Taylor, E. W. (2012). *Teaching adults in public places: Museums, parks, consumer education sites*. Malabar, FL: Kreiger Publishing Company.

Tesch-Römer, C. and Wurm, S. (2012) 'Research on active aging in Germany'. *The Journal of Gerontopsychology and Geriatric Psychology*, 25 (3), 167–170.

Thibodeau, J. (1979). *Adult performance on Piagetian tasks: Implications for education*. Paper presented at the Adult Education Research Conferences, Ann Arbor, MI, 4–6 April 1979.

Thistle, M. (1968). 'Emotional barriers to communication'. *Industrial Canada*, May.

Tisdell, E. J. (2000). 'Feminist pedagogies'. In E. Hayes and D. D. Flannery (Eds.), *Women as learners: The significance of gender in learning*. San Francisco, CA: Jossey-Bass.

Tough, A. M. (1979). *The adults' learning projects*. Ontario: Ontario Institute for Studies in Education.

Trigwell, K. and Prosser, M. (1991). 'Relating learning approaches, perceptions of context and learning outcomes'. *Higher Education (Special Edition on Student Learning)*, 22, 251–266.

Trigwell, K., Prosser, M. and Waterhouse, F. (1997). 'Relations between teachers' approaches to teaching and students' approaches to learning'. *Higher Education*, 37 (1), 57–70.

United Nations (2013). *World population prospects: The 2012 revision, key findings and advance tables*. New York: United Nations Department of Economic and Social Affairs/Population Division. Working paper No. ESA/P/WP.227.

United Nations, Department of Economic and Social Affairs, Population Division (2013). *World Population Ageing 2013*. ST/ESA/SER.A/348.

United Nations, Department of Economic and Social Affairs, Population Division (2015). World Population Prospects: The 2015 Revision, Key Findings and Advance Tables. Working Paper No. ESA/P/WP.241.

US Census Bureau (2018). *An ageing nation: Projected number of children and older adults* [Online] https://www.census.gov/library/visualizations/2018/ comm/historic-first.html

VanderArk, S., Newman, I. and Bell, S. (1983). 'The effects of music participation on quality of life of the elderly'. *Music Therapy*, 3 (1), 71–81.

Vanhoutte, B. (2012). *Measuring subjective well-being in later life, Research Briefing 2012*. Manchester: The Cathie Marsh Centre for Census and Survey Research.

Vygotsky, L. S. (1978). *Mind in Society: The development of higher psychological processes*. Cambridge, MA: Harvard University Press.

Wain, K. (2009). 'Lifelong learning and philosophy'. In P. Jarvis (Ed.), *The Routledge handbook of lifelong education*. London: Routledge.

Wenger, E. (1998). *Communities of practice: Learning, meaning and identity*. Cambridge: Cambridge University Press.

Wenger, E. and Snyder, W. M. (2000). 'Communities of practice: The organizational frontier'. *Harvard Business Review*, 78 (1), 139–145.

West-Burnham, J. (1992). *Managing quality in schools*. Harlow: Longman Group UK Ltd.

Williamson, A. (2000). 'Gender differences in older adults' participation in learning. Viewpoints and experiences of learners at the University of the Third Age (U3A)'. *Educational Gerontology*, 26 (1), 49–66.

Wilson, A. L. (1993). 'The promise of situated cognition'. In S. B. Merriam (Ed.), *An update on adult learning theory. New Directions for Adult and Continuing Education, No. 57*. San Francisco, CA: Jossey-Bass.

Wilson, R. S. (2002). 'Participation in cognitively stimulating activities and risk of incident Alzheimer disease'. *Journal of American Medical Association*, 287 (6), 742–748.

Withnall, A. (2010). *Improving learning in later life*. Abingdon: Routledge.

Withnall, A. (2012). 'Lifelong learning in long-term care settings'. In P. Jarvis and M. Watts (Eds.), *The Routledge international handbook of learning*. London/New York: Routledge.

Withnall, A. (2016). 'United Kingdom'. In B. Findsen and M. Formosa (Eds.), *International perspectives on older adult education, lifelong learning book series, volume 22*. New York: Springer.

Withnall, A. and Percy, K. (1994). *Good practice in the education and training of older adults*. Aldershot: Ashgate.

Wlodkowski, R. J. (1999). *Enhancing adult motivation to learn* (2nd edition). San Francisco, CA: Jossey-Bass.

Wlodkowski, R. J. (2008). *Enhancing adult motivation to learn: Comprehensive guide for teaching all adults*. San Francisco, CA: Jossey-Bass.

Wlodkowski, R. J. and Ginsberg, M. B. (1995). *Diversity and motivation: Culturally responsive teaching*. San Francisco, CA: Jossey-Bass.

Wolfe, P. (2006). 'The role of meaning and emotion in learning'. In S. Johnson and K. Taylor (Eds.), *The neuroscience of adult learning: New directions for adult and continuing learning, No. 110*. San Francisco, CA: Jossey-Bass.

Wood, A. (2010). 'Singing diplomats: The hidden life of a Russian-speaking choir in Jerusalem'. *Ethnomusicology Forum*, 19 (2), 165–169.

World Health Organisation (WHO) (2002). *Active ageing: A policy framework*. Geneva, Switzerland.

Wright, E. (2008). *The case for qualia*. Cambridge, MA: The MIT Press.

Yang, B. (2003). 'Toward a holistic theory of knowledge and adult learning'. *Human Resource Development Review*, 2 (2), 106–129.

Yin, R. K. (2009). *Case study research: Design and methods* (4th edition). Thousand Oaks, CA: Sage.

Zull, J. E. (2006). 'Key aspects of how the brain learns'. In S. Johnson and K. Taylor (Eds.), *The neuroscience of adult learning: New directions for adult and continuing* learning, *No. 110*. San Francisco, CA: Jossey-Bass.

APPENDIX A

The Third Age Trust (u3a) Vision and Mission Statement

Vision and Mission Statement

Our Vision Our Vision is to make lifelong learning, through the experience of u3a, a reality for all third agers.

Our Mission Our Mission declares our purpose as an organisation and serves as the standard against which we weigh our actions and decisions. It is to:

- Facilitate the growth of the u3a movement.
- Provide support for management and learning in u3as.
- Raise the profile of the u3a movement.
- Promote the benefits of learning in later life through self-help learning.

The Principles of the u3a Movement

The u3a movement is non-religious and non-political and has three main principles:

The Third Age Principle

- Membership of a u3a is open to all in their third age, which is defined not by a particular age but by a period in life in which full time employment has ceased.
- Members promote the values of lifelong learning and the positive attributes of belonging to a u3a.
- Members should do all they can to ensure that people wanting to join a u3a can do so.

The Self-help Learning Principle

- Members form interest groups covering as wide a range of topics and activities as they desire; by the members, for the members.
- No qualifications are sought or offered. Learning is for its own sake, with enjoyment being the prime motive, not qualifications or awards.
- There is no distinction between the learners and the teachers; they are all u3amembers.

The Mutual Aid Principle

- Each u3a is a mutual aid organisation, operationally independent but a member of The Third Age Trust, which requires adherence to the guiding principles of the u3a movement.
- No payments are made to members for services rendered to any u3a.
- Each u3a is self-funded with membership subscriptions and costs kept as low as possible.
- Outside financial assistance should only be sought if it does not imperil the integrity of the u3a movement.

APPENDIX B

A Sample of a [Golden Gates] Evaluation Form

GOLDEN GATES* EVALUATION FORM

CLASS ______________________ NAME (optional) ______________________

How would you describe each of the following? Tick one option for each description and offer any comments you may have					
	EXCELLENT t	*GOOD*	*SATISFACTORY*	*POOR*	*Your Comments*
EXAMPLE	✓				*TUTOR EXCELLENT ALWAYS PRO FESSIONAL*
Quality of sessions					
Tutor/speaker					
Venue					

By attending GOLDEN GATES activities have you been affected? Tick one option for each description and offer any comments you may have*					
	Strongly Agree	*Agree*	*Disagree*	*Not Applicable*	*Your Comments*
EXAMPLE	✓				*I HAVE MADE MANY FRIENDS HERE & FEEL LESS ISOLATED*
Improved health & well being					
Increased confidence					
Increased energy					
More new friends / social life					
More motivated					

Are there any new classes you would like GOLDEN GATES to provide? If so please list them here in BLOCK CAPITALS*

* The name of the organisation has been changed to Golden Gates to preserve anonymity.

APPENDIX C

The Final Quality Learning Questionnaire Used with Groups of Learners at the [Golden Gates] Charity

What Is Quality Learning?

The Institute of Education is undertaking some research with [Golden Gates] to identify what makes a 'quality' learning experience for those learning in later life. To help, we would be very grateful if you would complete this questionnaire.

Thank you for your help in this research

Think about a [Golden Gates] learning session or activity you considered to be of 'high quality'.

Please describe it briefly (e.g. language class, yoga, music group): ____________

Details: Size of Group ____ Time of Day ____ Did it have a teacher / tutor? _____

Thinking of the activity you have described, please respond to the following statements.

About You	*Strongly Agree 5*	*Agree 4*	*Neutral 3*	*Disagree 2*	*Strongly Disagree 1*
I definitely learned new things					
I found the group friendly					
I was challenged in my learning					
I had my individual needs met					
I was treated with respect					
I was, myself, motivated to learn					
I took part in the learning activities					
I encouraged others to learn too					

About the Tutor	*Strongly Agree 5*	*Agree 4*	*Neutral 3*	*Disagree 2*	*Strongly Disagree 1*
They made the learning interesting					
They let me ask questions					
They motivated me to want to learn					
They made learning fun					
They treated me with respect					
They were qualified as a teacher					
They are experienced in what they are teaching					
They involved learners in learning					
They challenged me to learn new things					
They asked for my opinions					
They gave me confidence					
They encouraged me to keep on learning					

About the Organisation	*Strongly Agree 5*	*Agree 4*	*Neutral 3*	*Disagree 2*	*Strongly Disagree 1*
The accommodation was suitable for our needs					
The atmosphere was safe and non-threatening					
The equipment worked well					
The group was not too large					
The group had a friendly feeling					
The organisation would listen to complaints					
The organisation selected the tutors with care					
The room was organised to enable everyone to see and hear					

Is there anything else you can think of that makes a learning session or learning experience high 'quality' for you?

____

____

____

____

____

Information about you as a learner while keeping you anonymous

I am male _______ female _________

I was born in the year 19 _________

I regard my ethnicity as ______________________________

The number of classes I attend each week is ___________

Do you hold any educational qualifications? (yes / no) ___________

If answered yes, what is the highest you have gained? _______________

Thank you for completing this questionnaire

INDEX

Note: **Bold** page numbers refer to tables and *italic* page numbers refer to figures.

For Product Safety Concerns and Information please contact our EU representative GPSR@taylorandfrancis.com
Taylor & Francis Verlag GmbH, Kaufingerstraße 24, 80331 München, Germany

www.ingramcontent.com/pod-product-compliance
Ingram Content Group UK Ltd.
Pitfield, Milton Keynes, MK11 3LW, UK
UKHW020009200926
475702UK00015B/2567

* 9 7 8 1 0 3 2 2 1 6 6 4 5 *